Beat the Crowd

Fisher Investments Press

Fisher Investments Press brings the research, analysis, and market intelligence of Fisher Investments' research team, headed by CEO and New York Times best-selling author Ken Fisher, to all investors. The Press covers a range of investing and market-related topics for a wide audience—from novices to enthusiasts to professionals.

Books by Ken Fisher

Debunkery
How to Smell a Rat
Markets Never Forget (But People Do)
Plan Your Prosperity
The Ten Roads to Riches
The Only Three Questions That Still Count
100 Minds That Made the Market
The Wall Street Waltz
Super Stocks
The Little Book of Market Myths

Fisher Investments Series

Own the World by Aaron Anderson
20/20 Money by Michael Hanson

Fisher Investments On Series

Fisher Investments on Consumer Discretionary
Fisher Investments on Consumer Staples
Fisher Investments on Emerging Markets
Fisher Investments on Energy
Fisher Investments on Financials
Fisher Investments on Health Care
Fisher Investments on Industrials
Fisher Investments on Materials
Fisher Investments on Technology
Fisher Investments on Telecom
Fisher Investments on Utilities

FISHER
INVESTMENTS
PRESS

Beat the Crowd

HOW YOU CAN OUT-INVEST THE HERD BY THINKING DIFFERENTLY

Ken Fisher
With Elisabeth Dellinger

WILEY

Cover image: City People Set © iStock.com/edge69; Multiple silhouettes of business people © 4x6/Digital Vision Vectors/Getty Images
Cover design: Thomas Perez

Published by John Wiley & Sons, Inc., Hoboken, New Jersey.
Published simultaneously in Canada.

Library of Congress Cataloging-in-Publication Data:

ISBN 978-1-118-97305-9 (Hardcover)
ISBN 978-1-118-97306-6 (ePDF)
ISBN 978-1-118-97307-3 (ePub)

Printed in the United States of America

10 9 8 7 6 5 4

Contents

Preface

True confession: I didn't want to write a preface for this book. It's too darned long already, and I wanted to spare you having to flip one more page. But alas, the powers that be require one—who knew!

Maybe that's fitting, because this is a book I didn't think I'd write. I was happy with 10 books. Ten is a round number, and plenty. I didn't think the world needed another Ken Fisher book. But ideas happen! An idea struck during a conversation with my former Wiley editor, Laura Gachko (still with Wiley, no longer saddled with my silly nonsense) and my co-author, Elisabeth Dellinger—one thing led to another, and next I knew, I was at it again. Eleven is a fun number, too.

The concept of contrarianism has run through my books since *Super Stocks*, way back in 1984, but I've never overtly addressed it. To me, contrarianism has always been about independent thinking, and my books have always demonstrated this (at least, I like to think so). But that fateful December day in 2013, it occurred to us that I'd never come out and explained just what the heck contrarianism is, isn't and how to practice it. I realized it was time, since contrarianism is misunderstood and misapplied by many and unknowingly practiced by some, who might like to know it.

Most assume being contrarian means doing the opposite of what "everyone" does—if "everyone" is mostly wrong most of the time, betting the opposite must bring success! Sometimes, that's true. But often not. Opposite-doers have a herd-like mentality, too, and the market loves fooling them as much as it loves fooling the crowd they're trying to game. Real life isn't "herd versus contrarians." It's the mainstream herd, the opposite-doing herd, and the independent thinkers—real contrarians. They see what both herds think, then weigh all extant factors—pluses and minuses—and reach their own conclusions.

This book is a how-to guide for anyone tired of rules of thumb, media hype and industry mythology and wants to think independently. It's a brain-training guide. Not foolproof! But foolproof doesn't exist. This book simply teaches the thought process that helped me be right more often than wrong for over four decades of money management. You can be right more often than wrong, too!

This book was a team effort. As said above, Laura helped generate the idea and provided early edits before passing the reins to Tula Batanchiev, who edited the lion's share along with Judy Howarth and the rest of their team at John Wiley & Sons. Vincent Nordhaus led production at Wiley. Wiley's team was diligent and patient as always, and I remain grateful to my excellent agent, Jeff Herman, for leading me to them. Jarred Kriz, Michael Olsen, Lauren Schekman, Eric Harger and Nathaniel Beeman—who have worked with me for years—also provided ideas. Thomas Perez designed another cool cover, capturing our theme perfectly. Jessica Wolfe, Chanddeep Madaan, Sam Olson, Michael Leong, Tim Schluter, Brad Pyles and Talia Hosenpud helped with research, while Jarred, Todd Bliman, Jill Hitchcock, Justin Arbuckle and Molly Lienesch weighed in on early drafts and helped steer us toward a sane path. Todd pulled triple duty, editing the entire book for content and shouldering most of Elisabeth's workload (and providing her unquantifiable moral support) while she shelved much of her day job of writing for my firm to devote her time to this project. Christopher Wong and Emily Dunbar—up-and-coming writers at my firm—helped with copy-edits. Last but not least, Fab Ornani, David Eckerly, Christopher Boaz and Theodore Gilliland led our PR and web marketing. To all of them and anyone I failed to mention here—and to my wife, Sherrilyn, and broad family—I give my deepest thanks.

And thanks to you, for reading! May you enjoy this as much as we enjoyed writing it.

Ken Fisher
Camas, WA

CHAPTER 1

Your Brain-Training Guide

Few truths are self-evident, but here's one as close as they get: In investing, the crowd is wrong much more often than right.

Most folks accept this. They remember pain from some of their own mistakes. More so, they recall market-bloodied friends, relatives, neighbors and co-workers. They've seen all the famous market gurus get egg on their faces. Academic studies show the wisdom of the investing crowd is folly.

Yet folks follow along anyway. For most, it's impossible not to! The financial blogosphere, websites and cable TV talking heads pound market groupthink into our brains 24/7. Without conditioning yourself to resist, it's all too easy to accept repeated falsehoods as fact, melt into the crowd and buy high, sell low—with the rest.

There is another way! Train your brain to battle the media, the crowd, your friends, neighbors and cocktail bankers and think differently. It doesn't take vast market knowledge, a finance degree, an economics PhD or endless rigorous study. Armed with a few basic principles, internal alarm bells and an instinct for independent thought, you can be a true crowd-beating contrarian investor.

Yogi Berra once quipped, "Baseball is 90% mental, the other half is physical." Might apply to investing! Mental discipline is key to success. See this book as your brain-training guide. You'll learn tricks you need to protect your brain from media hyperbole and some principles to outsmart the crowd.

What does being a contrarian mean? What's the secret to being right more than wrong? Prepare to find out. In this chapter, we'll start with the basics:

- Why Wall Street's definition of a contrarian investor is wrong
- The foolishness of conventional wisdom
- The true contrarian's gut-check

Wall Street's Contrarian Contradiction

Legend lumps all investors into two categories: bulls and bears. Those who think stocks will rise, and those who think stocks will fall. If the masses are bullish, Wall Street says anyone who's bearish is a contrarian. If the masses are bearish, bulls are the contrarians.

But this is wrong. It implies "everyone"—one big crowd who thinks stocks will do one thing—and "everyone else," another crowd thinking stocks will do the opposite. "Everyone else" often thinks they're contrarian. They think "everyone" is the herd, and the herd is always dead wrong. They've seen the countless academic studies showing the majority of investors are just terrible at making investment decisions, usually selling low and buying high. They believe doing the opposite of the crowd guarantees buying low and selling high.

Problem is, "everyone else" is as crowd-like as "everyone." Their opinions usually aren't unique, and their analysis often isn't any broader or better than the main crowd's. They look at all the same things, just with a dissenting, condescending sneer. People thinking this way and that they're contrarians aren't any smarter, any more discerning than you or me or the crowd. Their moves rarely pay off any better.

That's the bad news. Here's the good news: You can be a real contrarian! Once you know what leads the crowd or both crowds astray, it isn't hard to think better and act smarter. It's impossible to be perfect, but to be better than most isn't so hard.

The Curmudgeon's Conundrum

Two-herd contrarians see the world like an analog clock. They base bets on wherever the main herd expects the hand to land. If everyone says the clock will point at 1, the supposed contrarian herd bets it'll land on 7—roughly the mirror opposite direction. Just because it's the opposite! Contrary for contrary's sake. Much of the time, no real extra thought goes into it. Just a curmudgeonly instinct. "Everyone's cheery, so I can't be." It wouldn't occur to curmudgeons to consider other alternatives, like "Everyone's cheery, but maybe they should be even more so!" This isn't physics, where for every action there is an equal and opposite reaction. Assessing markets and events based on a false either/or could lead to big mistakes when you consider results are not binary.

Transferring our clock metaphor to stocks, if the crowd thinks stocks will rise 10% in a year, the curmudgeons bet on down. Perhaps not down 10% exactly—they'll bet on the opposite direction, but they might not bother guessing the magnitude. Their nature is to be ornery, but not ornery with precision. Simply betting the reverse direction is good enough for them.

We can transfer it to a recent scenario, too, like the Federal Reserve's quantitative easing (QE). The crowd thinks QE is good, propping up stocks. Contrarians think it's bad, risking inflation. Here is your false either/or! In my view, QE is bad because it is deflationary, an outcome neither the crowd nor the supposed contrarians consider. There is a century of economic theory and research supporting this notion, but the crowd buys the common narrative, which crowd-contrarians are so fast to categorically reject that they miss the truly big problem with crowd-think. There, too, they're just being an opposite crowd without much deep thought. (More on QE later.)

What's the problem? A clock doesn't have just two numbers! It has 12 hours, with 60 minutes in between. Even if the masses bet wrong, the curmudgeon has a 10-in-11 chance of being wrong, too. That's a 1-in-11 chance of being right. Same goes with markets. If everyone calls for a 10% year, stocks need not end down for them to be wrong. Flat returns would do it. So would up 20%, 30% or more, because most who envisioned 10% would have sold out by the time stocks hit 15%. The curmudgeons who bet on down could very easily be wrong—and often are. Not that being wrong would hurt if you called for 10% and stocks did 30%, if your positioning was right and you didn't sell too soon, but we'll get to that in Chapter 2.

There Is Always a But

The market is The Great Humiliator. TGH for short. Its goal is to humiliate as many people as possible as often as possible for as long as possible. Preying on the herd is its bread and butter—humiliates a whole bunch of investors at once! The crowd is the easy, typical prey, but TGH spares no one forever. Even true contrarians get whacked.

No approach works all the time, including assuming the crowd is wrong. Sometimes, they're right! The market usually doesn't do what everyone expects, but there are always exceptions. If TGH didn't let the crowd be right sometimes, there wouldn't be a crowd! Momentum investors—those whose guiding principle is "The trend is your friend"—would be proven wrong the moment they invest. Markets would slap most folks in the face as soon as they buy—or sell—and people would learn from their mistakes. Stocks wouldn't have anyone to fool, and fooling folks is one of the market's greatest pleasures.

People must be right sometimes, must feel good sometimes, or we'd never have a herd. They would just give up. The occasional rightness fosters false confidence, reinforcing the crowd's wisdom. It is plausible deniability for TGH. It is how TGH repeatedly sucks the crowd in, makes them ignore negatives, then doles out maximum pain and suffering. (TGH probably then enjoys a cartoon-villain-like laugh.) This is why seasonal myths like "Sell in May" and "September is the worst month" ring true. Even though they're wrong more often than not, they're right sometimes. Those times when May, summer and September returns look sad, coupled with below-average historical returns for May through September, keep the myth alive. Occasional and often dramatic rightness gives myths power.

Markets often let the crowd look right temporarily, before turning on them. Folks who believed the eurozone crisis would end the bull market in 2011 looked awfully right that October, when world stocks were at the bottom of a deep correction. But stocks bounced and the bull carried on in 2012, 2013 and beyond, shrugging off history's largest sovereign default in Greece along the way, ultimately proving the euro doom-mongers wrong (or very untimely, also effectively wrong).

Sometimes, markets' wobbles let folks think they're right, like when a correction comes after headlines warn some big evil will rock stocks. Corrections—sharp drops of –10% to –20% over a few weeks or months—come any time, for any reason or even no reason. But fear-mongers often assume conveniently timed corrections are proof that whatever they warned about was as big and bad as they said. This isn't fundamental rightness—just confirmation bias (seeing what you want to see), a dangerous behavioral phenomenon, but most folks don't bother differentiating between fundamental rightness and happenstance. (More on this in Chapter 9.)

Just as the crowd is sometimes right, true contrarians are sometimes wrong. Everyone is wrong sometimes! The goal is simply being right more often than wrong, as opposed to looking right at first but ultimately being wrong more often than not.

Why Most Investors Are Mostly Wrong Most of the Time

It isn't because they're uninformed. It isn't because they lack smarts. Very well-read, bright people who pay close attention to the market often make pretty bad investing decisions! There is usually one simple reason for this: They inadvertently get sucked into consensus views.

Groupthink can happen no matter how careful and studied your methods are. Many folks see investing as a discipline, art or science, which sounds good, but their methods morph into conventional wisdom—usually dangerous in investing. All operate on various sets of beliefs about what is and isn't good for stocks and when you should and shouldn't trade. Or they follow rules dictating the same.

Many doctors, lawyers and engineers are prone to this. Not because there is anything wrong with them as people. It isn't their fault! But their professional training leads them there. In their professional lives, they use a rules-based methodology, and there, it works. But in markets, it doesn't. For doctors to recommend a treatment, they need scientific proof it works—trials and controlled tests. They apply the same methodology to investing, looking for "rules" that have been back-tested and "proven" to work. Most lawyers are logicians by trade and nature—they expect markets to follow rules, processes and simple logic. Most engineers, too. They expect markets to be linear and rational, just like the systems they build and work with daily.

Rules-based investors usually use similar logic and reach similar conclusions. They use the same patterns, the same if-then assumptions. They end up expecting similar things, and it morphs into a consensus viewpoint. It usually appears very logical! But markets often defy logic, as we'll soon see.

Other folks take their rules and beliefs from academic theory and textbook curriculum. Theory and textbooks aren't inherently harmful. Principles and theory can be useful if you layer on independent thought. But many turn theory to dogma, textbooks to rulebooks. Whatever the literature says is good or bad for stocks must be true, always and everywhere. If the rulebook says high price-to-earnings ratios (P/Es) and high interest rates are bad, then they're bad! To fundamentalists, the canon is often truth. But canon is also widely read—more consensus! Markets price in the consensus pretty quickly and do something else. That "something else" is what the true contrarian wants to figure out.

Some investors use old saws and rules of thumb as a guide—the "playbook." Here, too, the approach might seem fine. The playbook is supposedly full of time-tested wisdom! If it didn't work, it wouldn't be in the playbook! But the more you base decisions on maxims, proverbs, and things everyone just knows, the less likely you are to think independently—and the less likely to have true contrarian views.

The playbook also doesn't pass a basic logic test—one of the true contrarian's favorite tools, as we'll see in Chapter 4. It includes familiar adages, like "buy on the dips"—when stocks are on sale, snap 'em up at a bargain! But that's also when the playbook would tell you to "cut your losses"—get out of that dog before it goes to zero, and get into something that's actually going up. One page tells you to "let your profits run"—if it's going up, stay in! It'll keep going! Yet the next page tells you to "take some profits off the table." Which do you choose? Both sound intuitive! If a stock is running, you want to let it run. But you know it could easily run off a cliff, plummeting with legs churning like Wile E. Coyote, so pocketing some of those gains seems wise! The playbook doesn't tell you which play to run.

Not all rules of thumb are based on price movement. One age-old playbook trick claims to have the secret for profiting off company announcements. You've heard it: "Buy the rumor, sell the news." If the rumor mill says Apple is working on a sexy new phone that operates telekinetically, opens your garage door, feeds your kids and locates distant planets all while you're on the phone with long-lost Aunt Sally (whom your phone found all on its own!), buy. Don't wait to find out if it's true! Get in before it's too late! Then sell when they announce it, after all the other suckers have piled in. As if it can't possibly go up more, as if the company has zero potential lift, will never do anything new and cool again ever, and maybe even do something else with another rumor right after that new phone is announced. How could you know?

All of these approaches rest on widely known information—and common interpretations of that information. No matter how intuitive and logical, they're what "everyone" does. The true contrarian moves beyond consensus views and conventional wisdom. Life is way more exciting there, in the wide-open air.

Love or Hate the Media, They Do You a Favor

Mass media reflects and also influences sentiment, and most of it has become steadily more groupthink, in my view, over the last two decades. Journalism today embodies John Maynard Keynes' old maxim: "Worldly wisdom teaches it is better for reputation to fail conventionally than to succeed unconventionally."

It wasn't always so. Pre-Internet, pre-cable, journalists often had distinct views. When you had three major national news networks and a handful of major national financial publications, pundits competed with insight. They wanted to be groundbreaking. Now, we have dozens of 24/7 cable news outlets, scores of financial websites and countless blogs—and every article and blog post has a comment feed where anyone and everyone can roast the author publicly and anonymously. Nothing attracts a roasting like an article far out of step with mainstream thinking. It drives the wing nut in the crowd into posting Internet terrorism, which cowers and moderates authors, melding a groupthink media. In some few realms, increased competition isn't always uniformly good.

But there is a big silver lining! Modern media makes it pretty easy to spot widely held beliefs and mass sentiment. The media will only rarely quote anyone outside the herd or anti-herd.

I experienced this firsthand whenever journalists asked my opinion about quantitative easing (QE). You've probably heard of it. It's a program the Fed launched during the 2008 financial crisis—an effort to boost liquidity and lower long-term interest rates so businesses and people would be eager to borrow. For years, the Fed bought Treasury bonds and agency mortgage-backed securities from banks and paid with newly created electronic "reserve credits." Well over $2 trillion of supposed new money! These purchases lowered long-term rates, and banks were supposed to use the new reserves as collateral to magically multiply money supply.

When journalists asked my opinion, I told them what they didn't like. Something outside the herd or anti-herd. When you reduce long-term rates while short-term rates are pegged near zero, you flatten the yield curve—shrink the spread between short and long rates. We have more than 100 years of evidence confirming a wider spread is the real magic. Why? Think about bank lending. Short-term rates are banks' funding costs. Long-term rates are their lending revenues. The difference—long rates minus short rates—mimics a bank's gross operating profit margin.

Banks aren't charities. They're for-profit. The more profitable lending is, the more they'll do it. The less profits, the less eager bankers are. They'll sit on their hands. Just like they did all through QE. For years, the herd thought the Fed was the only thing propping up growth. In reality, the Fed killed lending and gave us the slowest loan growth in decades, almost no growth in the quantity of money (aka M4)—a point almost no one noticed—and the slowest gross domestic product (GDP) growth since World War II.

I explained all this to reporters, in vast detail with data. It made sense, they said! But they didn't print it. If everyone said QE was a loose monetary policy, how could they publish some wacko saying it wasn't? They couldn't, because the wing nut part of the crowd would crucify them.

Major outlets wouldn't, couldn't print such a view on QE. In an age where seemingly every quoted expert, the Fed, the International Monetary Fund, the World Bank and every finance minister and central banker in the world said QE was a big economic lifeline and ending it was the biggest risk to the global economy, journalists would have to be out of their minds to differ. The commenters and bloggers would tear them to bits. It would be career suicide.

This makes it easier for real contrarians to sort through the media—there are always exceptions, but in general, it is pretty safe to assume that if headlines hype something, it isn't a contrarian view. It won't tell you anything you can act on. For that, you'll have to venture off on your own.

The First Rule of True Contrarianism

Here is the fundamental feature of true contrarianism. If you don't remember anything from the next nine chapters, remember this: If most believe something will happen in markets, the contrarian simply believes something else will.

This is what the curmudgeons mess up. Note, I didn't say the opposite happens. Just something different. Markets price in to today's prices what the crowds commonly conceive. If everyone is bearish because they see bad things, they might be right that they're bad—but bad might not mean bearish! Because everyone sees the bad things, and they're splashed all over the TV and Internet, they might be priced in. Those bad things might not matter at all. Or there could be some fundamentally big bad thing they aren't seeing at all, and things end up worse than they expect!

This is what happened heading into 2008. Then, everyone said housing, subprime and toxic mortgage-backed securities were trouble. They would cause a recession and make stocks fall. So many said it! So many saw it!

No one, me included, saw an even bigger, quiet problem: November 2007's implementation of the mark-to-market accounting rule (Statement of Financial Accounting Standards [FAS] 157, "Fair Value Measurements"), which could wipe a couple trillion dollars off bank balance sheets globally. No one fathomed that because every financial institution would have to mark every illiquid asset on its balance sheet at the going market price, whenever others sold a mortgage-backed security at fire-sale prices, everyone else would take a hit. Every bank in the US would have to take a paper loss on every comparable illiquid security it owned.

No one fathomed that this could cause pre-existing problems in subprime mortgages to eventually wipe out about $2 trillion from the US banking system in mere months. No one fathomed that the fear over these opaque, illiquid markets could cause markets to deny funding first to Bear Stearns, and then, six months later, to Lehman Brothers, triggering the demise of two of the five biggest investment banks. No one fathomed how the Fed, after lending JPMorgan Chase money to buy Bear, would deny funding to help Barclays buy Lehman, forcing the i-banking giant into bankruptcy. And no one fathomed how this would trigger sheer panic in the markets, making daily –8% drops seem the norm. Nor that, through it all, the Fed would forget how to function in a crisis, forget to do most of what central banks traditionally did in a crisis (presuming all of that wouldn't work), forget to boost traditional liquidity by any measure or act as lender of last resort.

If it were just subprime and housing in 2008, we'd probably have just gotten a big correction. It wasn't until around midyear, as the vicious circle of fire sales and write-downs picked up in earnest, that the real trauma started.

I missed it, too, which brings up the second big rule of contrarianism: You'll be wrong sometimes. Contrarians know it, accept it. But you don't have to be right all the time to do fine—a 60% or 70% success rate keeps you well ahead of most. As I've written in past books, if you're right 70% of the time in this realm, you become an absolute living legend. (Although it isn't impossible that all the snarky new bloodsucking ensures no new living legends ever emerge and endure ever again. Of course, a contrarian won't care about that—won't care about self-image. Despite what you may have read of me from my many critics, I care little about my image. Neither should you.)

The All-Seeing Market

Contrarians know when not to move and where not to go. How? They know markets are mostly efficient. Not fully, perfectly efficient at every moment—otherwise there would be no opportunities! Contrarians realize markets can be quite irrational in the short term. But over time and on average, prices typically reflect all widely known information. If it's out there, in the public domain, investors have already considered it and traded on it.

Rules, conventional wisdom and consensus expectations are all widely known. Ditto for ideological beliefs, biases and every "expert" view. Every textbook theory, rulebook and playbook ever published—markets know them inside and out. They know the rules, know the if-thens and know how most folks are likely to react to every news nugget. Markets know what the crowd will do before the people themselves know.

The same is true for seasonal myths and technical indicators. Dow Theory is perhaps the most extreme example. This indicator, around since the late nineteenth century, says that when the Dow Transports and Industrials hit new highs together, you get a lasting bull trend. If they hit new lows together, look out below. There is also a lot of mumbo-jumbo in between, but I'll spare you—the extremes are what matter. If Dow Theory were right, no bull market would ever end because the signal would keep on signaling, and stocks would keep on rising! Same in a bear market. But cycles always turn! Markets have priced all those Dow Theory expectations, and they'll ultimately do something different.

Different, Not Opposite

Whatever the rules say and the herd expects, you can bet the markets won't do. But that doesn't mean the opposite outcome happens!

Think back to our clock analogy. If everyone expects the hand to land on 1, the curmudgeon bets close to 7. The real contrarians remember markets are efficient, so they know the clock probably won't land between about 11 and 3—it would be too near where most folks expect. The contrarian can effectively rule out four possibilities. But there are still eight hours' worth of potential outcomes.

For example, if most expect stocks to rise 10% in a year, true contrarians bet stocks probably won't land in the 5% to 15% range. But that still leaves a big up year, flat returns or down.

Understanding how markets discount known information helps you narrow the range of possibilities. It doesn't tell you what will happen—that's where curmudgeons get messed up—it just tells you what probably won't happen and frees you to contemplate what might happen and improve your odds.

To narrow the field, the contrarian looks for things the herd and curmudgeons ignore—they branch out. Or they look at the same things but see them differently. Both actions let them find the risks and opportunities most others miss.

The Right Frame of Mind

Contrarians are patient—they think long-term. Short-term thinking makes you antsy, and that's when bad decisions happen.

You see it all the time when folks chase heat, piling into whatever is hottest purely because it is up the most. They might get bored with broad diversification during a rally and try to concentrate in a hot trend—they ditch long-term thinking for short. Think back to 1999 and 2000. Internet stocks flew high. Fiber optics was the Next Big Thing. The Nasdaq soared, and everyone wanted a piece of the new economy. Dot-coms seemed like the ultimate get-rich-quick magic.

It's an extremely short-term mindset, but it viraled. Few thought about where they needed to be in 10 or 20 years (of course, we're there now). Few looked a year ahead and considered whether companies with ultrahigh cash-burn rates and no revenues could still possibly be in business. They just wanted what was hot then, and they wanted as much as they could get. The bear market beginning in March 2000 was a rude awakening.

Panic-stricken people think short-term, too. Go back to March 2009, those violent final throes of that financial panic. People truly believed stocks could go to zero. Don't believe me? Do a Google search on "Can the stock market go to zero?" They asked it. Markets were tanking; zeroness felt real.

You're probably sitting there thinking, "That's not rational." But panic never is! Folks take those big losses and extrapolate them forward. They lose their grasp of history and reality. They forget the simple truths: Cycles always turn. Markets rise more often than not. As long as capitalism exists, businesses will find ways to profit and grow. New technologies will collide, bringing new growth and new sources of profits. This is what the steel-nerved contrarians believed in March 2009.

Steely contrarians also look past short-term market movement. They know daily drops, quick pullbacks and corrections are normal during bull markets, and reacting is dangerous. It usually means selling after stocks have already fallen, just when folks should hunker down and wait. Reacting to volatility is a good way to sell low, buy high.

The same goes for seemingly big short-term events, like geopolitical earthquakes. Skirmishes, minor wars, revolutions and saber-rattling have plagued us since the dawn of civilization—terrible as they are for lives and property of those in the line of fire, they usually aren't terrible (or even just plain bad) for stocks. Markets have dealt with conflict since before the first Dutch tulip changed hands, and only big, global and nasty conflicts, like the onset of World War II, have ever ended in bull markets. Life always goes on, and the going on is what matters.

Check Your Ego

As I said earlier, the contrarians know they won't be right all the time. Perfection is impossible.

Even a practiced contrarian should expect to be wrong fully 30% to 40% of the time. You needn't be right any more than two-thirds of the time to do fine and stay ahead of the pack. Simply being right more often than wrong is huge and exceptional. As said, a professional who is right 70% of the time in the long term becomes an absolute living legend—and had better also be used to being wrong 30% of the time. So you should be, too.

So how can you be right more often than wrong? I already told you: Remember markets will do whatever the herd doesn't expect! But there are many ways to apply this simple rule. I'll detail them. Read on!

CHAPTER 2

For Whom the Bell Curve Tolls

In terms of rites and traditions, not much matches New Year's. If you ever went on *Family Feud* and this category came up, you'd have a field day. Champagne toasts! "Auld Lang Syne"! Resolutions! Ryan Seacrest (Dick Clark for graybeards) counting down before a big glittery ball drops on national television!

Here's another: professional investors' annual market forecasts. Will they pop up in a game show? No way. But knowing and understanding them can help you make more money than game shows ever can, assuming a 50-show *Jeopardy* run isn't in your future.

Parsing professional forecasts can also help you develop one of the most basic principles of contrarianism: thinking different, not opposite. Wall Street strategists are far more gameable than retail investors. As my old research partner Meir Statman and I found in a 2000 study for the *Financial Analysts Journal*, professional forecasters are wronger stronger and for longer than regular folks. Most individual investors are less stubborn and flip with trends—they won't stand being wrong for too long before they flip. If they're skeptical, four months of strong returns can turn them into bulls. If they're getting optimistic, it just takes one big pullback to flip them back to skeptics. Amateurs often have less confidence in their views. As Meir and I found, when the media swings, individuals swing with them.

The pros are more stubborn. As we wrote then:

> Individual investors and newsletter writers form their sentiments as if they expect continuations of short-term returns. High S&P 500 returns during a month make them bullish. The sentiment of Wall Street strategists is little affected by stock returns. We found no statistically significant relationship between S&P 500 returns and future changes in the sentiment of Wall Street strategists.[1]

Pros don't flip like retail investors do. Their status breeds self-confidence—they're darned sure they know where markets are going and are willing to be patient. They don't give up the ghost, though they do mean-revert. If their forecasts for a year are too dour, clearly behind the mark halfway through, they'll revise them up—just a bit, and largely so they don't look ridiculous if the market finishes up strong. Many did this in 2014, pulling up their forecasts midyear when markets had already exceeded their full-year forecast for mid-single-digit returns—interestingly, the market then moved against them, with a third-quarter "stealth correction." That's The Great Humiliator (TGH) in action.

Armed with the knowledge that Wall Street pros are wronger stronger and longer—more often than not—we can game them. As we chronicled in Chapter 1, the curmudgeon posing as contrarian would say if all the pros are bullish, you should be bearish—and if they're bearish, you should bullishly rage on. But as we'll see, this is too black and white! Professional market gurus are wrong an awful lot, but not because the market always does the opposite of what they say. Understanding how and why they're wrong—and why the market does what it does instead—is the first step to being right more often than wrong.

In this chapter, we'll cover:

- Why most pros are mostly wrong most of the time
- What their wrongness *really* tells you about what markets will and won't do
- Why nailing a forecast on the head isn't important

Wall Street's Useless/Useful Fascination With Calendars

Wall Street's fascination with calendar-year return forecasts is largely foolish. Calendar-year returns don't matter. It's true! Market cycles are what matter, and market cycles don't care about calendars. Rare is the bull or bear market that turns with the calendar page. No Standard & Poor's (S&P) 500 Index bull market since 1926 began in January, and only one—1957 through 1961—ended in December. Maybe the next cycle aligns perfectly with the Roman calendar, or maybe it follows the lunar cycle. First time for everything! But nothing fundamentally changes when the calendar flips.

Yet Wall Street is fascinated with calendar years, and pundits like making yearly forecasts. They get headlines and eyeballs (always a good thing for a pundit). They're splashy and easy for readers to make heads or tails of—just a number! A very specific number for an individual index. This makes them easy to track and grade, giving the pundits the aura of accountability, even if few bother filling out their report cards and almost no one looks at report cards afterward.

Everyone gets in on the action. The big wire houses dedicate whole teams of economists and in-house gurus to the cause. Many fund managers do it with cult-like media following. Smaller pros may do it in their quarterly reports. Bloggers and columnists commonly tell you, to the number, where they think stocks will go.

Individually, none of these forecasts are much use to the average investor. Numerical forecasts aren't much use for these folks' clients, either. They're a sideshow! A pro's forecasting report card doesn't determine the returns their clients receive. Performance comes down to positioning. If they're positioned for a bull market, and it pays off for clients, that matters far more than whether they predicted 7% or 20% in an 18% year.

The trick for professional forecasts is to use them without using them. Nope, that isn't a typo! If you collect the whole batch of professional forecasts for a year, you get a marvelous snapshot of the general direction and magnitude Wall Street expects. And that gives you a pretty good idea of what the market likely discounts and hence won't happen.

Wall Street pros aren't the only ones fascinated with calendars—firms are, too! My father, Phil Fisher, always complained about this. He saw himself more as a business analyst than a stock market analyst, and he'd say publicly traded firms are way too focused on this year's or next year's earnings per share, always thinking in calendar years! If they were private, he said, they'd think much longer term. If they had the chance to make an investment with a sky-high return over 20 years, they'd care less about up-front costs, business cycles and the reality of short-term losses. They'd care much more about the total return at the end of those 20 years, net of all those occasional big losses.

When a business starts a plant, the project bleeds cash—planning, architecture and construction drain capital. Businesses hyper-focused on calendar-year earnings might not take the plunge, regardless of how much it could enhance growth and earnings down the line.

So how'd we get so taken with calendars? We bred it into ourselves centuries ago. It all ties back to our agricultural roots, where the calendar really does matter. Weather patterns are seasonal, harvest time comes every year, and in the nineteenth century, one year's results mattered. Whether we're talking farming, ranching or logging and milling, harvest time is harvest time. It comes once a year.

Go back to the dawn of markets, and most American employment was in agriculture. Manufacturing was tiny, and service was scant. You had merchants and banks, but not the huge service industries of today. Agriculture dominated and so did its mindset—so we applied calendars to everything with rigor. Survival depended on it. It evolved into our core. Those who didn't failed to pass their genes on.

Breaking free of Wall Street's love of calendars helps you think differently. Calendar-year returns aren't important. Whether a bull market lasts two years or 10 years, that's important! Returns in each of those calendar years, not so much. The overall return, net of all the corrections and pullbacks, is what gets you to your goals. If you measured market returns in rolling 14-month periods instead of rolling 12-month segments, it would be just as valid.

Professional Groupthink

Professional forecasters tend to fall into groupthink. They'll never admit it! They all swear their views are unique, smarter, superior. Some surely are. Yet professional forecasts have a remarkable tendency to cluster.

There are always outliers. Usually a few pros get it right each year, whether they're right for the right reasons or just plain lucky. But the bulk tend to fall in a pretty tight range, giving the market (The Great Humiliator) an easy target—a big chunk of experts to humiliate in one fell swoop, what TGH "discounts" into current prices.

The pros don't deliberately cluster, per se. But they all use the same information, and they tend to interpret it in similar ways. What they agree on—the consensus—is the crowd, the herd or whatever you want to call what the market discounts in pricing and what the contrarian must avoid. Fundamentalists all look at the same Federal Reserve policies, economic pluses and minuses, interest rates, valuations and politics, and they all make the same assumptions about what's good and what's bad for stocks—and most are pretty, well, conventional, one way or another. They all have the same tendency to mean-revert—betting on the long-term average by assuming small or down years follow big years. The technical analysts all use the same charts, patterns and rule sets. It's all the same widely known information the rest of the herd chews over daily. Dow Theorists follow Dow Theory. Those following Robert Shiller share the same broad interpretation of the wonky smoothed

10-year price-to-earnings (P/E) ratio he spearheaded (aka CAPE—Cyclically Adjusted P/E).

As a result, everything the pros agree on is priced. Their expectations for how events and developments will impact stocks? Priced! Perceived risks discussed in reports and articles? Priced! Market reality is exceedingly unlikely to occur as they expect. Even if certain events follow their predictions to a T, the market reaction probably won't.

Contrarians get this. They know most investors will share the pros' expectations. The media reports professional forecasts far and wide, and that influences most folks' outlooks. Investing-as-a-science folks will often agree with the gurus who use similar methodology, logic and theory. Technicians usually side with the pros who use the same chart patterns and rules. Contrarians also know the curmudgeons will expect the opposite direction.

How the Contrarian Uses Professional Forecasts

Contrarians know the bulk of professional forecasts are priced. Won't happen. But what, exactly, is priced? The actual number? If the consensus says 6%, would TGH hit them with 8%?

It might. But probably not! Wouldn't be nearly fun enough!

Here's the secret: The actual number isn't so important. Markets look more at the general bucket. A 6% forecast is really just a prediction for returns somewhere in the low to mid-single digits. The difference between a 6% and 8% forecast largely is without meaning. If that's where the bulk of professional forecasts fall, that's your clue the market probably won't land in that bucket. It might! TGH might decide to attack the curmudgeon anti-herd instead of the main herd—it has before (we'll get to that). But more often than not, the market will end up doing something very different than what the bulk of professional forecasters expect.

Tracking the pros is easier than you think. Just takes some Googling and basic Excel work—and if you don't know Excel, you can Google that too! (One of the Internet's many miracles is its vast volume of technical tutorials.)

So with minimal time and perseverance, you can do what we do at my firm. Though I warn you, few readers ever will because it is counter-sensical. Every year, my firm's Research staff rounds up all the professional forecasts for major countries' benchmark indexes—S&P 500 for the US, DAX for Germany, Nikkei for Japan. You get the gist. For each country, we throw all the numbers into a simple chart. Histogram, if you want to get technical.

On the horizontal axis, we break the return spectrum down into 5% ranges: 0% to 5%, 5% to 10%, 10% to 15% and so on. Then, in each range, we stack up every forecast that lands in it. It's like stacking Lego bricks with numbers on them.

What you usually end up with is a bell curve formation, with the fat part showing you the range where forecasts are most tightly clustered. If forecasts are clustered in the 0% to 5% and 5% to 10% ranges, that tells you most folks think markets will be up a little bit—single digits. Again, differences without distinction. If they're all in the low negative and low positive single digits, you know most expect a flattish year. If they're in the 10% to 20% brackets, folks expect a decent bull year. And if they're in the –10% to –20% range, most expect a bear market.

Once you identify the direction and magnitude the crowd expects, you know what probably won't happen. It's even easier to narrow than you think! In broad terms, markets really do only four things—go up a little, up a lot, down a little or down a lot. Four outcomes! Maybe five if you count "flat." Though, that's happened exactly once in the S&P 500's history—1947. As Casey Stengel said, you can look it up.

You can cross one of these broad outcomes off the list of potentials just by looking at the curve. Whichever of those four ranges the cluster lands in, you eliminate it.

This gives you three other choices. If everyone expects stocks to go up a little, TGH could surprise them with down a little, but it could also blow them away with up a lot or make them look foolish with down a lot. Curmudgeons, of course, would disagree with this. If the pros say up a little, curmudgeons assume down. If the pros say up a lot, curmudgeons plan for the apocalypse. Sometimes the curmudgeons are right! But banking on their assumptions won't work with any sort of repeatability. TGH likes to thwack them, too.

To figure out which outcome is most likely, you must figure out whether the pros are overlooking opportunities or risks—we'll cover this in the next few chapters. Listen to what the talking heads chatter about. What do they think are risks? What do they like? That tells you what's probably priced. Where aren't they looking? What are they misinterpreting? That's where you find real risks and opportunities. Then look for things the crowd might be missing. And look globally! Are most folks overlooking bad monetary policy in multiple major countries? The existence of bad monetary policy isn't enough—if everyone sees it, it is probably already baked into stock prices. You're looking for things very few others discuss. Are new tariffs and restrictions about to make trade nosedive, yet no one notices? Are nasty regulations about to pound profits—and not yet understood by most (as with 2008's mark-to-market accounting, implemented within weeks of the 2007 market peak)?

Of course, the sheer existence of these unseen risks isn't enough to make stocks fall a lot. Markets move on probabilities, not possibilities. You have to weigh the probability of whatever unseen risks you spot actually coming true and whacking the world. Being out of stocks is one of the biggest risks long-term growth investors can take. If they're wrong, and they're on the sidelines in a big bull year, that's a ton of lost ground to make up.

My January Ritual

I play the January game, too—it's an annual requirement in *Forbes*, and my clients want it. They know our forecast for the next 12 to 18 months drives our positioning, and they want to know why we're doing what we're doing. As well they should!

But I try not to play the numbers game. Numbers don't matter! Bull markets are bull markets. If I forecast 15% but stocks do 30%, was I wrong? Or was I right because the bull market continued and my positioning would have been the same either way?

So I forecast ranges. In my January *Forbes* columns and my firm's quarterly report for clients, the forecast is up a lot, up a little, down a lot or down a little. If you have to put numbers on it, you can think of up a lot as up 20% or more, up a little as 0% to 20%, down a little as –0% to –20% and down a lot as –20% or greater. But here, too, nothing is ironclad. If I said up a lot and stocks did 16%, I'd be feeling pretty good. We'd be positioned right, and 16% is a fine bull market return.

Bear markets add a wrinkle. Many bears don't feature full-year down-a-lot returns. You could very well have a bear market cover the last half of one year and first half of another—and see positive returns in both! Much of forecasting is simply about determining whether the cycle is likely to change. If you start the year in a bull market, what's the likelihood a bear starts at some point? If you start the year in a bear market, what's the likelihood a bull starts before year end?

Think of a year like 1987. It went from bull to bear and back again, all between August 25 and December. Full-year returns? Up a hair. If you predicted up a hair but missed the bear, were you really that good?

Not that most predicted that in 1987. When the year started, pros were uniformly bullish. Stocks were up about 150% in four years, and many forecasters extrapolated those returns forward—up, up and away! As I wrote in *Forbes* that January, sentiment was so high that my carpenter, John, was predicting a big up year. Why? Heard it on TV! He wasn't the only one. As I detailed in my June 1987 column, many investors were flipping from fear to greed, as the "extraordinary bull market has disoriented many folks' investment expectations."[2] We'd reached the stage where, as Bernard Baruch put it, "beggars and shoeshine boys, barbers and beauticians can tell you how to get rich." Euphoria!

(*continued*)

Most pundits cited ridiculous, unsupportable reasons for stocks to continue climbing—reasons you shouldn't heed warning signs. The contrarian in me didn't buy it. "If there is so much liquidity floating around to fuel higher stock prices, the way superbulls claim there is, then why the devil are interest rates rising? With excess liquidity, you would expect rates to be flat or down. Not so."[3]

The last straw—and the incident that made me move portfolios defensive—was when the folks from the *MacNeil-Lehrer NewsHour* called and asked if I was bearish. At the time I'd made some minorly bearish writing and public comments, and I told them, Yeah, I'm minorly bearish. They said they were planning a segment with noted bull Dan Dorfman, and they wanted a bear to debate him with an interviewer moderating. Sure, sounds like fun! But I had to ask: Why me? I wasn't famous, just a West Coast guy with three years in *Forbes* and a book. What did they want with a non-celebrity?

Their answer? They couldn't find anyone else to do it! They found people who said they were bearish but didn't want to go on TV and say so. No one would stand up in public, oppose a bull as big as Dorfman and say why his argument was wrong. This was a huge, scary sign that sentiment was too euphoric.

Sure enough, by October, with most pundits just clueless about rising rates and the liquidity crunch they signaled, it seemed clear what was then a small pullback was about to get worse. It did! And then it quickly got better.

In 1987 it was all about positioning. Getting the direction right as the year evolved. Pre-year forecast? Schmorecast.

Even the Best Fall Sometimes . . .

As with pretty much every forecasting trick, there is a "but." If it works well, eventually people catch on, they use it, and it gets priced and doesn't work anymore—at least for a while, until they forget. That happened several years ago with this trick. It worked too well! Then it didn't. But then the not working got priced. So now it works again. Someday, folks will catch on again, and as awareness that the sentiment bell curve is unpriced spreads, it will again be priced.

This isn't unusual. I'll get to this more in Chapter 5, but most investors have very short memories. I wrote a book about this very thing in 2011: *Markets Never Forget (But People Do)*. True then, true now. When something doesn't work for a while, folks forget it, and it regains its mojo. I call this the "elephant in the room"—the thing that's always there, always has been there, but isn't always seen. If an elephant is in your living room, that's a big deal! When you first see it, you probably fall over! It's an elephant! But after a while, if he stays, you might get used to him. Elephants are gray, so he probably blends in. You walk by and don't notice. That gives him power to surprise you again if he starts moving. It's the same with markets. If investors become too aware of something, whether it's a trick or a risk, it loses surprise power. It's just there, part of the long-term backdrop, nothing special. But once folks forget, it packs a punch again.

For several years, gaming professional forecasts was my secret trick, and it worked marvelously. In the old days, it was easy—we'd just use the professional forecaster surveys *BusinessWeek* would publish every December. That one page was all you needed to assess Wall Street sentiment—it was a good enough sample. Gaming one page let you game the herd! These days, with that publication no longer printing that page of assembled forecasters and owned by *Bloomberg*, rounding up professional forecasts takes more effort—scouring *Bloomberg*, *Barron's* and other outlets. Doable, but harder than in the simple days of gaming one page in a magazine.

The following pages show professional forecasts and actual returns since 1996. These aren't new—1996 through 2003, in Figure 2.1, are straight from my 2006 book, *The Only Three Questions That Count*. As I mentioned there, they all use forecasts from that one page of *BusinessWeek*. The charts from 2004 on are new to you, but they're all from my firm's research archives and use the same methodology—just with broader sourcing after *Bloomberg Businessweek* ceased printing that page.

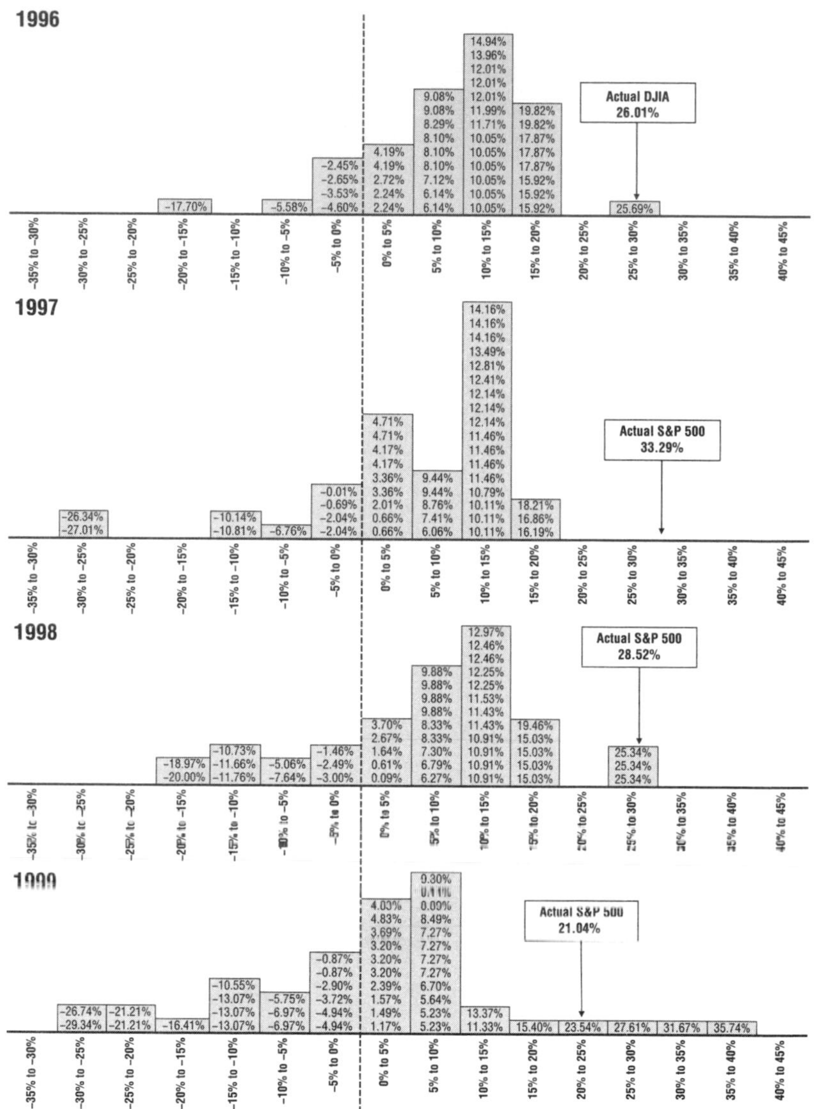

Figure 2.1 1996–2003

Sources: BusinessWeek, FactSet, Fisher Investments Research.

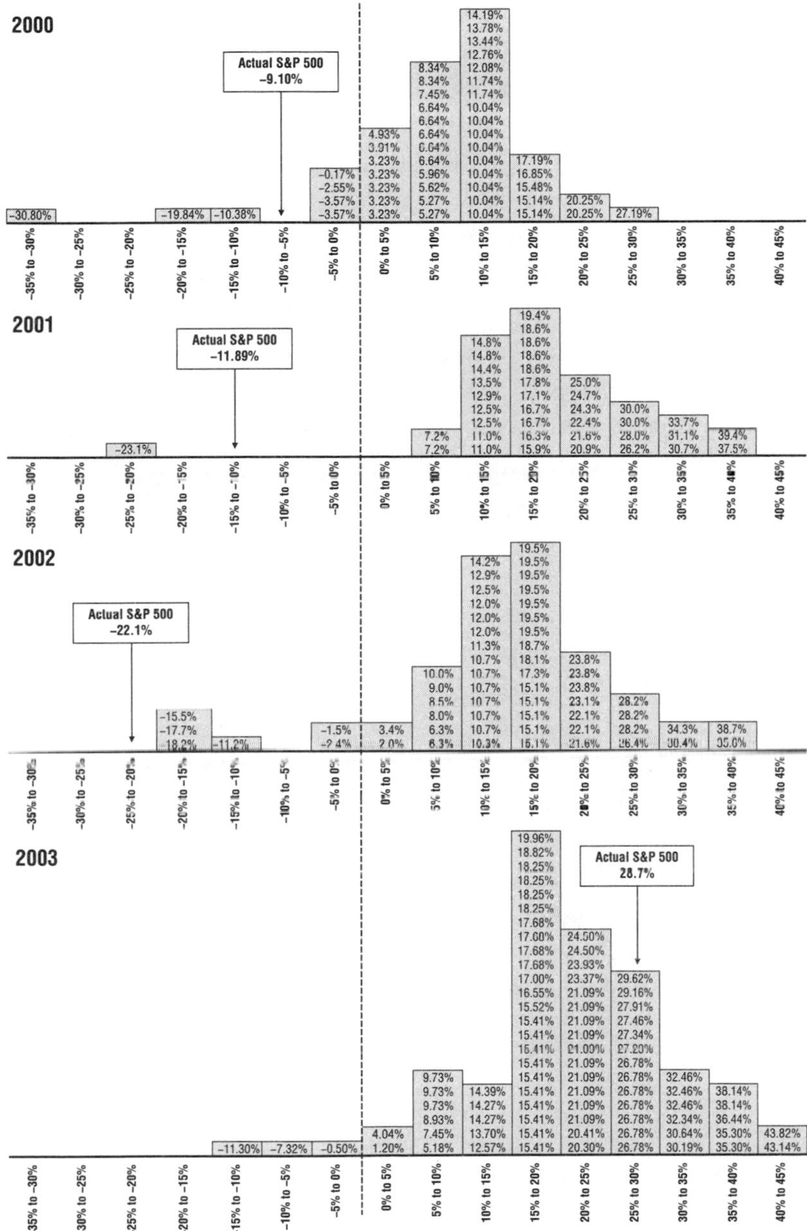

Figure 2.1 (*continued*)

As you'll see, from 1996 through 2002, the actual return fell far outside what most expected. In 1996, 1997, 1998 and 1999, the pros said up a little. Stocks did up a lot. In 2000, the pros got more bullish, but stocks fell. They got even more bullish in 2001 and 2002, but stocks fell even further. Those seven years, the market's actual return fell near-perfectly outside the curve. Fully off the chart three of those times!

But in 2003, the pros called for up a lot, and that's what the market did. The S&P 500's total return, 28.7%, fell smack in the middle of the curve. When this happens, it's tempting to brush it off. It's random! My trick works! It can't not work! But that's pride talking—a deadly sin in investing. When the little voice in your head starts trying to rationalize wrongness, run away. Turn it off. Stop rationalizing, start thinking rationally. You (and I and everyone else) will be wrong often. The greats are wrong about a third of the time! That's a lot of wrongness! If you rationalize, you can't learn from these eventual errors. Learning from your mistakes keeps you a contrarian.

That's what I did after 2003. Something had to be amiss, there had to be some fundamental reason the pros were right. I didn't sweat it that hard—again, positioning matters, and we were full bull ahead. Plus, because professional forecasters are big-time mean-reverters, it went without saying they'd predict a big up year in 2003 after 2002's nightmare.

But by the end of 2004, it was abundantly clear the bell curve trick needed to hibernate (Figure 2.2). That year, most forecasts clustered in the high single digits and low double digits. The S&P 500's actual return fell smack in the middle, 10.9%. Then, too, Wall Street caught on! Some of the pros started publicly admitting they were now using something like this to game the herd, waiting till everyone else had made their forecasts so they could pick something outside the mainstream and have a better shot at being right. They were all tired of being wrong and wanted some of the glory for themselves. So like all new capital markets technology, it spread around, got popular, got priced in. Everyone was looking at the elephant, so it was time to look somewhere else.

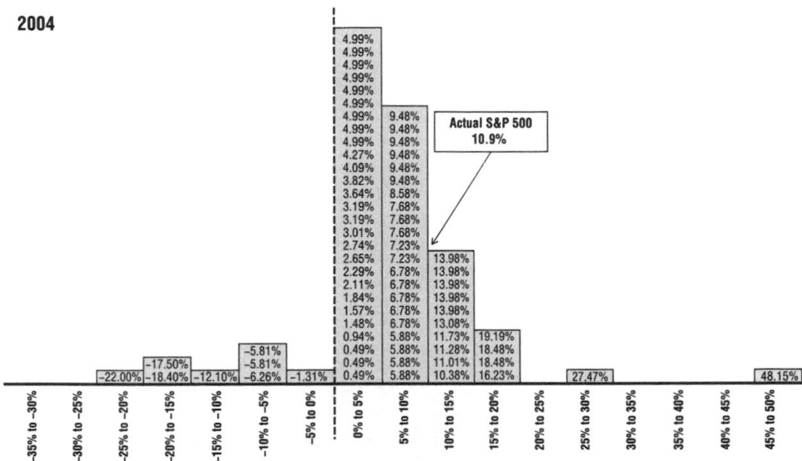

Figure 2.2 2004

Sources: BusinessWeek, FactSet, Fisher Investments Research.

As you'll see in Figure 2.3, it stayed broken for several years. Most of 2005's forecasts were in the single digits. The S&P 500 delivered 4.9%. In 2006, predictions concentrated in the low to mid-teens. The actual? 15.8%. In 2007, forecasts clumped in the single digits, and the S&P's 5.5% made them look smart.

In 2008, the pros were wrong (Figure 2.4). Most forecast S&P 500 returns between 10% and 20%. I was wrong, too. We all got TGHed. After 2008, it would be tempting to say, Hey! It's working again! But that's another mistake—correlation without causation! There has to be a why.

The why behind professional forecasters' wrongness in 2008 was simple and didn't reveal whether the bell curve trick was working again. We all just missed the impact of the mark-to-market accounting rule before it was too late (as discussed in Chapter 1). As the year wore on and banks kept writing down assets, few could fathom that the Fed and Treasury would respond so inconsistently if more banks went under. That's why stocks and the economy tanked, a huge bad that had not been priced.

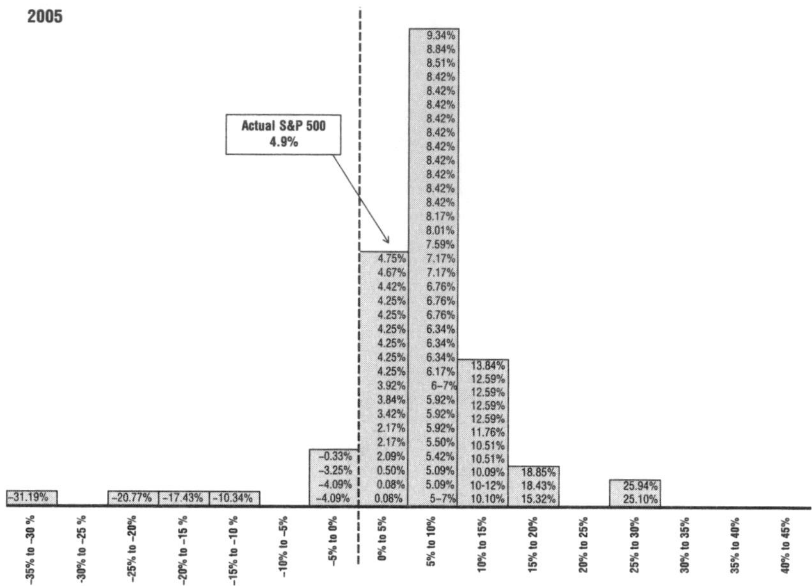

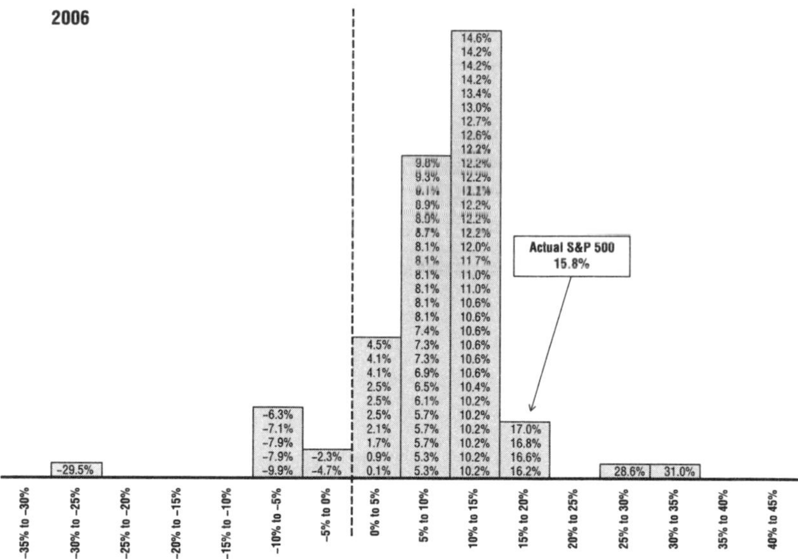

Figure 2.3 2005–2007

Sources: BusinessWeek, FactSet, Fisher Investments Research.

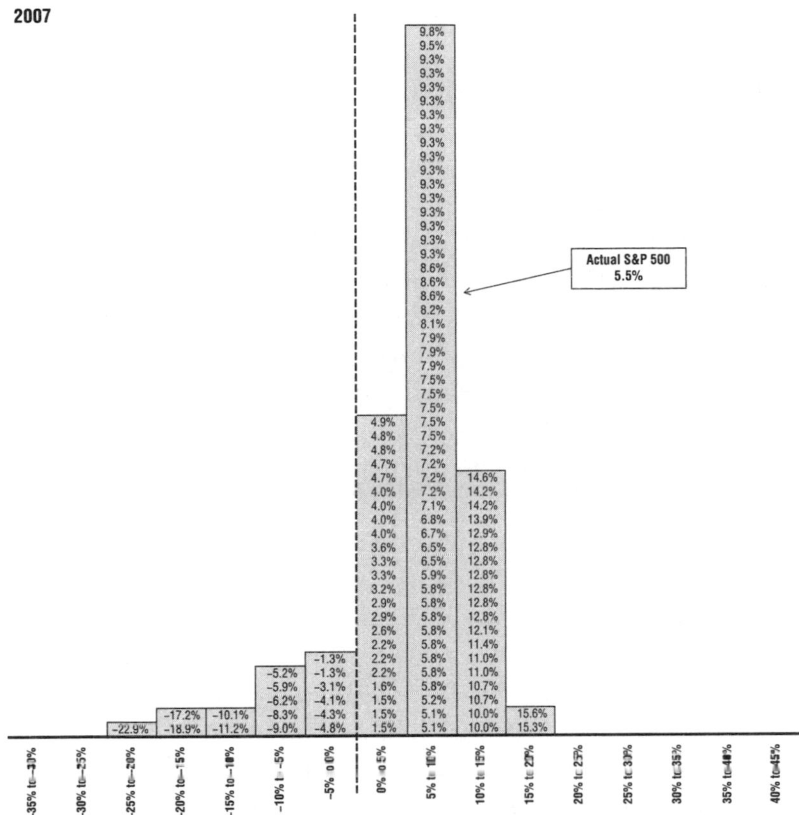

Figure 2.3 (*continued*)

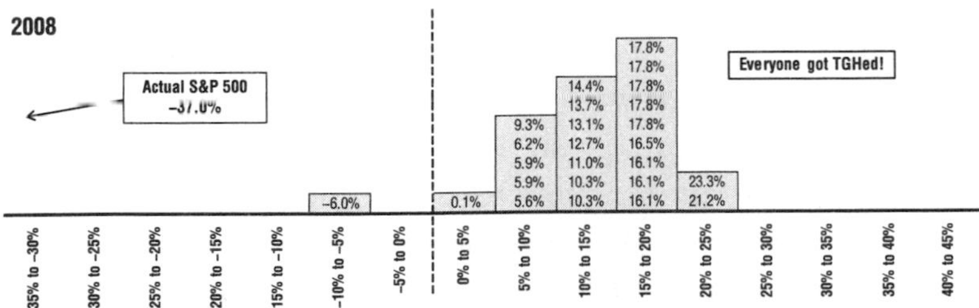

Figure 2.4 2008

Sources: BusinessWeek, FactSet, Fisher Investments Research.

I knew that going into 2009—I knew there was probably nothing magical about the pros being wrong the prior year. I also knew we were probably closer to the bear's end than the beginning, so it would be foolish to position my clients' portfolios for more bear market. Not when stocks bounce so high off bear market lows! So when a bunch of professional forecasters called for returns over 20%, I didn't blink at joining them. Yes, they were all mean-reverting after a big down year—just like 2003—but even mean-reverters can be right sometimes. The chance of a down year was almost nil. Had to be a big up year—though many individual investors thought the opposite—and it was.

But something else happened in 2009. Even though a bunch of pros were right, the S&P 500's actual return fell outside the bell curve's biggest hump.

It happened again in 2010. (See Figure 2.5.) Then, forecasts clustered in the single digits, which just seemed wacky less than a year into a bull market, and with fundamentals firing on all cylinders. Only five of the gurus we tracked saw a down year, with only two predicting a nasty one.

That was a good sign: They were still mean-reverting! Assuming a blah year had to follow a great one because, um, averages! Seemed to me they weren't using the old bell curve trick anymore. They were grouping in an irrational place, and they seemed ripe for wrongness, ripe to be TGHed.

Here, the curmudgeon would say, with dozens of pros calling for up, it has to be down! But the economy was coming back, Emerging Markets were blazing, post-midterm gridlock seemed assured with the Democrats losing favor, and headlines were deeply pessimistic. Bad news was everywhere. Good news was ignored, couched as something that couldn't last, or dressed up as bad. Slowish growth was a sign of a "lost decade." Monetary and fiscal stimulus boosting demand was really just storing up impossible debt burdens for the future, or hyperinflation, or, or, or. With a wall of worry that big, big down looked least likely.

For Whom the Bell Curve Tolls

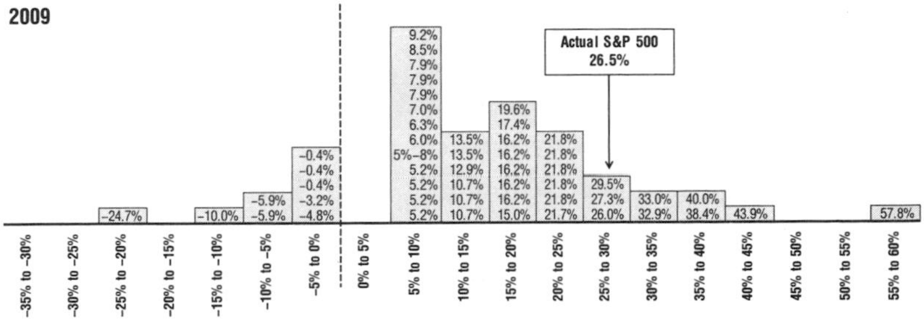

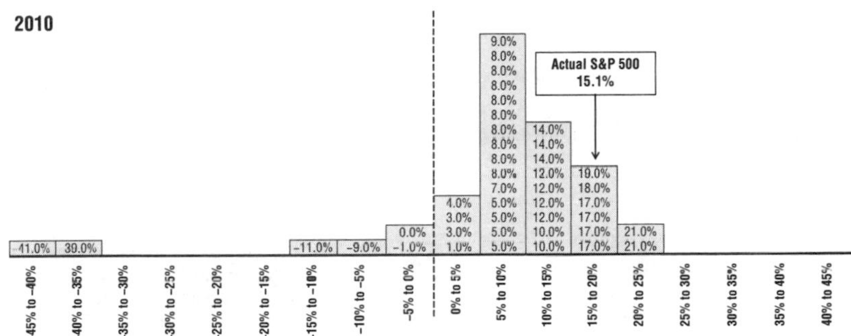

Figure 2.5 2009 and 2010

Sources: *BusinessWeek*, FactSet, Fisher Investments Research.

With the pros muted and the pundits dour, stocks seemed primed to go up more than most expected. And they did! Like 2009, the actual return—15.1%—wasn't fully outside the curve, but it was outside the hump and moving toward more extreme.

How to Beat the Street

With returns now falling outside the bell curve's hump again, it's pretty well clear the pundits are all back to their old groupthink ways. Bad for them. Good for you!

Of course, eliminating the pros' forecasts is only the first step toward figuring what stocks *will* do. Again, it simply narrows possible outcomes from four to three. I don't have a crystal ball, so I can't tell you what you'll need to look at next year, the year after that or 20 years from now. But I can show you what I did the past three years. You can learn the approach, then apply it in any year you want—you simply need to know how to see and how to think.

In 2011, forecasting started with sentiment—see the below box which highlights my observations in the February 2011 issue of *Forbes*. The pros again hovered between the mid-single digits and low double digits, and the bull market was still in its early stages—ordinarily, prime pickins. But broader investor sentiment was wacky. Retail investors—my clients—and journalists seemed split.

"A Year for Stock Pickers," *Forbes*, February 14, 2011

My advice now is more somber than it was last year. This year will frustrate bulls and bears alike—without a big directional trend. On Feb. 8, 2010 I proclaimed we were bogged in the "pessimism of disbelief," a post-big-bear-market mental state where folks overemphasize the bad, ignore the good or sniff for whiffs of more bad. My view was 2010 would be great for stocks and pessimism would decrease.

My research now shows there are too many optimists out there. That's bearish! But wait, the research indicates that there are also too many pessimists lingering about—many longtime, heels-dug-in doomers—as well as newly converted acrophobics. They are fearful mostly because of the last two years' heady rise. That's bullish.

It's a standoff between gloomers and bulls—a barbelled sentiment bifurcation. I've regularly referred to the market as "The Great Humiliator," a nearly all-powerful spiritual entity existing solely to humiliate as many people as possible for as many dollars as possible for as long as possible. It's after you and me and your aged aunt. It now accomplishes its goal best by frustrating bulls and bears alike in a year where the stock market ends up or down just by a hair.

Half thought 2011 would be amazing. Disaster hadn't happened in 2010. No double-dip recession. Greece was going down the tubes and Ireland had to get a bailout, but the widely feared euro collapse never happened. After a correction midyear, stocks rallied hard. So the public's mood improved some, with formerly cautious forecasters morphing to outright bulls—they just extrapolated the recent trend forward without an actual thought to the future. Never a rational move—and often something TGH likes to punish.

But better fundamentals didn't sway all the steadfast doom-and-gloomers. They stuck to their bearish guns despite the many signs of improvement; 2011 would be the year the cratering eurozone periphery would *really* take down the world, or the US would double dip, or China's luck would run out. The "perma-bear" contingent was larger. It also had more credibility after 2008—lots of "I saw it coming! I was right!" even though they were all bearish for the wrong reasons. Didn't matter. Media bought the narrative. Perma-bear Nouriel Roubini was a global celebrity. Their influence, along with newly minted acrophobes scared by stocks' rapid rise off the bottom, made a big down year unlikely. No fun for TGH!

So we eliminated the pros' picks (Figure 2.6) and the two extremes. That left flattish. Now, this probably sounds bizarre for a young bull market, but it's actually fairly normal. It was year three—often time for a pause, like 1994. All the signs said flattish returns were most likely—up or down a wee bit.

The year itself was a roller coaster. Stocks started off nicely, then went through a nasty correction in summer—but gained a lot of it back, finishing up just a hair (after having been down –11.3% in early October).[4]

The year 2012 was more cut-and-dried (Figure 2.7). Once again, the herd was clustered in the single digits, with the average and median professional S&P 500 forecast at 7.3%. But a fair amount expected small negative returns—they were spooked after 2011's wild ride. A handful saw low double-digit-positive years, and only one was wildly bullish. With

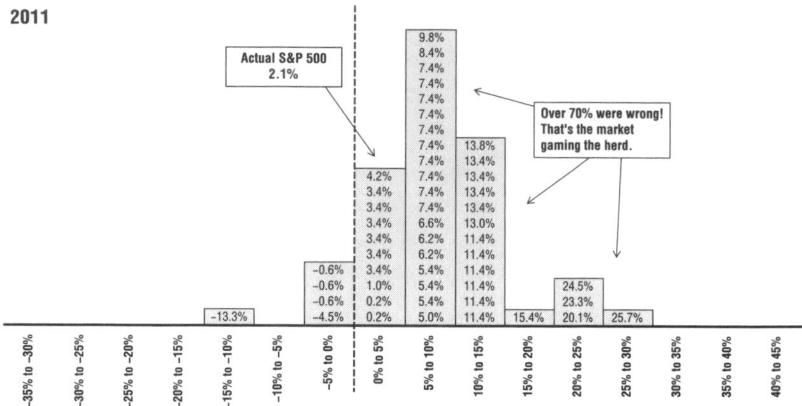

Figure 2.6 2011

Sources: Bloomberg Businessweek, Barron's, FactSet, Fisher Investments Research.

2011's pause out of the way, economic fundamentals still strong, election-year gridlock keeping legislative risk low and sentiment building a big wall of worry, stocks seemed poised to surprise to the upside—and they did!

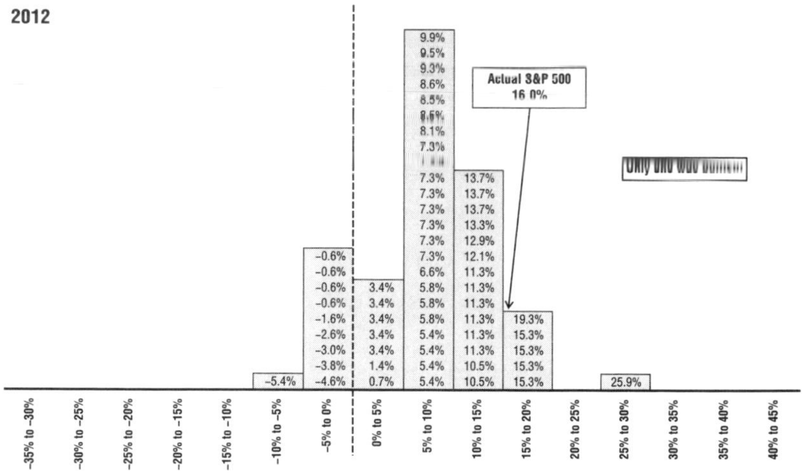

Figure 2.7 2012

Sources: Bloomberg Businessweek, Barron's, FactSet, Fisher Investments Research.

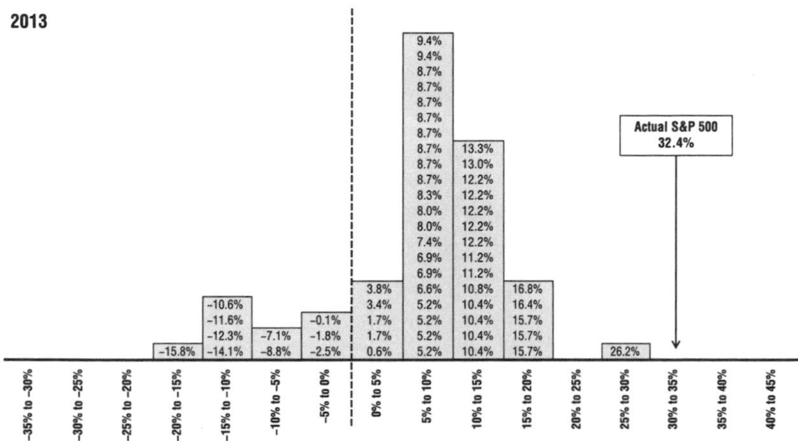

Figure 2.8 2013

Sources: Bloomberg Businessweek, Barron's, FactSet, Fisher Investments Research.

In 2013 (Figure 2.8), the pros clustered between 5% and 15%—they expected an average year. When everyone expects average, that makes markets want to be extreme to shake them out of boredom—extreme up or extreme down. But there wasn't any reason for stocks to tank. Bull markets usually run on until they lose steam or get walloped by a huge, unseen negative. Sentiment was still pretty dour, so losing steam didn't seem likely—bulls lose steam when sentiment is super euphoric after climbing the proverbial "wall of worry." Nor were there any wallops, as far as we could see. Just the same old cud folks had chewed over and over since the bull began—a big fat wall of worry. That meant a big fat year was most likely. So did the improving global economy, still-growing earnings, continuing gridlock and all the other good news folks continued ignoring. Stocks didn't disappoint—they doubled the pros' projections.

Professionals clustered even tighter in 2014 (Figure 2.9), as the dug-in bears got less bearish and fear of heights made the bulls less bullish. After a gangbusters 2013, the bears became

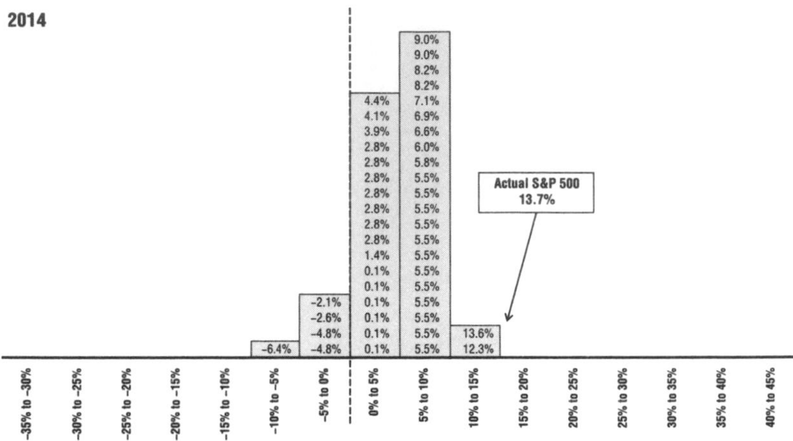

Figure 2.9 2014

Sources: Bloomberg Businessweek, Barron's, FactSet, Fisher Investments Research.

tired of being wrong. They'd spent years calling for 2008's crisis to return, and it hadn't. Most stopped believing them—boy-who-cried-wolf syndrome, as I explained it in *Forbes.* Meanwhile, the bulls were convinced stocks came too far, too fast in 2013. Only two predicted full-year returns above 10%.

The average S&P 500 forecast was about 6%, which meant you could discount low positive US returns. As I told *Forbes* readers in the January 20 issue: "When sentiment clusters like that my research shows stocks almost always do much better or much worse. Expect better!"[5] I elaborated in the following issue: "To my study of history, that 19-percentage-point spread [between the highest and lowest forecast] is what is now discounted into pricing. Hence the market is most likely to continue booming, up 20%-plus, or officially correct, down more than 10%. All or nothing, embarrassing basically everyone. The downside happens if new, undiscussed big bad forces emerge. Shy of that the surprises are all on the upside. For now, believe in that."[6]

In the end, no big bad shocker emerged. Nor did stocks officially correct, though an autumn dip came close. The S&P

500 finished up 13.7%, higher than the crowd anticipated, but not as high as I expected—TGH wanted to poke me, too![7] Again, gaming professional forecasts doesn't tell you exactly where stocks *will* go, just where they likely won't. That worked fine in 2014, even if we didn't get that booming 20%-plus year. Besides, a portfolio positioned for a 15% year shouldn't look different from a gangbusters year. A bull market is a bull market. The expected direction, not magnitude, should drive positioning.

Different, not opposite. That's the key to using professional forecasts—and the key to being a contrarian. And as we'll see in the following chapters, thinking differently can be as simple as asking, "Why are you thinking about that?"

Notes

1. "Investor Sentiment and Stock Returns," Kenneth L. Fisher and Meir Statman, *Financial Analysts Journal*, March/April 2000.
2. "What Goes Up . . . ," Ken Fisher, *Forbes*, June 15, 1987.
3. "Double Damned," Ken Fisher, *Forbes*, October 5, 1987.
4. FactSet, as of 8/19/2014. S&P 500 Total Return Index, 12/31/2010–10/3/2011.
5. "A Big (Bull) Surprise for 2014," Ken Fisher, *Forbes*, January 20, 2014.
6. "All or Nothing in 2014," Ken Fisher, *Forbes*, February 10, 2014.
7. FactSet, as of 1/2/2015. S&P 500 Total Return Index, 12/31/2013–12/31/2014.

CHAPTER 3

Dracula and the Four Horsemen of the Media Apocalypse

As the last chapter said, you want to look for the elephant in the room—the big thing the herd overlooks. But we're not quite there yet. Before knowing what to look for, you must know what not to look at! The media fails miserably at this. They most often look in the wrong place—leading most investors to look at the wrong things, too.

You can't spot the elephant if you don't look in the room. Yet very few folks do! Most stare out the window, looking at far-off specks that may never come. They gaze at sociological issues, peripheral chaos and academic debates—unimportant for markets. Or they peek just around the corner, always scared of what's lurking.

None of this matters. Not the far future! Not sociology! Not what just happened! Not things everyone says could happen tomorrow! Markets aren't far-sighted or myopic. They look about 3 to 30 months ahead and look hardest 12 to 18 months ahead. If we knew for a fact, with perfect 20/20 vision, the world would end on December 31, 2020, stocks wouldn't start pricing it until about 2018 at the earliest. That's the market's version of 20/20 vision. Further out than about 30 months is to the market a blur not to be believed. It simply disbelieves.

Think of this chapter and the next as a primer on how to read your newspaper, peruse the Internet or watch CNBC, starting with how to know real news from short-term noise.

How to slay vampires and battle the four horsemen of the media apocalypse. Or to put it less fancifully:

- How to tell what's short-term noise and what's something stocks might actually care about
- How to battle media hype with simple logic
- How to tell when headlines are crying "wolf!"

The Media's Flawed Financial Eyesight

Ok, maybe that section header is a bit harsh. Journalists aren't blind—they can see near and far! But they are writing for a customer market that isn't capital markets based. They aren't writing for the 1%, that's for sure. They aren't even writing for the 3%. Their eyes naturally drift to what seems important to their pressing reader but isn't important to markets. The too-near and too-far.

Most headlines look at the wrong timeframes. That's where the noise is loudest, and noise sells. Especially bad news! If it bleeds, it leads. Most of the time, it leads investors astray.

Open any financial paper or website, and you'll see: The stories will nearly all fall into two categories. The super-short-term and the ultra-long-term.

On page one, you always get the obligatory story about what stocks did that day (or yesterday, if it's your morning paper). Five hundred words pinning volatility on some event or economic report. Even though 99.9% of it is garbage, hey, it's breaking news. Extra! Extra! Stocks fall on retail sales and Janet Yellen's haircut! It's all useless. Usually, you can't tie the market's daily moves to any one thing, and it's always backward-looking. And no one knows, at all, who was buying or selling that day, much less why. Media simply summarizes what yakkers were yakking about. Besides, what happened to stocks yesterday has no bearing on what they will do over the next year.

You'll also get stories dissecting data releases. Gross domestic product (GDP)! Consumer spending! Retail sales! Unemployment! Inflation! Factory orders! Factory output!

Trade deficit! Jobless claims! Home prices! Bored yet? You should be. It's all yesterday's news, which should be a snooze, but you're still guaranteed to get a few hundred words on why any and all of these (and more!) rose or fell in any month or quarter, and too much speculating on what it means. This includes quotes from analysts and economists telling you why it's all important, anything to be quoted in print. Sometimes you even get a preview story a day or two before, guessing at what the results will be—and then analyzing the implications of that guess. Mindless myopia.

Same goes for big earnings releases. Preview stories predicting big bellwethers' results, then the actual news. Then stories moaning about or cheering over the results and guidance, and all the sell-side firms' analysts updating their buy/sell recommendations. All it takes is one look at a chart of the stock's intraday price movement to see that none of that news is actionable—it's priced within microseconds. But that doesn't stop the town crier.

The Fed is featured regularly, too. Any time a Fed member gives a speech, you get a bunch of media blather guessing at what the comments mean for future rate moves. They whip out their decoder rings and look for hidden messages in vague comments and off-the-cuff remarks, then try to tell you what it all means for rates, and what rates mean for stocks. It's all entirely unknowable. You can't game the Fed! Really, you can't. But pundits never stop trying.

Then there is the event-related chatter. If there is strife or war in any part of the world, and there usually is, stories speculate about the impact on stocks. This goes double if the conflict is in the Middle East—then you get oil, too! Heck, any time oil prices move big, headlines hit it hard, telling you it means something for markets. If oil prices move and stocks don't, they tell you the stock market is broken, not pricing in some big risk. It's all a bunch of malarkey. Markets are markets! All liquid markets are forward-looking and relatively efficient. Don't waste time seeking hidden meaning in the gap between stocks' wiggles, bonds' waggles and commodities' wobbles.

That's just some of the short-term drivel you'll see on any one day—there is loads more. From the ridiculous to the sublime! But there is also the other end of the spectrum: the super-long-term forecasting.

A lot comes from government agencies like the Congressional Budget Office (CBO) or supranationals like the World Bank, International Money Fund (IMF) and Organisation for Economic Co-operation and Development (OECD). You get 30-year potential growth forecasts. Estimates of the long-term consequences of climate change. Or debt. Or income inequality. Shrinking populations in the developed world. Baby Boom bust. Obamacare driving health care spending through the roof and dooming us to decades of despair. Innovation stopping. China taking over the world. You name it.

You get the forecasts and the warnings. Then you get the talking heads arguing over the forecasts. It's all static. All of it! Whether life is amazing or dismal in 50 years has nothing to do with the next 30 months and nothing to do with what the markets do now. And markets don't believe one darned thing about 10, 20 or 50 years from now.

Yet headlines hover over all of these stories and more, which makes normal folks obsess and falsely presume significance. "It must be important if I keep reading about it." If you read a few dozen times that something is critically important for markets or the economy, it's near-impossible not to believe. The repetition is too powerful. This is why you don't need to take a survey or hold elaborate focus groups to figure out what is on most investors' minds. The media performs that service for you almost for free. Again, go to any financial publication's website now. (You can put the book down for a second. It's ok. I'll wait.) My bet is nearly everything they claim will influence the broad market is either myopic or super-long-term. Go to any investor conference, and the Q&A concentrates on whatever has been big in the media or documented in the last month—and hence already priced—or the super-long-term (we're too indebted, society is going to hell, Social Security is bankrupt).

Markets have already dealt with all those short-term issues and couldn't be bothered with the long-term ones. Any number of things could happen between now and then to make those long-term forecasts look downright silly, no matter how wise they might seem now. (More on this in Chapter 4.)

Dracula Around the Corner

One such short-term media obsession is what I call "Dracula around the corner": some big, evil, scary thing with superpowers that promises a future of death and destruction, just lurking there ready to bite. A ticking time bomb about to blow.

Now, don't get me wrong. If Dracula were in your house, that'd be bad. Bloodsucking and all like that. But if he's really there, sooner or later he must show himself. Otherwise, he's just a ghost story. Ghost stories can scare you—and sometimes markets briefly!—but they can't bite you.

Terrorism is one example. Most assume first-world terrorist strikes are automatic negatives, pointing to 9/11. The S&P 500 lost –11.6% the first five trading days after the attacks and finished the year down –13%—"proof" terrorism knocks stocks hard.[1]

Or is it? Always be skeptical of anecdotal "proof." Ask: What else was going on then? In 2001, the answer would be "a raging bear market." That –13% full-year return had far less to do with 9/11 than with the bear market beginning 18 months prior, on March 24, 2000, as the tech bubble burst. Stocks were already down –17.3% year-to-date through September 10, before the planes hit. After the immediate –11.6% drop, the S&P 500 rallied, regaining pre-attack levels 19 trading days after markets re-opened, and rose through year end (a brief bear-market rally before deep fundamental negatives resumed their hold over stocks in 2002).[2]

Stocks have weathered several terrorist attacks since the 1980s. Most saw some volatility in the surrounding days, though to a smaller extent. Each time, the reaction was quick—no terrorist attack ended a bull market. See for yourself in Figures 3.1 through 3.8.

Fundamentals support this as well as history. Terrorism whacks sentiment, but usually only briefly. That hits stocks in the short term, but forward-looking markets soon resume weighing future economic growth, earnings and political factors, which aren't much disrupted by the attacks. The 9/11 attacks occurred six months into a recession, but recovery began in November. The attacks impacted politics via the Patriot Act and Afghanistan War, but they had nothing to do with Sarbanes-Oxley—the chief political negative as markets dove through October 2002.

Figure 3.1 Pan Am Flight 103

Source: FactSet, as of 9/11/2014. MSCI UK Price Index, 12/21/1987–12/21/1989. Shaded period includes the day before the attack and the following 10 trading sessions.

Figure 3.2 First World Trade Center Bombing

Source: FactSet, as of 9/11/2014. S&P 500 Price Index, 2/26/1992–2/25/1994. Shaded period includes the day before the attack and the following 10 trading sessions.

Figure 3.3 Tokyo Sarin Gas Attacks

Source: FactSet, as of 9/11/2014. MSCI Japan Price Index, 3/21/1994–3/20/1996. Shaded period includes the day before the attack and the following 10 trading sessions.

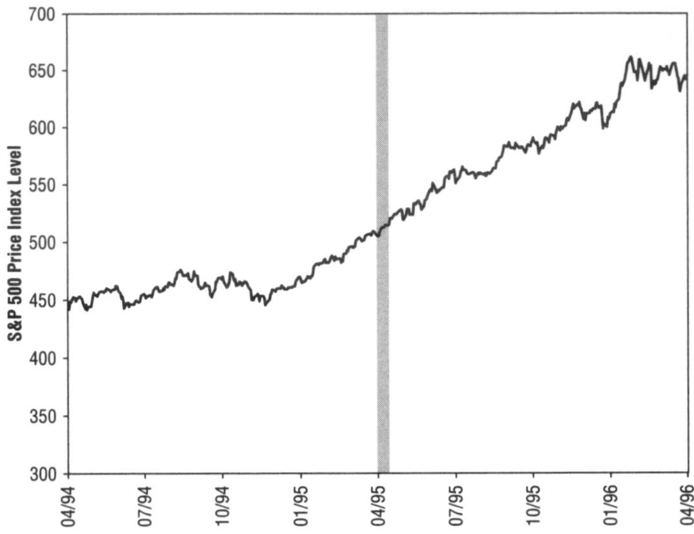

Figure 3.4 Oklahoma City Bombing

Source: FactSet, as of 9/11/2014. S&P 500 Price Index, 4/19/1994–4/19/1996. Shaded period includes the day before the attack and the following 10 trading sessions.

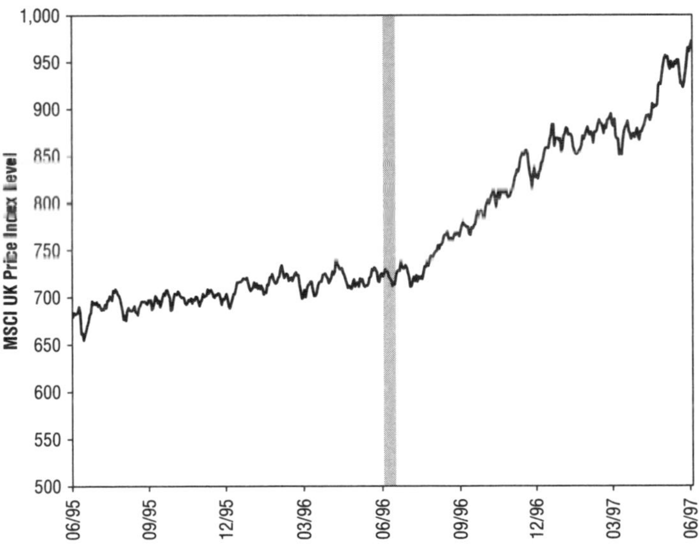

Figure 3.5 IRA Attacks on Manchester

Source: FactSet, as of 9/11/2014. MSCI UK Price Index, 6/15/1995–6/13/1997. Shaded period includes the day before the attack and the following 10 trading sessions.

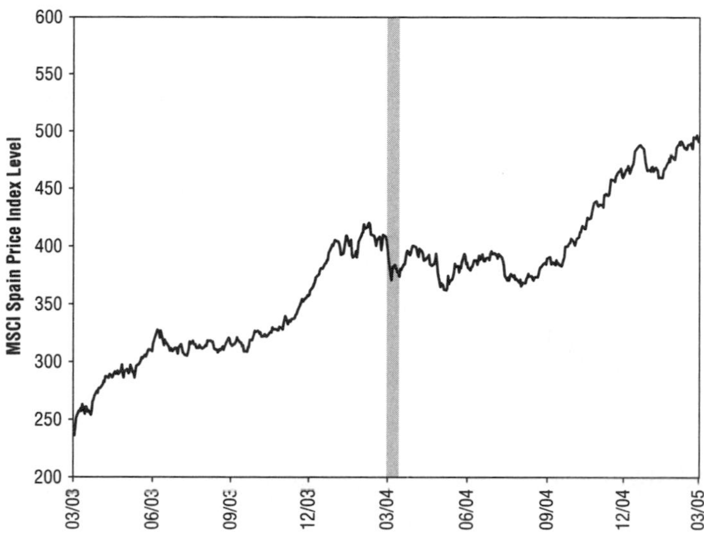

Figure 3.6 Madrid Train Bombings

Source: FactSet, as of 9/11/2014. MSCI Spain Price Index, 3/11/2003–3/11/2005. Shaded period includes the day before the attack and the following 10 trading sessions.

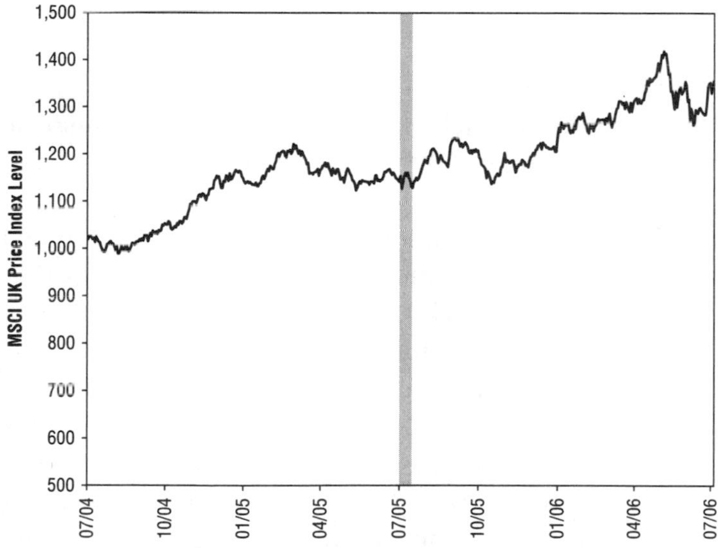

Figure 3.7 London 7/7 Transport Bombings

Source: FactSet, as of 9/11/2014. MSCI UK Price Index, 7/7/2004–7/7/2006. Shaded period includes the day before the attack and the following 10 trading sessions.

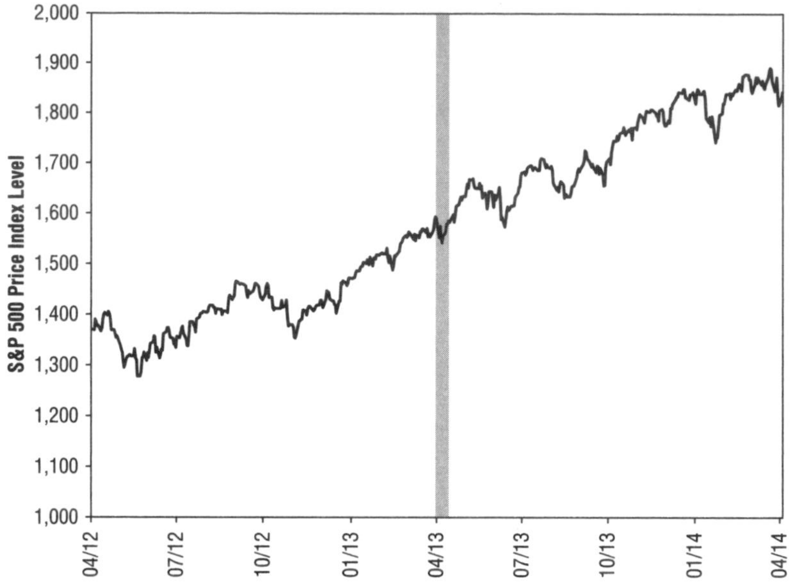

Figure 3.8 Boston Marathon Bombing

Source: FactSet, as of 9/11/2014. S&P 500 Price Index, 4/13/2012–4/15/2014. Shaded period includes the day before the attack and the following 10 trading sessions.

Investors don't quickly forget attacks. On a human level, they're always with us. But as time passes, folks realize the economic impact is small. They see growth continuing, companies profiting and their country's spirit too strong to be broken by evil. These realizations give stocks relief from the jolt they received in the attack's immediate aftermath.

Terrorism is just one Dracula. War is another, as we'll see in these pages. But perhaps the biggest, oldest vampire tale of all is pandemic pandemonium. Every few years, some big flu scare comes along, and headlines warn that millions of people could die, taking the economy and stocks to the grave with them. In 2009, it was swine flu: Innocent Mexican piggies were going to infect humanity with the virus to end all viruses, killing huge chunks of the global population. In 2005 and 2006 it was avian bird flu (which is, of course, redundant and double-stated in the scare for emphasis). Chinese chickens destroying the world. In 2003 it was SARS, severe acute respiratory syndrome, again from China. As I write, folks fret an Ebola outbreak in Africa will infect America and markets. Dracula is back!

Don't fall for any of this. For one, none of these ever resulted in more than a few hundred or thousand deaths—tragic, but too small for cold-hearted markets to care about at all. Two, during the one modern pandemic that did pack a punch—1918's Spanish flu, which infected about a third of the world's population and killed roughly 100 million—stocks rose nicely, amazing and hard for most to believe as that is! But markets really are hard-hearted and cruel and don't care about human suffering—only wealth. There is zero evidence disease and pestilence are market risks. Zero! The fear can cause volatility in the short term—bird flu fright caused a correction in 2005—but in that magic 12- to 18-month range, it's a false factor.

These are ghost stories. When you're a kid, and you hear a ghost story around the campfire, you get scared. You think it's real. You can't sleep. But then you realize it isn't real! It's a myth! It's ok to relax! It can't get you! Vampires and monsters aren't real! Same thing can be said about markets. When the media tells you Dracula's there and he's real and about to kill you, that's scary, and that fear impacts markets. Stocks can behave pretty darned irrationally over short periods. But it doesn't last. Investors realize whatever they feared wasn't real, markets bounce back, and life goes on.

As long we have markets and media, we'll have Dracula. He'll never go away. But now you know better—no need to run for cover! Or arm yourself with a stake and holy water! Dracula isn't ever real. You can wait it out and game it, knowing that false fear will flip and markets will be a-ok.

Looking for Growth in All the Wrong Places

What's another misguided media obsession? Economic data. It's an easy story to write—growth good, drop bad, add 600 words and call it a day. Every darned time a report comes out, headlines react, assuming it means something and has magical predictive powers.

Normal economic expansions have normal but meaningless volatility within them. The masses often debate whether a certain statistic is good or bad, whether a dip is a blip or a trend, but it isn't about which side is right and which is wrong. The debate is entirely noise. Static. Meaningless noise. You can just tune it all out.

One of contrarians' biggest strengths—and advantages—is their ability to filter out the noise and keep things simple. Simplicity is power. One, it's usually right. Two, it keeps you sane. Getting hung up on any and every economic data release will drive you crazy—and get you nowhere. Fast. Even—and especially—GDP.

GDP is supposedly the mother of all economic data—the big report folks spend months trying to guess at, the one that adds up all the small data releases throughout the quarter and finally brings them meaning. But GDP is a look back at that which has already been priced—a rough tally of everything that happened over a three-month window that closed a month (or more) ago. It isn't a terrible tally, but it also isn't the economy! It isn't stocks. You don't buy a share in GDP. You buy a share in publicly traded companies' growth and earnings (or lack thereof).

GDP captures some of this through business investment and to an extent government and consumer spending, which can result in revenues. But it misses tons. It counts imports as a negative, even though imports reflect demand and help keep businesses' costs low. If imports tanked, you can bet Wal-Mart would be in bad, bad shape. But GDP might look great! GDP also counts government spending as an economic positive, which even the strictest Keynesian would agree isn't exactly correct. It could also represent places where government agencies are crowding out private businesses. There, too, it counts bad as good.

Maybe you think none of that matters—a rough snapshot is better than no snapshot so we may as well use it. Fair enough. But even then, GDP is useless to you as an investor. It's past-tense. Markets don't care about the past. GDP simply aggregates things stocks have already anticipated, lived through and priced in. In July 2011, for example, headlines were atwitter over revisions to the depth of the 2007–2009 recession, which was very meaningful in 2007–2009, but less than worthless for investors two years after growth returned. Stocks look forward, not backward. Last quarter's output doesn't tell you where the economy will go.

Most media does the same with every other data release, big or small. The reports are all the same—random numbers that vary hugely from month to month. They come out every darned month or quarter, telling you what happened in a narrow past space over some short period that has already been priced by markets. Industrial production, retail sales, consumer spending, manufacturing output, exports, imports—all snapshots of past activity. None are leading indicators; none carry magical, hidden insight. Recessions don't start because auto sales are down.

Yet because we're bombarded with stories claiming these things are significant, many investors can't stop overthinking them. The noise never stops. Everyone searches for meaning in these silly stats, and the media provides plenty of fuel. Like kids with cereal box treasure maps and decoder rings, they look for hidden meaning in every release, not realizing it's all just backward-looking noise. "U.S. industrial production rose in March, moving beyond a lackluster winter and showing potential to gain strength in the coming months."[3] "Retail sales barely rose in April, tempering hopes of a sharp acceleration in economic growth in the second quarter."[4] "The [consumer spending] report added to data ranging from employment to industrial production in suggesting there was momentum in the economy at the tail end of a very difficult first quarter, which provides a springboard for faster growth in the April–June period."[5] "Exports hit one of their highest levels ever in March, but the trade deficit didn't shrink as much as expected, leading economists to predict that first-quarter GDP will be revised down."[6] All pre-priced.

That last one should be on someone's top-10 list of the most bizarre interpretations of an economic release. The quote comes from *The Wall Street Journal*, but they weren't the only ones saying it; most mainstream outlets warned the wider-than-expected trade deficit in March 2014 would cause Q1 GDP to get revised from low growth to a small drop (it eventually did, but that isn't the point). They fussed over a statistic—the trade deficit—that says zilch about an economy's health, and they were worried it would make already-old GDP numbers look uglier. Who cares? It doesn't matter! All that mattered was both exports and imports went up in the month, which means demand was great at home and abroad. Good, not bad, but none of it forward-looking. You can read it, say "That's nice, pre-priced," and move on.

The Magic Indicator

You don't need to parse dozens of narrow stats to see which way the world is going. Overthinking is an unnecessary headache. I hate overthinking. You should too. Pointless. There is a simple, quick way to see if economies are heading up or down over a meaningful timeframe—the next several months out.

What is it? The Leading Economic Index, better known as LEI. It's simple and usually magical.

The LEI is old, born in the post–Great Depression United States, when economic stats and national accounts became all the rage. Everyone knew, intuitively, that the country had been through hell, but it was all qualitative. Arthur Burns and Wesley C. Mitchell, economists at the National Bureau of Economic Research (NBER), had a hunch that if they could aggregate the many stats in NBER's treasure trove of historical time series, they could measure how much the country had shrunk—and find patterns through history to help predict the next downturn. What they found, of course, was the business cycle.

In their analysis, which was later picked up by another NBER economist, Geoffrey H. Moore, they identified which variables moved ahead of the pack, which moved coincidentally and which lagged. Moore packaged these into leading, coincident and lagging business cycle indicators, and they debuted in 1950, exactly midway through the last century. Thus, LEI—a composite of a handful of the most forward-looking economic variables—was born. Coincidentally, just when I was. A long time ago by human standards. NBER administered LEI at first, but the US Census Bureau took over in 1961. The Commerce Department's Bureau of Economic Analysis picked it up in 1972, and The Conference Board adopted it in 1995. The Conference Board still administers it today, along with LEIs for 11 other major countries and the eurozone.

Today's LEI doesn't much resemble the original. The components changed over time as data and understanding improved and the United States evolved. The original series reflects 1940s understanding and a 1940s United States. It included liabilities of business failures, the Dow Jones Industrial Average, durable goods orders, residential and commercial/industrial building contracts, the average manufacturing workweek, new incorporations, and wholesale commodity prices. Exactly what you'd expect in a postwar, manufacturing-heavy economy.

Over the next 30 years, the broader, more structurally correct, capitalization-weighted Standard & Poor's (S&P) 500 replaced the narrow, industry-heavy, price-weighted Dow. Construction permits replaced building contracts. Industrial metals prices replaced broader commodity prices. Then prices fell out entirely, along with business incorporations and failures—these weren't predictive. Supplier delivery times went in, then got replaced by factory orders—more forward-looking. M2 money supply and the 10-year US Treasury yield appeared for a while, as Milton Friedman's influence spread, and in 1996 The Conference Board added the interest rate spread (10-year minus federal-funds rate)—the most meaningful, forward-looking thing you can look at. More than 100 years of economic theory and evidence show that a wide interest rate spread is growthy and marvelous for stocks. We've known this since God created little green apples. Economists had argued for its inclusion in LEI since the early 1980s. It just took a while to get there (as tends to happen when bureaucratic government agencies administer anything).

The last major change occurred in 2011, when The Conference Board added its Leading Credit Index—a snapshot of credit availability. The current series has 10 variables (Table 3.1), and The Conference Board has computed it back all the way to 1959. As you'll see in Figure 3.9, it's a wonderfully accurate read of the economy's future direction. Not its short-term wibbles and wobbles—the broader, longer-term trend. LEI trends usually precede reality by several months. No recession in the last 55 years has occurred during a rising LEI trend—they all started after LEI had fallen for some time.

To see which direction the world is headed, just look at the big-country LEIs. America, Britain, China, Japan, eurozone. Simple! No overthinking required!

Table 3.1 LEI Components

Components of the Leading Economic Index
1. Average weekly manufacturing work hours
2. Average weekly initial jobless claims
3. Manufacturers' new orders for consumer goods and materials
4. Manufacturers' new orders for nondefense capital goods ex-aircraft
5. ISM New Orders Index (manufacturing)
6. Building permits for new private housing units
7. S&P 500 Index (monthly average closing price)
8. Leading Credit Index (The Conference Board's proprietary gauge of credit conditions)
9. Interest rate spread (10-year US Treasury minus fed-funds rate)
10. Average consumer expectations for business conditions (from University of Michigan and Conference Board surveys)

Source: The Conference Board.

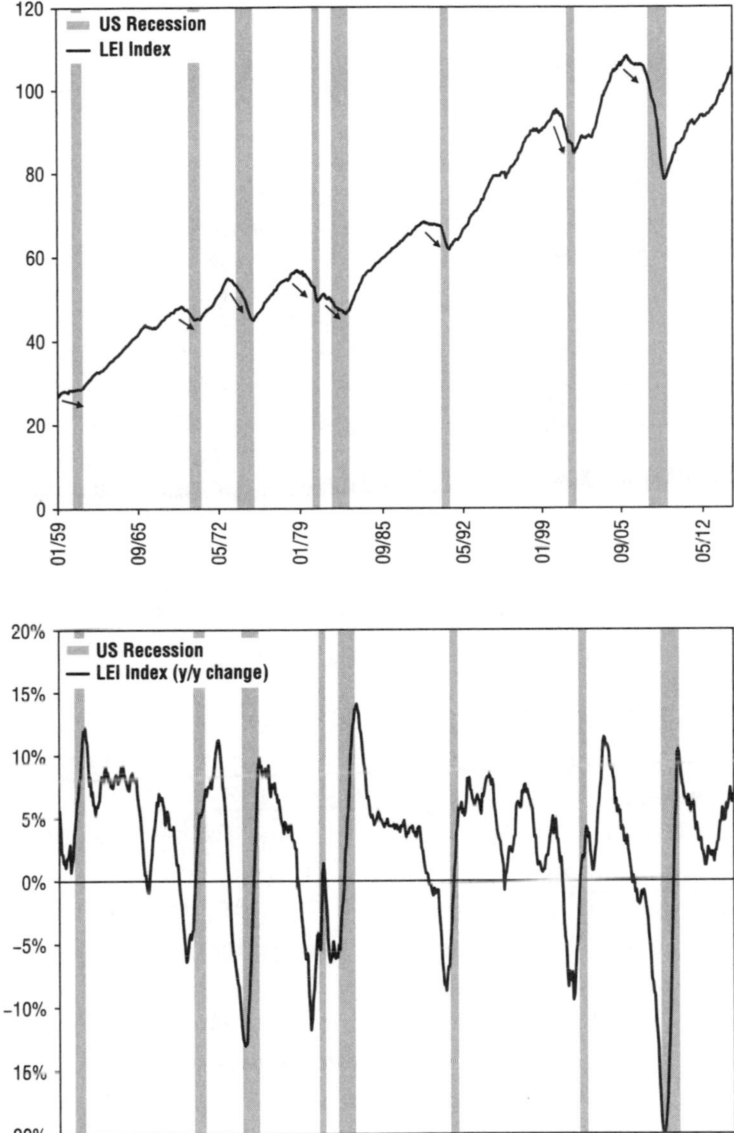

Figure 3.9 LEI and Recessions

Source: The Conference Board and National Bureau of Economic Research (NBER), as of 12/9/2014. The Conference Board Leading Economic Index, January 1959–October 2014. Shaded areas indicate recessions as dated by NBER.

If you look at these graphs and wonder how could everyone miss that big LEI drop pre-2008, you aren't alone! The answer, quite simply, is LEI didn't look like that in 2008. That drop is the 2011 series, backdated. The old series didn't fall through the floor. It was largely flat in 2006 and 2007, falling only incrementally as 2007 ended—one reason for the decision to revise the components. The Conference Board realized LEI didn't work great before a recession preceded by squeezed credit, hence the creation of the Leading Credit Index. You can see all this for yourself in a paper on The Conference Board's website, "Comprehensive Benchmark Revisions for The Conference Board Leading Economic Index for the United States." There, the authors observe: "Of note, the lead of the new LEI during the last cyclical peak was 21 months, much earlier than the five-month lead of the current LEI. However, an above-average lead in retrospect is in line with the experience of the economy heading into the recession. The new LEI declined much more sharply during the last recession, falling about 20% from peak to trough compared to a 7% peak-to-trough fall for the current LEI."[7]

Just look at recent trends, don't get caught up in any one month, and you'll be fine. Often, usually, just seeing America's is enough.

LEI works. Yet few look at it—not flashy enough, perhaps not complicated enough. But good enough. The best in simplest form. Perhaps it's that journalists would rather cover the splashier, individual data points that make up the whole. By the time the aggregation is done, the others have already had their myopic moment in the sun. Few news outlets even cover it. LEI's guardian, The Conference Board, issues a press release on every update, and occasionally it gets reposted on some of the news aggregators. But it rarely hits the A-block on *The Wall Street Journal* or *Bloomberg*. Talking heads don't dissect it on CNBC. Few even realize there are LEIs for all major countries. LEI's power lies partly in their ignorance—it isn't widely discussed so its conclusions frequently aren't fully discounted. If folks broadly expect the economy to dip, dive or stagnate based on their reading of past data, and LEI still points up, that's something you can work with.

Most of LEI's power comes from its components. No one stat perfectly captures the entire economy. But by gathering 10 variables, LEI casts a pretty wide net—not perfect, but better than otherwise. It gives a broad snapshot of future manufacturing conditions, consumer spending, construction and credit, and it includes the two most powerful leading indicators—stock prices and the yield curve spread.

Because LEI includes stock prices, it isn't a direct market forecasting tool. Stocks don't predict stocks. The LEI doesn't predict stocks because its components, too, are pre-priced. But it takes worries about the economy's direction off the table. As Forrest Gump told you, "one less thing."

LEI can be noisy. That's just normal—some of its components are pretty volatile. Manufacturing orders, building permits, manufacturing hours and the employment variables drop often and irregularly during an expansion, usually without strong discernible trends. Consumer expectations are less variable, but they aren't terribly forward-looking. Consumer confidence surveys reflect people's feelings about the present and recent past, making them a coincident indicator at best. Stocks are the ultimate leading indicator, though sentiment-driven pullbacks can make that component noisy, too.

But the Leading Credit Index and interest rate spread are consistent and forward-looking. Their trends are long, and turning points typically occur before a recession begins. This shouldn't surprise anyone. There is a world of evidence showing that a negative rate spread—or inverted yield curve—is a strong indication of future recession, and deteriorating credit conditions often presage a fall in investment. When the other components wobble, it's a fair bet you can look past them and make your judgment based on the Leading Credit Index and yield spread.

Looking at LEI is a great way to see whether most investors' economic expectations are right or wrong—whether heeding media's warnings of recession will lead you astray. Back in early 2010, everyone feared a double-dipping US economy. Several indicators had slowed or dropped, and many were sure a recession relapse was nigh—the economy hadn't achieved "escape velocity," so gravity must naturally take hold.

Economies aren't spaceships. If the pundits predict something based on liftoff, escape velocity, momentum or gravity, you can discount it. Laws of physics don't apply to markets—only the laws of supply and demand. So when headlines fret about economies losing steam, just look at LEI—LEI is all about supply and demand!

The whole time double-dip fears reigned supreme, LEI headed up. Look back to Figure 3.9. LEI believers were rewarded. LEI ignorers who fled stocks because they overthought a few teetering backward-looking data points missed world stocks' 11.8% gain in 2010.

LEI works internationally, too. Each country's LEI components are different—no two economies are exactly alike, so no two countries' leading indicators are twins. China has a command economy where the government dictates credit growth, so China's LEI doesn't include the yield curve spread; it wouldn't make sense. Credit conditions are harder to pin down in India, so India's LEI uses M3 money supply growth instead of a Leading Credit Index. But the many decades of lessons and analysis that underpin the US LEI inform the foreign LEIs, too.

Look at the eurozone. After the region exited an 18-month recession in June 2013, growth was anemic and everyone feared a "weak recovery"—just an iteration of those old US double-dip fears. There, too, many monthly indicators reeled. The herd dreaded a relapse. No one noticed LEI had almost perfectly predicted the past year's economic directions. It started rising months before the recession ended—normal.

Then it dipped a bit, a few months before GDP slightly slowed in the recovery's second quarter. After that, it went on a tear, suggesting growth was accelerating. LEI was right! No one noticed.

Same thing in France. In late 2013, everyone said France was the "sick man" of Europe. Europe always has a "sick man"—one of the continent's quirks. No one would ever say Michigan is the "sick man" of America. But Europe is just funny like that—they've had "sick men" since the Ottoman Empire. (Which included Greece—another recent "sick man"!)

The French "sick man" claims came from a few lousy Purchasing Managers Index (PMI) readings in Q4 2013. Media loves PMIs. They come out early and claim to give you a near-instantaneous read on whether a country or sector grew in a given month. Any reading above 50 is considered growth, anything below 50 a contraction.

PMIs are somewhat useful at best, but they aren't amazingly accurate. They're surveys—never the most reliable. Read Darrell Huff's classic, *How to Lie With Statistics* (WW Norton, 1954; pap. 1993), to fathom the unreliability of surveys. (More in Chapter 8.) PMIs also measure, specifically, the number of firms reporting an increase in overall activity, demand, employment and other categories during that month. But they don't give you the magnitude of that growth. In real life, if only a minority of firms grow, but they grow at a fast rate, they can tip the whole country into growth.

So look past headline PMI results and focus on the key components, like new orders, export orders and order backlogs. If these are over 50, that means demand is probably growing—and today's orders and backlogs become tomorrow's production. And then look at LEI! Even while France was supposedly the sick man, its LEI was rising. Not what you get if France is really sick. There, too, LEI was right. France grew. Not so sick!

In all these examples, LEI would have given anyone a very simple, quick way to see whether warnings would be right. It's easy to find—just go to The Conference Board's website. The splash page shows every single one. You can go look it up now at www.conference-board.org/data/bci.cfm. Do it, and you'll be one of the few who use the power of the magic indicator. There are other producers of "LEIs," but only The Conference Board's are reliable. They are the gold standard.

High-Frequency Trading

Sometimes, folks fret about things having zilch to do with the market outlook. Like high-frequency trading, or HFT—a hot topic ever since the infamous Flash Crash in May 2010.

HFT, at its simplest, refers to computers using algorithms and superfast data connections to trade at light speed—they execute transactions in microseconds. They'll move in and out of a stock in the blink of an eye, with the goal of making maybe half a cent per share. But they do this thousands of times per day, racking up good-sized profits.

Those profits—billions a year across the entire HFT industry—have driven accusations of HFTers skimming off the top. The rap goes something like this: Either by locating in (or close to) an exchange's matching engine or by paying for a nonpublic feed of order flow, between the time you hit "buy" on your computer screen and the "transaction complete" page loads, a computer can see your order, buy the stock and sell it to you at a penny or so (or less!) higher. You see nothing—you get the stock just about where the ticker said it was trading—but the HFT computer makes a few cents. Cents that could, should have been yours!

That's one side. The other side says HFT has put the old human market makers out of business and boosted liquidity, narrowing bid/ask spreads to pennies or less and making trading cheaper and easier for all of us. The half a cent or so the HFTers make per share is just the fee we pay for that service—way smaller than the implicit fees we used to pay through wider spreads.

By now, it's probably pretty clear to you this issue has nothing to do with where stocks go. It has to do with how markets function. Interesting! Related to investing! But not anything that would impact whether a bull becomes a bear. Hyperbolic claims of a rigged market are just noise—it's fine to have an opinion! But you don't need to get caught up in the debate over market impact.

There is another segment of HFT haters who claim the practice does move markets. Because the computers are running thousands of algorithms simultaneously, with all manner of price moves, economic news and earnings reports triggering automatic trades, some argue HFT magnifies volatility, making markets unstable and triggering events like the Flash Crash.

But this, too, is noise! One, there is no evidence the theory is right. Markets are less volatile today, not more—we had enormous intraday moves in the 1930s (and so many more of them!), before anyone dreamed of HFT. Two, even if it were true, it doesn't matter. The dips are so, so short-term—we're talking minutes, not months. Plus, if you accept that algorithms can trigger a cascade of sales, you must also accept that at some point, "buy" algorithms kick in, bidding the market back up where it was. No net loss unless you sold out at the wrong time. Even a Flash Crash–sized move has no bearing on stocks' long-term returns. Or yours, if you stay cool.

War—What Is It Good For?

Absolutely nothin' . . . except stocks! Ok, that's beyond a tad oversimplified. Bullets aren't bullish. But there is no—zero—evidence showing a regional conflict ends bull markets. Even if the United States is involved. You often get some volatility in the run-up to a conflict as fear hits the market—normal—but it fades fast. Sometimes the conflict defuses. Other times bullets fly but investors quickly realize it doesn't have much scope—terrible as war is for those directly involved, market life just goes on as normal for the rest of the world. Business doesn't stop, trade doesn't stop. This realization is a relief for stocks.

Many investors can't get past this—and here, too, the media bears much of the responsibility. With every geopolitical skirmish and potential armed conflict, no matter how far-flung or small, headlines warn of the toll it will take on stocks and the economy. If it's in the Middle East, you get the oil-stocks double threat.

It's easy to see these stories and freak out. War is hell, after all. But freaking out of stocks is rarely profitable. You must stay cool and think rationally! To do this, use two tools: history and scale. History shows no regional conflict has ever caused a bear market. Usually, conflict is simply too fleeting and centered in too small a section of the global economy to take a big bite out of commerce and profits. Ukraine and Iraq were 2014's hot spots—0.2% and 0.3% of world GDP, respectively.[8] In 2013 it was Syria—0.1%.[9] In 2012 it was Egypt—0.4%.[10] Tiny fractions of global output and trade. Unless the conflict turns to World War III, it probably isn't a market risk.

Rarely will the media look at history, which makes history a powerful tool. I mentioned earlier that when the media makes sweeping claims, you should demand supporting evidence—and then go look for it yourself. Usually, market history is a great way to do this! Even if you don't have a fancy stock market database, you can find old S&P 500 returns pretty easily. Yahoo! Finance has daily S&P 500 Price Index returns back to 1950—publicly available and free for your use. Whenever the media says such and such is horrible for markets, think of times when such and such happened before, and look up what markets did then. History never repeats perfectly! But as Mark Twain said, it sure as heck rhymes, and it is a marvelous way to determine the probability of a certain event impacting markets. Often what's convention and the media says happens simply never does.

So let's be contrarian and look at history! Pick a skirmish—any skirmish—and you'll see it didn't whack stocks. Even in the Middle East! Folks always fear Middle East conflict—they think it's the world's powder keg. Or where all the oil is. Or a hair's breadth away from a nuclear strike. Or, or, or . . . But conflict has raged on and off there since pretty much always. It has been near-constant since the dawn of modern markets. Never has the conflagration gone global or been anywhere near major enough to put global commerce at risk. Markets are just used to it—it's part of the background, with us in bull and bear markets alike. Not once has a Middle Eastern conflict caused a cyclical turning point.

Don't believe me? Look at Figure 3.10, which shows the S&P 500 during four big Middle Eastern conflicts. None derailed a bull market. Some saw stocks wobble as the initial uncertainty drove fear, but markets resumed rising well before the conflicts ended.

Anti-herd contrarians might think, "Sell the fear, buy the bullets," but short-term timing is a fool's errand. There's no guarantee fear triggers a drop. It didn't when folks feared America would bomb Syria in 2013 or when Russia invaded Ukraine in March 2014. Re-entry is also difficult to time. Sometimes markets rise when shots are first fired, sometimes weeks later. Even if you do time it well, transaction costs and taxes might offset your savings. More often than not, you're best off waiting it out.

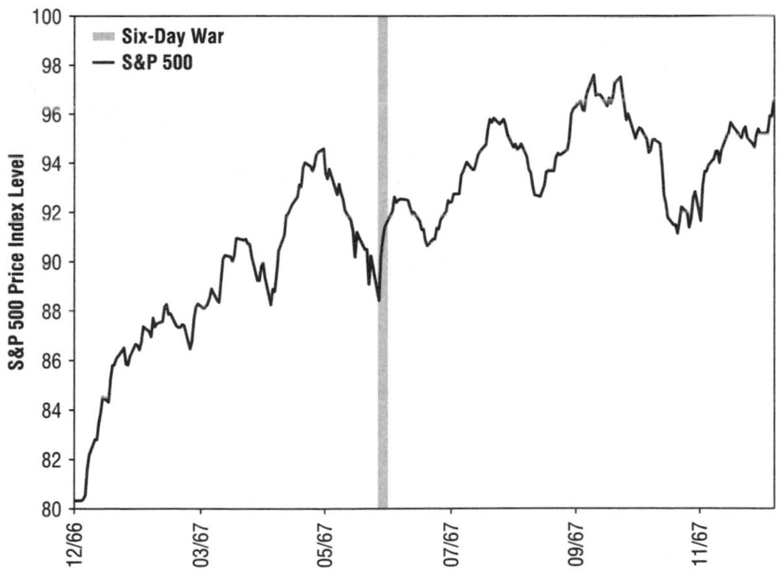

Figure 3.10 Middle Eastern Conflicts and Stocks

Source: FactSet, as of 7/15/2014. S&P 500 Price Index, 12/30/1966–12/29/2006.

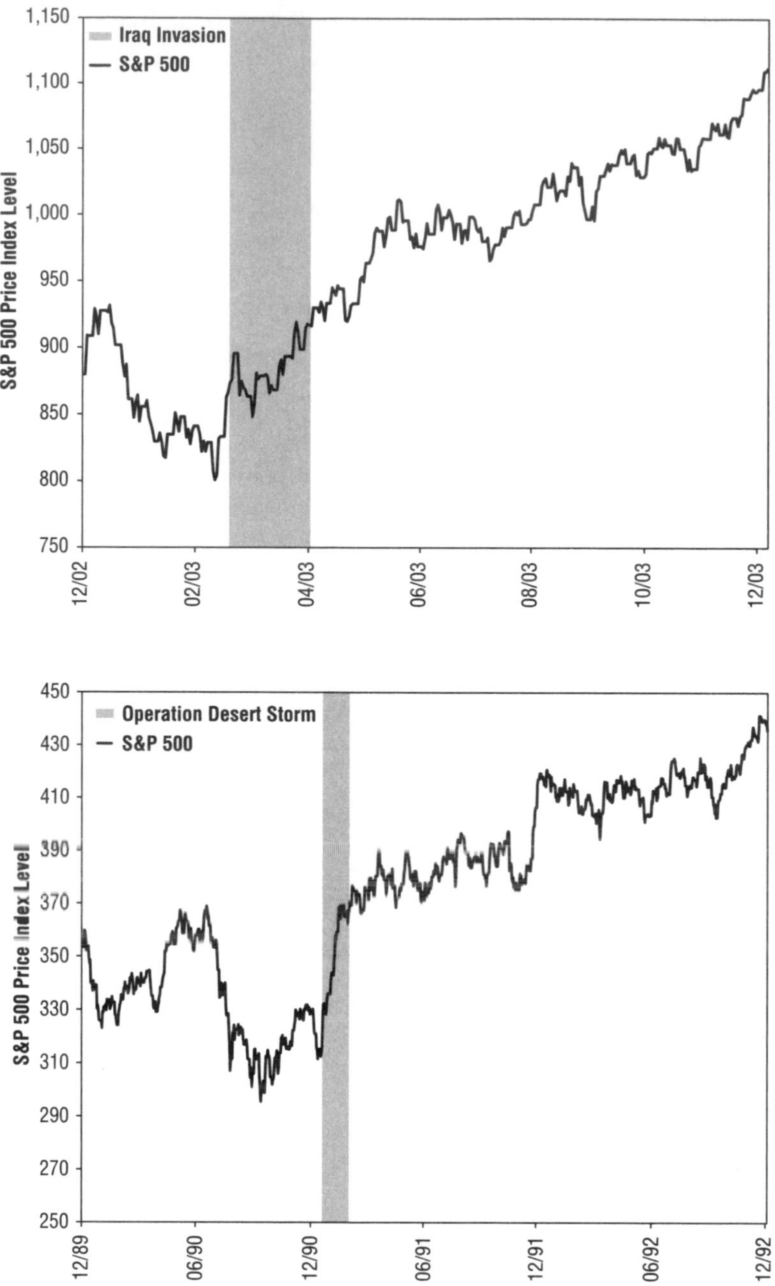

Figure 3.10 (*continued*)

Figure 3.10 (*continued*)

Those are just four examples. Here are more! The S&P 500 suffered a quick correction at the dawn of the Korean War, losing 14% between June 12, 1950—about two weeks before the war's official start—and July 17, 1950.[11] But stocks were back in the black by September 22. Over the entire conflict, from June 25, 1950, through July 27, 1953, the S&P rose 25.8%.[12]

The S&P 500 fell in the run-up to the Cuban Missile Crisis in 1962 but bottomed on October 23, the day after President Kennedy's television address informing the nation of the naval blockade. Stocks *rose* on October 24, the day Soviet ships neared the blockade as Soviet Premier Khrushchev called the move an "act of aggression." By the time the Soviet ships turned around on November 5, the S&P had gained 9.1% since the low.[13] The nascent bull carried on another three-plus years.

Stocks were choppy in the run-up to the US's involvement in the Bosnian War in 1994, but the S&P 500 bottomed shortly after the NATO airstrikes on Croatia began—and gained

36% by the war's end on December 20, 1995.[14] Another example? The years 1973–1974, which contained a bear market. Folks are convinced the Yom Kippur War, which began in October 1973, was the trigger. But the bear began January 11, 1973. Not in October. Not even close. The Organization of Petroleum Exporting Countries (OPEC) embargo was from October 16, 1973, to March 16, 1974. So even if you lump in this protectionist measure as a reaction to US support of Israel, it's hard to see how those dates match up with a bear market that ran from January 11, 1973, to October 3, 1974.

Only once in history—once!—can conflict be identified as the proximate cause of a bear market. In 1938, Hitler's invasion of the Sudetenland made his territorial ambitions abundantly clear, forcing the world to start pricing in the likelihood of massive, destructive global conflict—World War II. This truncated a young bull market (more on this in Chapter 5). Even then, stocks didn't sink right away. They lulled along sideways until May 1940, when markets got a shocker: France fell. The S&P 500 Price Index lost nearly 25% in the first three weeks of May as Germany made a farce of the Maginot Line, forcing stocks to price in a much deeper, longer, more destructive European conflict.[15] Among others, historian Niall Ferguson claims in his book *The Ascent of Money* (Penguin Press, 2008) that World War I had a similarly crushing impact on stocks. Which is possible or even probable, but the data from this time period are very shaky and unreliable (more on this, too, in Chapter 5). Either way, it would merely emphasize the point: World wars matter; regional ones don't.

It takes a huge war, with major powers facing off against each other across a global theater, for capital markets to suffer heavy enough losses to cause a bear market. When you know that, determining whether a conflict can sink stocks is easy. Just ask yourself: How likely is it that this becomes World War III? It will always be possible—anything is possible always! But possible isn't probable. Only if you have a mountain of evidence suggesting a skirmish will become a global eruption should you act.

Conflict will always be with us. As I type this section, news has just broken that a civilian aircraft carrying 298 passengers and crew members—including US citizens—from Amsterdam to Kuala Lumpur was shot down over a conflict zone in Eastern Ukraine. A terrible, tragic loss of life! An international incident! Headlines are already saying it will sink stocks. But I remember history. I remember when Korean Air flight 007 was shot down by Soviets in 1983, and everyone was sure the Cold War would turn hot. It didn't, and the nascent bull market continued.

Don't Be a Cow, Be a Contrarian

Everything we've covered in this chapter has something in common besides myopia: They're all cud. Issues investors chew and rechew, sometimes for years.

Think about what cud is: a mass of semidegraded food a cow regurgitates and then chews over and over for comfort. It has little nutritional value. It can't do much of anything for them. They mostly just cud it for fun—like gum for cows, only they don't blow bubbles.

News cud is the same. It doesn't drive stock returns. Stewing over it doesn't help investors make better decisions. Folks chew and rechew it because the media hypes it—bad news sells!—but it has no nutritional value for investors. Markets are too efficient! Again, if something is widely known, it's either wrong or powerless to move stocks. The longer a fear circulates—the more cud-like it becomes—the more you can know for sure it is already priced in.

Investors chewed a lot of cud during the bull market that began in March 2009. China is a prime example. From 2010 on, folks feared China's slowing growth would snowball into a hard landing, taking down the world economy and stocks globally. Every slowing PMI, every drop in trade, every slowdown in retail sales or industrial production caused crash fears. Each year, when full-year GDP grew fine, pundits said "Yeah, but next year the bottom will fall out." If they were wrong about one hyped hard-landing trigger, they just moved on to another—fearing the same outcome, just with a different cause. For a while they feared a property bubble would spell doom. That was wrong, so they moved to collapsing manufacturing. That was wrong, so they moved to the banking system. That was wrong, so they moved back to property markets.

China slowed all the while—they were right about that!—but the hard landing still isn't here. China hasn't tanked the world economy, and global stocks fared fine. Markets don't mind a slower-growing China! But the cud-chewing continues.

The eurozone debt crisis was terrible for many but was also big-time cud. Headlines started chewing in late 2009, when Greece started wobbling. For all of 2010 and 2011, folks feared Greece, then Ireland, then Portugal, then Italy and Spain would default, splinter the euro and send the world into chaos. When Greece actually did default in February 2012, fears were so baked in, markets didn't blink. When Greece defaulted a second time late that year, almost no one noticed! Meanwhile, euro collapse fears morphed to fears the bloc's recession would go deeper and global. When that didn't happen and the eurozone started recovering mid-2013, slow-growth fears took over. In 2014, fear flipped to a "lost decade" of deflation and shrinking nominal GDP.

The specific fears morphed for five years, but the underlying issue didn't. Whether folks feared a collapsing currency, deepening recession, sluggish growth or deflation doompocalypse, they really feared Continental Europe would be a black hole in the world economy. They've chewed on this for five-plus years, and stocks overall rose the whole time. Have the cud chewers been right about some things? Sure! They were right about Greece! They were right about recession! Right about just enough to drive confirmation bias. But their deeper fears were already priced in, so these small negatives didn't knock stocks.

You should see all this cud for what it is: priced-in pointlessness. Even if you think the crowd is right about whatever bad thing will happen, efficient markets have probably already discounted that outcome. This is why an 18-month recession in Continental Europe couldn't sink stocks globally. And as we'll see in Chapter 6, it's why stocks barely blinked at the Affordable Care Act.

But we aren't ready to talk politics yet. We're still just getting to know each other! And we haven't even covered cud-like far-future fears that hoodwink investors! Time to turn to Chapter 4, the second part of our financial media user's manual.

Notes

1. FactSet, as of 11/31/2014. S&P 500 Price Index, 8/31/2001–9/30/2011.
2. FactSet, as of 11/30/2014. S&P 500 Price Index, 12/31/1999–12/31/2002.
3. "US Industrial Production Rises in March," Sarah Portlock, *The Wall Street Journal*, 4/16/2014. http://online.wsj.com/news/articles/SB10001424052702303626804579505150315991462 (accessed 5/14/2014).
4. "US Retail Sales Rise Slightly, Far Below Expectations," Staff writers, *Reuters*, 5/13/2014. www.nytimes.com/2014/05/14/business/us-retail-sales-rise-slightly-far-below-expectations.html (accessed 5/14/2014).
5. "US Consumer Spending Surges, Boosts Growth Outlook," Staff writers, *Reuters*, 5/5/2014. www.hawaiireporter.com/us-consumer-spending-surges-boosts-growth-outlook/123 (accessed 5/14/2014).
6. "Trade Data Indicate Economy Contracted," Ben Leubsdorf, *The Wall Street Journal*, 5/6/2014. http://online.wsj.com/news/articles/SB10001424052702304101504579545522484566420 (accessed 5/14/2014).
7. "Comprehensive Benchmark Revisions for The Conference Board Leading Economic Index for the United States," Gad Levanon, Atamam Ozyildirim, Brian Schaitkin and Justyna Zabinska, The Conference Board, Economics Program Working Paper #11–06, December 2011. www.conference-board.org/pdf_free/workingpapers/EPWP1106.pdf (accessed 12/9/2014).
8. World Bank, as of 7/17/2014. Nominal GDP of Ukraine, Iraq and the world, 2013.
9. World Bank, as of 7/17/2014. Nominal GDP of Syria and the world, 2013.
10. World Bank, as of 7/17/2014. Nominal GDP of Egypt and the world, 2013.
11. FactSet, as of 7/17/2014. S&P 500 Price Index, 6/12/1950–7/17/1950.
12. FactSet, as of 7/17/2014. S&P 500 Price Index, 6/23/1950–7/27/1953.
13. FactSet, as of 7/17/2014. S&P 500 Price Index, 10/23/1962–11/5/1962.
14. FactSet, as of 7/17/2014. S&P 500 Price Index, 12/8/1994–12/20/1995.
15. FactSet, as of 1/21/2015. S&P 500 Price Index, 4/30/1938–5/31/1938.

CHAPTER 4

Not in the Next 30 Months

When you were a little kid, what did you want to be when you grew up?

Pretty much every tyke has some fanciful vision of their adulthood. Maybe you wanted to be a firefighter, princess, astronaut or baseball player! Maybe a doctor, movie star, builder, action hero or train conductor. Perhaps a pirate! At some time, most kids have wanted to be one of these or something similar—something they idealized for whatever reason.

Rarely do any of these dreams come true. Some do! But usually, hopes, dreams, possibilities and plans change as we age. Wanna-be athletes grow up to be mathletes. Wanna-be astronauts discover they hate studying physics. Kids who played Operation—that board game where you poke at a plastic patient's ailments with tweezers—might grow up squeamish at the sight of blood. Those who idealized train conductors may learn *Thomas the Tank Engine* isn't real life.

Countless things change between ages 5 and 30, and no five-year-old can know what their adult life will look like. They can imagine! But real life usually goes differently in ways we can't predict. Kids can know what'll probably happen in a rough way over the next two years or so of their life—what grade they'll be in, what teachers they'll probably have, how old they'll be, what milestones they'll hit. But not much further out. A nine-year-old might expect to end up at the local high school, but what if their parents move? Or another school opens? We have to live life, experience the changes firsthand, and see how it goes.

Same for markets. We can't know the far future today! Too much change to fathom! Stocks know it, and they don't look more than about 30 months ahead. Anything further out is sheer guesswork—possibilities, not probabilities, and markets move on probabilities.

Yet headlines continually bombard us with slowly developing super-long-term trends, claiming they'll be our eventual doom. Like high debt, China taking over the world, global warming—you name it. Countless academic studies use fancy formulas claiming to predict how these and many other issues will play out. Pundits take their hypotheses as fact and hype them ad infinitum. Many take it a step further, warning these big, bad long-term things could doom stocks today and for the foreseeable future.

You can use an easy trick to identify this far-future unknowable pointlessness and tune it out. Simply ask: "Is any of this a material risk impacting economies in the next 30 months?"

This will sound Pollyannaish and dismissive, but it's true: If whatever big, bad, terrible thing the media warns about won't happen materially in the next approximate 30 months, it doesn't matter for stocks. Even if the terrible horrible prediction ends up true eventually, way down the road! Stocks don't look that far ahead. Ok, maybe 32 months sometimes, but not the far distant future.

This doesn't mean you shouldn't consider possibilities. Thinking about them—seeing what the crowd is saying, and considering what they're overlooking or not imagining—can help you figure out whether the long-term picture is really so dire, and that can help you sleep at night. All good! But for your investing decisions, you need only assess what is most likely to happen over the next 30 months.

The "not in the next 30 months" test is a top trick. You can apply it to pretty much every long-term issue the headlines hype as America or the world's eventual socioeconomic downfall. Even if they say we have to ACT NOW to prevent our eventual doom! If doom isn't likely within the next 30 months, markets won't worry about it today, and neither should you. This simple trick helps tune out a cacophony of frightful noise.

In this chapter, we'll cover how to use "not in the next 30 months" to:

- Separate political and social issues from economic ones.
- Dazzle your next dinner party when the conversation turns to US debt.
- Skewer every long-term terror the media wants you to fear today.

Baby Boomer Bomb?

For over a decade now, folks have obsessed over the Baby Boomers. What happens when they all retire? Who will be left to buy stocks?

Who knows? Not me! Not you! Not the famous champions of Boomer doom and gloom! We can't know—none of us—because it's all too far out. Sure, the first Boomers turned 65 in 2011. But the last of them won't get there until 2029. No one can see that far into the future. The average Boomer retirement is still far out. Stocks know this and don't even bother trying—not in the next 30 months is good enough for markets!

But thanks to efficient markets, we can be darned sure about this: Boomers' retirement won't move markets. It will play out too slowly—over an entire generation!—and nothing about it is a surprise. Markets have known when Boomers will retire since they were born—that's not foresight, just math. Fears started circulating about a decade before the first Boomers turned 65. They've been retiring in earnest for more than four years, and that doesn't count the many who took early retirement. The world hasn't ended. To presume markets won't discount things like this is to insult The Great Humiliator (TGH). Never smart!

Contrarians know all of this. They also know all the fears surrounding Boomer retirement are just opinions, based on the assumption Boomers will swap stocks for bonds when they retire, denting demand for stocks and putting less pressure on prices. Maybe! But if it does come true, it's a structural factor—stocks can still do fine, and cyclical factors can swamp.

Then again, this presumption of sagging demand for stocks ignores so many other possibilities. Maybe Boomers sell their businesses and invest the proceeds in stocks, and demand gets bigger! Private equity for public equity. Maybe their kids—a boom of their own—enter their prime working years and plow a ton of money into their 401(k)s, driving demand even higher! Maybe we see a combination, plus some other variables we can't dream up today.

The ultimate Boomer retirement endgame is simply too far out to game today. So don't even try. No point! Remember it isn't a surprise, an automatic negative or a big market mover.

What About Social Security and Medicare?

A subset of Boomer doom is the fear this massive increase in America's above-retirement age population will bankrupt Social Security and Medicaid. The Social Security Administration predicts that over 25% of Americans will be above the retirement age by 2029. The Social Security Board of Trustees' Annual Report to Congress claims the Old-Age and Survivors Insurance and Disability Insurance, combined, will be depleted in 2033. It also suggests Social Security will be able to pay only 75% of its scheduled benefits by then unless something changes.

This is the subject of media hype regularly, and the general conclusion is: Panic! But contrarians don't blink, and neither should you.

Why? One, it's not in the next 30 months! Two, these fears don't pass a basic logic test—one of a contrarian's favorite tools, as I mentioned in Chapter 1. If a claim or forecast is based on a bad assumption, it's bunk.

Social Security and Medicare depletion fears are based on long-term forecasts government agencies make using straight-line math—just take current conditions or historical averages and extrapolate them out to eternity. How is that rational? Why would the future ever look exactly like the past? Back in 2000, the Congressional Budget Office (CBO) predicted perpetual federal budget surpluses. In 2003, it predicted we'd have a $508 billion surplus and a 14.4% debt-to-GDP ratio in 2013. In real-life 2013, America ran a $680 billion deficit, bringing the debt-to-GDP ratio to 72.1%. The CBO gets the inputs wrong, too. In 2002, the CBO assumed 10-year US Treasury yields would hover near 6% for the next decade. This was nowhere close to true! Figure 4.1 shows just how wrong that projection was.

Figure 4.1 The CBO's Comical Interest Rate Projection

Sources: FactSet, CBO, as of 12/4/2014. 10-year US Treasury yields (constant maturity), 12/31/1991–12/31/2012; CBO projection of 10-year US Treasury yields from 2002 to 2012 (issued January 2002).

Is the CBO right sometimes? Sure! That's how TGH keeps us guessing, and it's how the CBO still has some fragment of credibility after all these years. Plus, like the professional market forecasters we covered in Chapter 2, the CBO has a long time to revise its forecasts to catch up with reality—it updates twice a year. Table 4.1 shows how the CBO's forecast for 2013's fiscal stats evolved over time. Between 2003 and early 2013, it gradually morphed from massively wrong to largely right.

Table 4.1 The CBO's Evolving Projections for Fiscal 2013

Date Projection Issued	Spending ($ Billions)	Revenue ($ Billions)	Surplus or Deficit (-)	Debt ($ Billions)	Debt-to-GDP
Jan-03	3,167	3,674	508	2,565	14.4%
Aug-03	3,422	3,634	459	5,438	30.7%
Jan-04	3,457	3,441	-16	6,409	37.0%
Sep-04	3,547	3,471	-75	6,675	37.8%
Jan-05	3,389	3,474	85	5,884	32.6%
Aug-05	3,561	3,481	-80	6,691	37.0%
Jan-06	3,506	3,546	40	6,032	32.9%
Aug-06	3,631	3,555	-76	6,469	35.4%
Jan-07	3,391	3,550	159	5,089	28.3%
Aug-07	3,583	3,619	36	5,730	31.5%
Jan-08	3,524	3,585	61	5,701	31.6%
Sep-08	3,766	3,619	-147	6,968	38.6%
Jan-09	3,610	3,353	-257	8,516	50.0%
Aug-09	3,759	3,221	-538	10,870	65.5%
Jan-10	3,756	3,218	-539	11,056	66.3%
Aug-10	3,760	3,236	-525	11,422	68.4%
Jan-11	3,794	3,090	-704	12,386	75.5%
Aug-11	3,692	3,069	-510*	11,773	72.8%
Jan-12	3,573	2,988	-585	11,945	75.1%
Aug-12	3,554	2,913	-641	12,064	76.1%
Feb-13	3,553	2,708	-845	12,229	76.3%
May-13	3,455	2,813	-642	12,036	75.1%
Actual 2013	**3,454**	**2,774**	**-680**	**11,982**	**72.1%**

*Assumes $113 billion in additional savings under the Budget Control Act of 2011.
Source: Congressional Budget Office, as of 12/4/2014. Baseline Budget Outlooks from the CBO's semiannual *Budget and Economic Outlook* reports published from January 2003 to February 2014.

We now know the CBO is often wrong, but we can't dismiss it out of hand just because it's the CBO! So we turn to another faulty premise: The presumption Social Security is a "lockbox," to use the term popularized by Al Gore and *Saturday Night Live* during the 2000 Presidential campaign. The "lockbox" myth assumes the Social Security and Medicare trusts are money set in store for our retirees and maybe, one day, us. Nope! Of every tax dollar we pay into Social Security, 85 cents goes immediately to fund current benefits. The other 15 cents goes to the "trust fund," which pays people with disabilities and their eligible family members. This trust isn't locked away. Surplus funds, by law, are lent to the federal government for general use through the purchase of special issue Treasury bonds. The money is spent.

And all that chatter about "unfunded liabilities"? Meaningless! *All* of Social Security's liabilities are technically unfunded! The Treasury isn't borrowing to pay them! This system is entirely pay as you go. Workers pay in, the feds pay out.

What Boomers collect from entitlements over the next few decades will be paid, right then and there, by Gen X and the Millennials—and despite all those "aging population" fears, there are about 15 million more Millennials than Boomers. When they reach retirement age, their kids and grandkids—Gen Z or whatever snappy name they get—will fund their benefits. It's the circle of life. (Even if Elton John never writes a song about it.)

Here, you might say, "Yeah, but what if the Millennials never grow up?!" What if they're a disaster in their prime working years? Well, think about the basis for that question. Folks fear Millennials will never grow up because they see them as a bunch of self-entitled brats. It's a "kids today!" argument. I have a lot of Millennials working for me. They're no worse than Gen X, who were supposed to waste their lives drinking coffee and wearing grungy flannel—they grew up. They're no worse than my generation, which was supposed to be anti-corporate drugged-out good-for-nothing turn on, tune in, drop outers—we grew up. Maybe the "kids today!" crowd is right this time, and the Millennials do turn into a bunch of 60-year-old brats who never did anything. Or maybe, just maybe, the kids are alright. But none of this is an issue in the next 30 months—always and everywhere what matters for stocks.

If natural population growth, immigration, and naturalization aren't enough to maintain the programs, Congress can just change them. None of this is set in stone! It's all legislation! Social Security and Medicare were created by Congress, and they can be tweaked by Congress. Yes, we've all heard this is the third rail of American politics, but Congress grabbed that third rail several times during the twentieth century, tweaking the inputs and outputs to preserve the program's solvency. Way back in the 1970s, Trustees estimated Social Security would be unable to fully cover benefits by 1979! But a few small fixes in 1977 took care of it. It doesn't take much to astronomically extend full funding. This issue can easily remain outside of markets' forecasting horizon in perpetuity.

But What if the "Lost Generation" Stays Lost?

Some say the kids surely won't be alright because the student loan bubble warped all their personal balance sheets into debt-heavy disaster. All for some degree that will never pay off!

This is another "not in the next 30 months" thing. Heck, it might be a "not in the ever" thing.

Let's do the numbers. Student loan bubblephobia headlines hype the nearly threefold rise in outstanding debt since 2006. When that year began, total student debt was around $500 billion, according to the New York Fed. By Q1 2014, it was $1.3 trillion. Add in most student loans' exemption from bankruptcy protection, and headlines can easily convince you student debt is a mounting, unshakeable burden on the Millennial generation.

Here, the skeptical contrarian asks questions. Who's paying that $1.3 trillion? How many borrowers? How old are they? How much does each person pay?

You can get all the answers at the New York Fed, which keeps a running tally of the demographic breakdown of outstanding student debt. There, you'll see the following:

- Nearly 40 million people share that $1.3 trillion in outstanding student loans.
- Using simple math, the average amount owed is $32,500.
- As of 2011 (the latest published figure as I'm writing this), the median amount owed was about $12,000. Half owed more, half owed less.
- One-third of the total was owed by the under-30 crowd.
- Another third was owned by folks aged 30 to 39.
- The rest was owed by the over-40 set.

It seems exceedingly difficult to argue Millennials are disproportionately impacted here. A lot of these folks owe the equivalent of a car loan. Most student debt is owed by folks in their prime working years.

Chances are Millennials can afford their loans. After all, the result of a student loan is a college education! College grads are mostly at the top of the food chain in labor markets. According to the US Bureau of Labor Statistics, the employment/population ratio for college grads has averaged 74.5% since 2004.[1] For the total population, it averages just 60.6%. Job growth for college grads was over five times faster than total job growth during this period.[2] The unemployment rate for college grads peaked at 5% after the 2007–2009 recession; it peaked at 10% for everyone.[3] College grads' median weekly earnings are about 30% higher than the broader population's at both the high and low ends of the spectrum.[4]

Might some indebted Millennials have to delay a home purchase for a few years while they pay this down? Sure! Might those who racked up six figures in debt gunning for careers in academia have a tougher time? Sure! But none of that is a gigantic negative in the next 30 months.

Could student debt eventually spiral into the massive negative the media (and politicians!) say it is? Maybe! But college costs would have to hit the stratosphere, and job prospects would have to crater. Possible, in theory—but not in the next 30 months!

There is almost no one alive who doesn't know college degrees boost employment opportunities. It's like how everyone knows cigarettes cause most lung cancer. You'd have to grow up in the upper Amazon basin or some other out-of-touch place not to get this. But the media would never point it out—too politically incorrect!

Why? Because if they went there, they'd have to point out the obvious: If the unemployment rate for college grads topped out at 5% during the so-called Great Recession, it really wasn't all that terrible for educated folks. This means the recession was mostly a purge of less skilled workers. The hysteria about unemployment wasn't something to be quite so hysterical about. Is it cruel that these folks were unemployed? Of course! But this is a social issue, not an economic or market one. You can lead a horse to water, but you can't make it think. You can show people the benefits of education, but you can't make them get one. People make a choice, and they're employed only in the best of circumstances as a result.

Again, the media will never admit this, because it is a cruel thing to print—and a lot of their readers aren't college grads and are instead simply gullible. But for you, dear reader and budding contrarian investor, this truth can help put things in perspective when unemployment hysteria hits maximum.

What About Debt?

Nowhere does "not in the next 30 months" help you more than with the endless warnings that America will be bankrupt by some random year, usually decades in the future.

Most of this is based on total outstanding debt—either as a percentage of GDP or as just a gigantic absolute number. Trillions upon trillions of dollars America owes the world. The debt doom-mongers say our government is spending and borrowing us into oblivion, saddling our children and their children and their children with debt they'll never be able to repay.

Children and children's children? That's not in the next 30 months.

This probably sounds too dismissive, so let's go through the proof. Always demand evidence!

The CBO's 2014 forecast (them again!) says US net public debt (which excludes all the money America owes itself) will hit 106% of GDP by 2039.[5] Once again, the CBO uses straight-line math and a bunch of random assumptions—just fantasy.

But maybe they're right! What then? Armageddon? Debtpocalypse?

Probably not. There is no evidence in history that debt at 106% of GDP leads to poor economic performance, default or stock market mayhem. America had more than that in the aftermath of World War II. We were fine. Britain had more than twice that amount during much of the industrial revolution—fine there, too. The empire flourished. No bankruptcy there! (Of course, they got to rape, loot and pillage, which may have buoyed the "animal spirits" in ways that no longer apply.) Japan has double that *as I type this*. Now, the Japanese economy isn't the greatest, but it isn't due to debt—it's more tied to their bizarrely nineteenth-century mercantilistic take on capitalism.

Besides, total debt—whether at an absolute level or as a percentage of the economy—is a pretty arbitrary number. Tells you nothing about solvency. Think about your mortgage.

You might have hundreds of thousands, even millions of dollars in mortgage debt! Big numbers! But those big numbers don't matter—what matters is that monthly mortgage payment. Can you afford it? Yes? Then you can afford that big number over time.

Same with America. Just the same! All that matters is whether the Treasury can afford interest payments. Today, the interest on our debt is more affordable than almost ever—near historic lows relative to GDP and tax revenue, as shown in Figures 4.2 and 4.3. Lower than levels seen in much of the 1980s and 1990s—wonderful times for stocks. Even as total debt has risen in recent years, total interest payments have fallen. Interest rates have been at generational lows, and the Treasury refinanced a huge chunk of maturing debt at these low rates. Meanwhile, tax revenue is up with the growing economy.

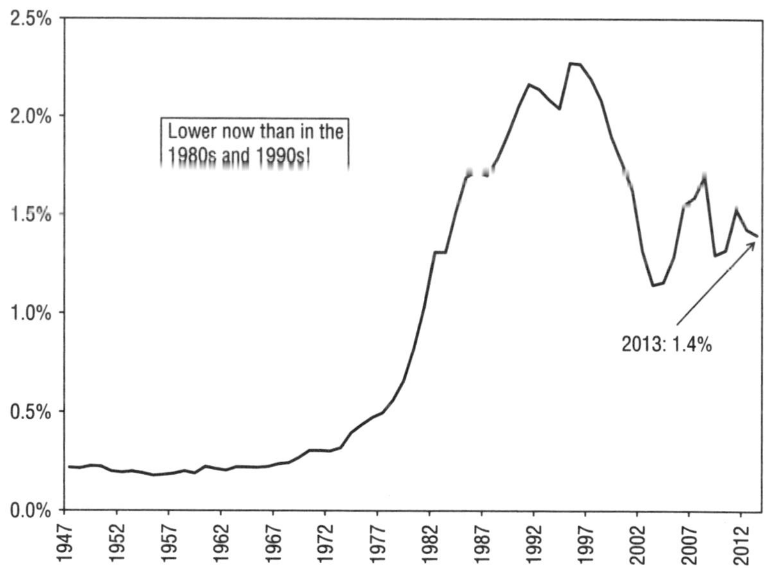

Figure 4.2 US Federal Interest Payments as a Percentage of GDP
Source: Federal Reserve Bank of St. Louis, as of 11/28/2014.

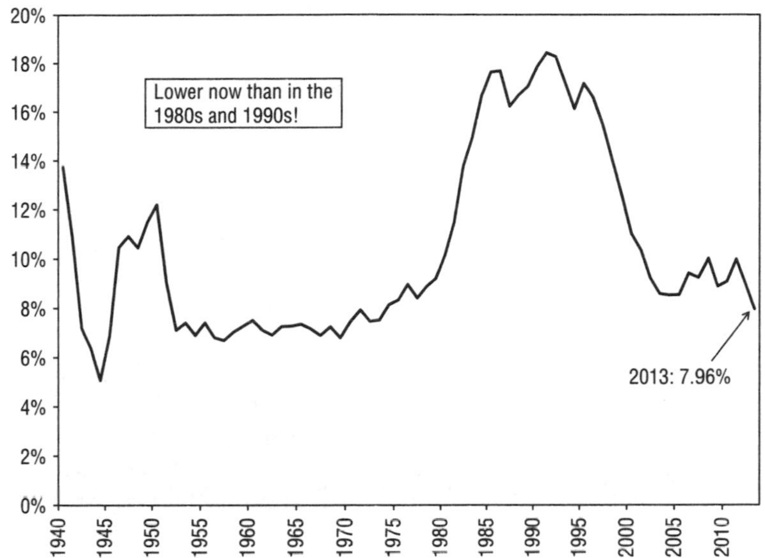

Figure 4.3 US Federal Interest Payments as a Percentage of Tax Revenue

Source: Federal Reserve Bank of St. Louis, as of 11/28/2014.

For debt to become a problem, interest rates would need to rise to nosebleed levels and stay there for years. Rates directly matter for the federal government only at issuance—the primary market. That means they have to stay high as the federal government rolls over a lot of debt. Today, the average maturity is more than five years. Rates need to rise high and stay there long enough to move average payments to those levels. Could it happen? Sure. But not in the next 30 months! That blip of high rates in the early 1980s wasn't anywhere near big or long enough to sink us. We'd have to get into fiscal trouble of Grecian proportions and mafia duration for the world to see us as a big enough credit risk to demand significantly higher payments. Possible? Sure! But not in the next 30 months.

We Might Never Pay It Off, and That's Ok!

By 2014, the worst of the eurozone crisis was past, but the PIIGS countries' (Portugal, Italy, Ireland, Greece and Spain) debt was still climbing. Even after two defaults, Greek debt jumped from 129.7% of GDP in 2009 to 171.5% when 2013 ended.[6] Ireland from 64.4% to 123.7%.[7] Portugal from 83.7% to 129%, Spain from 54% to 93.9% and Italy from 116.4% to 132.6%.[8] Partly because they all still ran deficits (just smaller deficits), partly because GDP was down (denominator effect) and partly because interest costs and tax revenues went in opposite directions for years.

Based on this seemingly dismal reality, pundits started arguing the eurozone could never fully recover without widespread debt forgiveness—a massive do-over. They claimed high debt was a huge overhang on the economy, and countries would never be able to grow their way out because high debt prevents growth! And if years of so-called austerity couldn't get debt under control, forgiveness was the only solution.

Will they ever pay down their debt? I don't know! But they probably don't need to. Debt doesn't drag down growth. You don't have to pay it off.

How can we know? Easy! History! Once upon a time, a certain country's net public debt ballooned from $42.8 billion to $241.9 billion over six years, hitting 106.1% of GDP. This country managed to pay off about $18.4 billion over the next two years, and the Treasury took another $9.2 billion in bonds out of circulation, but austerity didn't last. Debt resumed rising. It spiraled to $12 trillion over the next 65 years! Yet this country also grew into the world's biggest, most competitive, dynamic, innovative economy. It is still a powerhouse today.

This country is the US.

Between 1940 and 1945, America borrowed over $200 billion—mostly to pay for the war effort. Gross debt jumped from $50.7 billion in 1940 to $260.1 billion in 1945. The country piled on another $10 billion in 1946. Net debt, which excludes the Treasury's holdings, clocked in at $241.9 billion, as noted above. If you owe yourself money, it basically cancels, and the government has always owned a lot of its own debt—from one pocket into another.

Net debt fell about $27.5 billion from 1947 to 1949—$18.4 billion matured and was retired, and the Treasury took on the rest.

But borrowing ticked back up in 1950, and America never really looked back. You can see all this history—all these numbers—at the White House Office of Management and Budget's website.

Think this through—and bear with me while we do some math. World War II added about $192 billion to net debt. Repayment and Treasury maneuvering shaved off about $27.5 billion of it. The rest we never paid off and still carry, plus nearly 70 years' worth of compounding interest payments. If you take that $192 billion, subtract $27.5 billion, and then compound using the average interest rate on our debt—a crude calculation, but illustrative—you end up with roughly $1.5 trillion by year-end 2013. That's $1.5 trillion of America's $12 trillion net debt that might be considered attributable to World War II. Again, a crude estimate! But it's something that shows the point—and not insignificant. We never paid it off. It spiraled higher for decades as interest piled on. It is still with us today. Along with over $10 trillion borrowed for other purposes. And yet we're fine.

Countries rarely have to pay off debt. They just have to manage it—pay interest and roll over maturing bonds (issue new debt to pay off existing bondholders). A growing economy makes it fairly simple to manage debt. The UK still carries debt from the South Sea Company's 1720 collapse, the Napoleonic and Crimean Wars and Irish famine relief in the mid-nineteenth century! They're paying some of it off now, along with World War I debt, but only because the bonds were open ended and were more expensive than current market interest rates. Replacing them with bonds with set maturities and lower rates is good financial sense.

Debt doesn't prevent growth in competitive, private-sector-led economies. Growth, at its simplest, is a function of four variables: resources, labor, capital and technology. If the government is directing traffic—providing the capital—then debt can matter. But in a free market where banks—the private sector—create most capital (lending off the monetary base, which comes from the central bank), a high government debt load doesn't matter as long as it is affordable. This is how the US grew by leaps and bounds in the twentieth century despite that high debt load. It's how net public debt dropped from 106.1% of GDP in 1946 to 23.1% in 1974 even though we never paid it off. It's how the US is still considered the world's most stable, deepest, dynamic market today—even though we never paid it off.

But What if Debt Causes Runaway Inflation?

Debt "causes" inflation only if you monetize it. Could it happen? Maybe! But not in the next 30 months.

Governments generally monetize debt only if they can't afford interest payments. If you monetize the debt, you deliberately cause inflation to rise so those interest payments get cheaper—the total dollar amount stays the same, but it's worth less. There are just more dollars sloshing around.

For the United States to monetize the debt, we'd have to see interest payments on debt skyrocket—we just covered that. Not happening in the next 30 months. Could the United States pile on debt endlessly over time and get to a point where we have to monetize? Maybe! But maybe Congress turns thrifty and at some point decides to let the debt slowly mature, and it falls out of the monetary base. Or, maybe debt keeps rising, but the growth of society pays for it, just like always. Maybe we keep getting more productive. Maybe technology keeps getting better, faster, more powerful, driving advances we can't even imagine today—and entire new economic frontiers. Again, none of that is about the next 30 months.

But long-term straight-line forecasts can't account for any of that. Again, those government stat-heads delivering dire warnings of debt doom just chart-out the recent past forward. Analysis that tries to account for technological change requires imagination and an ability to quantify unknowable wonders. That's no knock on CBO crunchers—just a knock on standard projections.

But What if America Stops Innovating?

It might! But not in the next 30 months!

Most technological advancement comes from an opportunistic business consumer's realization of the collision of four factors:

1. *Moore's Law:* The theory that the number of transistors you can fit on a microprocessor doubles about every two years. Intel founder Gordon Moore hypothesized this in 1965, and so far, it has held true far longer than anyone ever envisioned decades back. Moore's law is why technology has become exponentially more powerful, smaller and awesomer over time; it's why your smartphone does way more than an Apple IIe or an old IBM PC.
2. *Koomey's Law:* The theory that energy efficiency in computing doubles every year and a half or so—it takes less battery power to perform the same computations. This, too, has made devices smaller, more powerful and longer-lasting. It's why your smartphone keeps a charge longer than your old flip phone, even though it's smaller and does things your flip phone never dreamed of. (*If* flip phones dream. Maybe they dream of electric sheep.)
3. *Kryder's Law:* The theory that the amount of data you can fit in one inch of disk drive doubles every 13 months. This is why smartphones a fraction of the size of a 10-year-old laptop can store vastly more information.
4. *The Shannon-Hartley Theorem:* The theory that as long as you can create channels with greater bandwidth—which is theoretically limitless—you can transmit information more clearly and faster. Decades from now, fiber optics will look slow.

Most—if not all—of America's tech industry now revolves around these four rules, and all are running full-steam ahead. Could they peter out one day? Maybe! But not in the next 30 months. And as these wind down, who knows what new advances will take their place, otherwise driving technology ever forward.

Then, too, as long as America is where the tech companies are, America will be where innovation happens. Most inventions don't happen at the firms making the processors, batteries, hard disks and wires made possible by those four rules.

Innovation comes from the creative users who figure out new ways to use these gizmos. These inventive users tend to flourish near where these components are created. It's like the adjacency effect in science—the optical phenomenon where two close-together objects affect each other in ways they otherwise wouldn't. It's like the very recently discovered fourth state of water. Beyond solid, liquid and gas. Look it up. I'm not kidding. It's EZ. (EZ water; EZ stands for exclusion zone.) Same with technology! Nearness counts. You get the former employee at a semiconductor firm who has lunch with a nanotechnology geek and dreams up a contact lens that takes pictures.

America has the edge here. Nine of the 10 biggest tech firms by market capitalization are in the U-S-of-A. Could we lose this advantage? Maybe! Nothing lasts forever! Japan once had an edge here, but it doesn't now. But Japan didn't erode overnight. It took decades. So maybe America erodes too! But not in the next 30 months. There is a big bugaboo in America right now about firms moving for tax purposes, but this isn't a hollowing-out. Only the address moves. All the normal operational facilities—the entire R&D—that all stays here. Along with the many R&D centers foreign firms operate here.

But What About Global Warming?

Global warming is a classic case of the media telling investors to look for risk in the wrong places. It is a scientific debate that gets misapplied to economics by politicians, and folks get caught up in the chatter. They fret over which side is right. They get caught up in academics and politics. And they lose sight of—what else!—the next 30 months.

You see this with pretty much every hot-button issue. Government spending. Debt. Most things political. Investors get drowned in rhetoric and ideology, so they can't see the likely market impact.

Now, I'm not a scientist—I have no clarity on whether global warming is real and, if so, whether it will exponentially increase the frequency of natural disasters. Or raise the oceans and put the entire Eastern Seaboard and Gulf Coast under water in 60 or 70 years. I can't tell you whether Houston is going the way of Atlantis.

Problem is, neither can the scientists. That's why the debate remains so loud and distracting! The global warming alarmists rely on "consensus science," arguing a glut of research shows temperatures have risen (or become more extreme on either end of the thermometer) in tandem with carbon emissions. Policymakers tout this as the defining issue of our time, then use all the science to justify all the laws they wanted to pass anyway, like taxes on certain activities or sectors. Stuff like carbon cap-and-trade—it's just a tax grab dressed up as environmental policy. Massive subsidies for wind and solar energy firms are just spending boondoggles couched as environmental necessity. It's all a shell game of environmental concern. Not for the scientists! But for the politicians. Fact is, consensus science has been wrong most of history, and basing investment decisions on the consensus of scientists is too far-sighted to work, ever.

So the other herd argues consensus science is just wrong—just because everyone says something is true doesn't mean it's right. If the science herd were always right, they say, we'd still think the world was flat. In science, too, being right can mean being lonely. This might make you, as a budding contrarian investor, prone to side with the "global warming isn't real" crowd. Be careful—that's bias talking! Allow your sympathies to drift to either side, and you let ideology seep in, and that's dangerous. Contrarians shun bias. But sometimes, many times, consensus is right. After all, is gravity real or not?

So, how should the contrarian think about global warming? Here's an easy three-step process:

1. Remember you aren't a scientist. Unless you are a scientist—then you can skip to step two. Otherwise, you are not a scientist and therefore not an expert, and you

don't know anything that hasn't already been discussed ad nauseam by the scientific crowd—you don't know anything markets aren't already aware of.

2. Accept that no one knows which side of the debate is right, because neither side has seen the scientific method through—they hypothesize, observe, analyze and deduce, but they lack a control group. The warmists can show rising temperatures and carbon emissions till the cows come home, but they will never have a counterfactual. Same goes for the anti-warmists. None of it proves anything.
3. Accept that it doesn't matter which side is right. Because even if the warmists turn out to be correct, even they admit the world won't turn into a full-time natural disaster with ceaseless flooding and droughts in the near future. That potential is all very, very far-future. Not in the next 30 months!

What About Income Inequality?

This is another debate and an entirely social one. It isn't for the market practitioner to be an expert on what's good or bad for society in 30 years. My standard line when asked about this is: "I don't do sociology." What's great in the far future could be really great, and what's bad could be terrible, but neither impacts pricing today.

It's fine to have and discuss opinions about sociological and political matters. Many impact daily life! Questions like, what's the right long-term structure to educate our children? Vital to our future. But this isn't my field. I don't do sociology. Lots of people who chime in about sociology know nothing about it. People with no education, no background, no experience at age 19 think they know everything about sociology—and have a higher likelihood of being wrong. And I'm convinced most PhD sociologists know nothing about sociology either. But that's another book. This is a book about markets! Your sociology is up to you, and you can believe whatever you want. But whatever your opinions, the issues are outside markets' sphere and shouldn't impact stocks now.

With income inequality, to be a contrarian, stay above the fray. This probably sounds callous, but it's true: If the gap between haves and have-nots really is widening, it doesn't matter for stocks. Some say inequality is a destructive political force that will be America's downfall, but if that were true, America would have fallen during the Gilded Age.

Stocks don't really care who has wealth as long as whoever has it keeps bidding prices higher. Inequality becomes a market issue only if politicians try to "fix" it through some massive redistribution scheme. And maybe they will! But not in the next 30 months.

Now, you're probably a nice person, so you probably find all that a bit dismissive. Maybe you want more evidence so you don't have to feel callous for not trying to guard your portfolio against income inequality. Well, here you go!

Those who argue inequality is (a) real and (b) a problem rely mostly on a study by Emmanuel Saez and Thomas Piketty, which claims to show that the highest earners take home an ever-larger share of US income.[9] But glaring issues cast doubt on their conclusions. The figures cited most to support their premise are pretax and pre-benefit. They don't account at all for the progressive income tax system this country has used since 1913 to address the very issue they raise. They also count capital gains on investments as "income," which the US tax code hasn't done for decades—and rightly so. Capital gains are a function of wealth. Wealth might come from high income, but it might also come from judicious saving and wise investing.

Another shortcoming: The Saez-Piketty study looks at household income, essentially pitting households with two or more earners against single filers, ignoring demographic trends. Today's proportion of households with multiple earners is simply lower than in 1980—about when Saez and Piketty show the gap widening. If you're pitting more divorced and single heads of household against multi-earner families, you're going to get a bigger gap regardless of how much an individual earns. Then, too, Saez and Piketty don't account for age. Of course a 24-year-old in his or her first job will earn far, far less than an otherwise comparable 58-year-old who has built up a high salary over an entire career. It's not just me saying all this, either. Noted economists like the University of Michigan's Mark J. Perry have done some excellent work on demographics and income. According to Dr. Perry:[10]

- In 2012, households in the top quintile of incomes had, on average, 2.04 earners. The bottom quintile had 0.45 earners.
- 77.5% of the top quintile were married-couple households, compared to 17% of the bottom quintile.
- 79.5% of the top quintile included one or more earners in their prime working years, ages 35 to 64. Only 47.3% of the bottom quintile had an earner in this age range.

From this angle, it becomes clear this is a sociological debate. Higher divorce rates and more single parents are political issues. Nothing a contrarian should think about in investing. And of course, who do you suspect has higher income on average: drug addicts or non–drug addicts? Sociology.

Inequality would be a problem if the economy were a fixed pie—if the 0.01% having more meant everyone else had less. But household incomes at all levels of society are up over time. Ditto for household net worth. Everyone is making more. Some folks are just making a lot more. Another study, whose authors include the very same Emmanuel Saez, shows social mobility is the same today as it was 50 years ago—opportunities are the same![11] Only the payout for success is bigger. Shouldn't that provide more incentive? Who knows?

As long as Bill Gates' billions don't prevent any other American from striking it rich, widening inequality doesn't matter. Might there one day be a ceiling? Could Congress legislate America into a fixed pie where Bill's big slice means the rest of us get less? Maybe! But not in the next 30 months.

What if the Dollar Loses Its Place as the World's Reserve Currency?

What happens to America if foreign countries start completing transactions in their own currencies? Will the dollar suffer if it's no longer the king of foreign exchange reserves? Who knows! But it won't happen in the next 30 months.

Folks have fretted over this one for decades. China's occasional rumblings about diversifying away from dollars drive jitters anew. The noise spikes any time countries chatter about pricing oil in something other than dollars, as if America benefits from the dollar being a trade intermediary.

But America gets nothing from the dollar being used in international trade. We don't get a brokerage fee. It's also a big hassle for the other countries. They don't trade in dollars because dollars are awesome—they just do it because it happens to be the world's most convertible currency. Some currencies, like China's yuan, aren't directly convertible to many others. If a Chinese manufacturer wanted to sell gadgets to a Polish retailer, the Polish firm just has to convert its zlotys to dollars, buy the gadgets in dollars, and let the Chinese firm deal with the hassle of converting those dollars to yuan.

If the dollar is used less in international trade and finance, it just means more currencies are more directly convertible. That's good! It probably means more trade happens over time. Great for everyone!

As for currency reserves—the real lightning rod—look closely at the evidence and you'll see there's nothing there. The media hype says if the dollar loses market share in foreign exchange reserves, US Treasury bonds will have fewer buyers, interest rates will skyrocket, and Armageddon will ensue. Bad! But not true, and we have proof.

First up, it's time for the logic test. This fear is based on the assumption that reserve-currency demand is what keeps US borrowing costs low. So ask: How do US borrowing costs compare with non-reserve-currency nations?

Answer: Middle of the pack, at best or worst! Figure 4.4 shows benchmark 10-year government bond rates for America and six other major developed nations since 2009—about when dollar-losing-reserve-currency-status fears amped up. US rates about match Britain's. Australia is higher. Germany, France, Japan and Canada are all lower. Being the world's favorite reserve currency doesn't let America borrow more cheaply than everyone else. Other variables play a huge role.

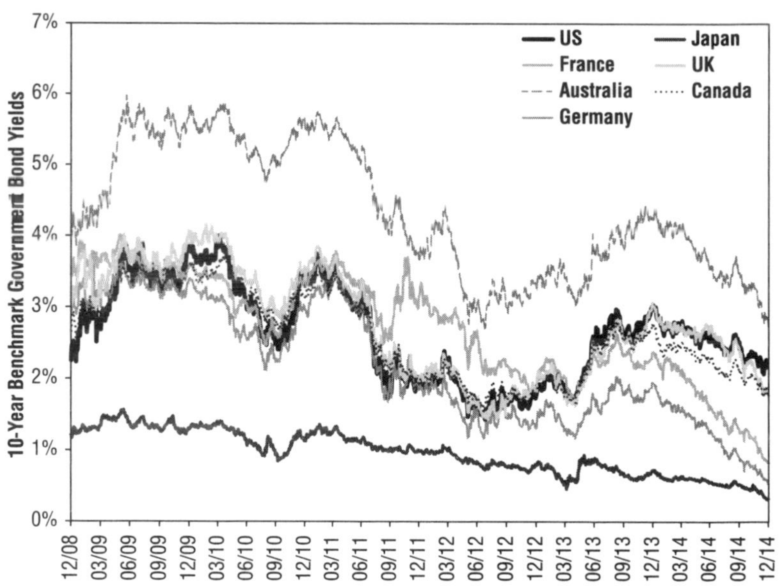

Figure 4.4 Benchmark 10-Year Government Bond Yields

Source: FactSet, as of 1/5/2015. Select 10-year benchmark government bond yields, 12/31/2008–12/31/2014.

Second, we can look at the actual foreign exchange reserves! The International Monetary Fund publishes them. You can download the full dataset at its website and see how much of each currency is held in reserve each year.[12] Do this, and you'll see two things:

1. The dollar's market share fell from 71% in 1999 to 61% in 2012.
2. The total amount of dollars held in reserve jumped from about $980 billion in 1999 to over $3.7 trillion in 2012.

The reserve pie got bigger! So countries diversified. They still buy tons of dollars, but they buy euros, yen, sterling and a handful of others, too.

Losing market share has been just fine for America. Treasury demand is still sky-high. Interest rates are nice and low. The world is turning. Dogs and cats aren't snorting coke.

As long as the United States has the world's biggest, deepest and most liquid capital markets, it's a safe assumption the dollar plays a big role in global currency reserves. There is a dearth of alternatives. The euro is on the rise, but as we learned in the PIIGS crisis, it has stability issues. UK gilts are great, but there aren't many of them. What about China? As long as the yuan doesn't trade freely or have market-set interest rates, it isn't ready for prime time.

Counterintuitively, the same US debt load many fear is exactly why we're the world's reserve currency. Many believe cutting debt is the only way to shore up our reserve currency status, but this would just cut supply and force countries to look elsewhere for reserve assets. The solution would compound the supposed problem. Strange, but true! Tiny countries with tiny debt loads can't be reserve currencies—too illiquid to matter. One of those perverse, overlooked ironies you should train yourself to see.

Could something happen to make foreign governments want to sell off dollar reserves all at once? Sure—anything is always possible! But probable? Not so much. It would take something catastrophic and heretofore unseen. A heated debt ceiling debate in 2011—complete with Standard & Poor's downgrading America's credit rating—saw Treasury demand *rise,* not fall. Budget bickering, a government shutdown and default threats from the US Treasury didn't dent demand in late 2013. Big bear markets and recessions in 2000 and 2008? Foreign governments didn't blink. Debt? Japan's debt is way bigger than America's as a percentage of its economy, and international yen holdings are rising.

Absent an asteroid hitting earth, this probably remains a very, very slow ebb. Not a disaster, not a surprise. We've seen it for 15 years now, and it's certainly not an issue in the next 30 months.

What the Markets Know

If you take just one thing from these last two chapters, it should be this: When you read the news, watch CNBC or listen to the chatter at your favorite watering hole, and they're yammering on about something big and bad, always remember the relatively efficient market.

As a contrarian, your best friend is the relatively efficient market. Know it. Love it. Remember it. Send it a birthday card.

The market is your weapon against media hysteria. Because you know how quickly markets work, you know all those short-term data and developments decried as instant doom are priced in. You've seen how quickly markets move on surprising earnings reports and economic releases—microseconds. You've seen how markets yawn when news isn't a surprise—they already expected it, and expectations are pre-priced.

And because you know markets only look about 30 months out, you know all those annoying, noisy academic ideological and sociological debates don't matter for markets right now.

Maybe they do matter 20, 30, 40 or more years from now! Or maybe life changes in unimaginable ways and makes all those straight-line forecasts null and void. Or maybe sociological and weather-related issues never become actual economic concerns. But you can't know any of that exactly today, and neither can markets. So for now, you can just breathe easy! If you can push it beyond the next 30 months, you don't need to fear.

The herd will always fear myopic and far-future doom. Headlines always need something to chatter about! Just let 'em. If they're all doom-filled, you know you don't need to worry about whatever they're hyping. How? Because hysteria can't be the elephant in the room! Everyone sees it! The market sees it! None of it is a surprise ever.

So while the crowd stares at static, it's time for us to go elephant-spotting. What tools will you need for this living room safari? Flip to Chapter 5 and find out!

Notes

1. Bureau of Labor Statistics, as of 6/21/2014. Employment/population ratio for college graduates and total civilian labor force, January 2004–May 2014.
2. Bureau of Labor Statistics, as of 6/21/2014. Growth in nonfarm payrolls for college graduates and total civilian labor force, January 2004–May 2014.
3. Bureau of Labor Statistics, as of 6/21/2014. Unemployment rates for college graduates and total civilian labor force, December 2007–June 2010.
4. Bureau of Labor Statistics, as of 6/21/2014. Median weekly earnings for college graduates and total civilian labor force, Q1 2004–Q2 2014.
5. "The 2014 Long-Term Budget Outlook," Congressional Budget Office, July 2014.
6. Eurostat, as of 10/3/2014. Greek government debt as a percentage of GDP, 2009 and 2013.
7. Eurostat, as of 10/3/2014. Irish government debt as a percentage of GDP, 2009 and 2013.
8. Eurostat, as of 10/3/2014. Portuguese, Spanish and Italian government debt as a percentage of GDP, 2009 and 2013.

9. "Income Inequality in the United States, 1913–1998," Thomas Piketty and Emmanuel Saez, *The Quarterly Journal of Economics*, Vol. 118, No. 1 (February 2003): 1–39.
10. "Explaining Income Inequality by Household Demographics," Mark J. Perry, *AEIdeas*, 12/6/2013. http://www.aei.org/publication/explaining-income-inequality-by-household-demographics/ (accessed 2/24/2015).
11. "Is the United States Still a Land of Opportunity? Recent Trends in Intergenerational Mobility," Raj Chetty, Nathaniel Hendren, Patrick Kline, Emmanuel Saez and Nicholas Turner, *NBER Working Paper Series*, Working Paper 19844, January 2014.
12. Currency Composition of Official Foreign Exchange Reserves, International Monetary Fund (IMF). www.imf.org/External/np/sta/cofer/eng/index.htm (accessed 10/31/2013).

CHAPTER 5

Take a Safari With Jack Lemmon and Walter Matthau

Throw on your khakis, grab your binoculars and don't forget your hat: It's safari time!

Yes, we're going on an elephant hunt. Not a *real* one—we're trading stocks, not ivory! This is an observation-only expedition. Elephants are our friends.

As we saw in Chapters 3 and 4, markets are pretty efficient at pre-pricing all known information and widely discussed opinions. When everyone stares at something, and they chatter endlessly about their opinions and expectations, it can't surprise. But if folks stare at one thing, they overlook something else. That something else may be the proverbial elephant in the living room—some huge truth that, for whatever reason, everyone ignores or forgets. Spot the elephant, and you can get an edge.

The elephant in the room is jam-packed with surprise-power mojo. It's the big thing that has always been there, and everyone knows about, but they've forgotten (humans don't have elephants' awesome memories). If you ask someone about the elephant, they might nod politely—they might know of it!—but they'll assume it's too old, too familiar to be any good. They've discounted it and forgotten how much it works, just like we saw with professional forecasts in Chapter 2. Or they brush you off because they're too busy looking for Dracula around the corner. Or they think the elephant is too boring. The latest headlines are way more exciting!

So what is the elephant?

Simple: Walter Matthau and Jack Lemmon in 1993.

Stay with me here. If you turned back time and asked your best buddies what they thought about Jack and Walter in early 1993, they'd probably say, "Those old guys? Lemmon was good in *Some Like It Hot,* and Walter was a riot in *The Odd Couple,* but I haven't seen 'em in ages. They still at it?" If you then told your pals that Jack and Walter would headline one of the year's biggest comedy hits—with Ann-Margret their leading lady—they'd have called the men in white coats to take you away. Those old geezers? Leads in a blockbuster romantic comedy? Get real! Could never happen!

But it did! *Grumpy Old Men* was the surprise hit of the year. It out-earned action studs of the day Sylvester Stallone and Arnold Schwarzenegger, hauling in over $70 million at the box office (big back then!). It was so big they made a sequel—another smash! No one saw it coming. But the producers who bet on it doubled their money.

To beat the crowd, you want to be on a perpetual hunt for Jack and Walter. Things everyone knows in the back of his or her mind but ignores. Things nearly everyone forgets, overlooks or assumes lack power. Things staring everyone in the face, but mostly unseen. Things hiding in plain sight.

Think of this chapter as your elephant-spotting living room safari guide. We'll cover:

- Where the elephant in the room gets its mojo
- Some elephants with blockbuster power
- Where elephants hide in plain sight

How the Elephant Got Its Tusks

The average elephant lives about 60 years and has a steel-trap memory. Humans live longer but remember far less.

Our financial memories are particularly terrible. We remember really big things! The great and terrible times from our own lives and the things our parents and grandparents always talked about. Folks know the Great Depression. Nixon oil shock. Dot-com bubble. The 2008 global meltdown. But most other economic events, recessions and even old panics are gone. History students might learn about the biggies, like the Panics of 1873 and 1907, but most of it fades over summer vacation.

Few folks see the importance of knowing economic history. Have you ever looked at one of those "What happened in (insert year here)" things online? They're all pop culture. Celebrities, scandals, politicians—the fun stuff. They ignore the stock market.

Try it and see for yourself. Google "1990 year in review" or "What happened in 1990?" You'll get pop culture overload! Sports champions, Miss America, top-10 movies and TV shows and a snippet of the "I've fallen and I can't get up" commercial. You'll learn Chuck Berry was accused of being a peeping tom and supermodel Elle Macpherson was one of the year's "hotties." Some sites give you basic economic stats like average home prices, inflation, gas prices and the cost of an IBM PC—all to show you the cost of living. Some give you full-year gross domestic product (GDP) and government debt. One, "The People's History," mentions the US had a "major recession." None mention the bear market. None even give full-year stock returns.

Old market volatility is going away. Old corrections. Old bear markets and their causes. Old tricks of the trade. All gone.

Let's do another one: 1981! If you were alive then, you know President Reagan was shot. You know the shooter was John Hinckley Jr., and he had a crush on Jodie Foster, the actress. You may also remember MTV was born, Natalie Wood died, and Prince Charles and Lady Di got hitched. Even if you don't remember "Bette Davis Eyes" was the number-one single, you can probably hum a few bars. But do you remember the capital gains tax hike? Do you remember markets did fine? And do you recall which parts of the market did best? Of course not. Our brains don't work that way.

Things everyone lived through, feared or loved at one time, then forgot—those are the elephants in the room. Forgotten knowledge! Reliable truisms that aren't priced! They should be, in theory, because they were once widely known. But they aren't, because they're forgotten and unseen. Humans' terrible economic memories empower elephants.

Dumbo, Gross Margins and Other High-Flying Elephants

Here's an elephant with blockbuster power: gross operating profit margins (GPMs). A business's revenues minus cost of goods sold, as a percentage of revenues. A quick, easy way to see how profitable a firm is at its core.

Few folks today bother with gross margins. Post-tax earnings win the popularity contest. Those are the headline earnings numbers firms report every quarter. They report the absolute total in dollars and dollars per share. Big number good! Growing number good! Small number blah. Negative number bad.

Earnings are a fine statistic. They're what you buy when you buy a stock! But earnings aren't the most telling about a company's profitability and ability to invest in the future. Earnings are skewed by accounting and other jiggery-pokery. Depreciation, write offs, stock buybacks, one-off legal and regulatory factors—they all tell you little about the health of a firm's core business. Earnings also don't tell you how big a buffer a profitable firm has—how much room to invest more, absorb higher costs or weather a temporary demand drop.

Gross margins tell you this. In the old days, they were all the rage. When I was young, you didn't have every possible piece of data about a company at your fingertips. All you had were company reports. Sales and cost of goods sold were right there. Everyone could calculate the gross margin. Just subtract and divide. No accounting skills required! Today, investors have information overload. The more data you have, the more you get bogged down in minutiae—more overthinking. Folks forget the simplicity and beauty of the old ways.

Table 5.1 Gross Margins and Returns

	Annualized Total Return in 1st Half of Bull Market		Annualized Total Return in 2nd Half of Bull Market	
Bull Start	Low GPM	High GPM	Low GPM	High GPM
8/12/1982	32.2%	32.9%	24.7%	36.3%
12/4/1987	35.5%	26.6%	11.3%	22.8%
10/11/1990	18.8%	21.2%	13.8%	26.1%
10/9/2002	32.2%	29.7%	16.6%	15.9%
Average	**30.2%**	**27.6%**	**16.6%**	**25.3%**

Sources: FactSet, Bloomberg and Compustat, as of 1/6/2015. S&P 500 daily total returns and gross profit margins, 12/31/1978-12/31/2007. The Financials sector is excluded as traditional gross profit margins do not factor into Financials firms' business models. "Low GPM" includes firms with bottom-quartile gross profit margins. "High GPM" includes firms with top-quartile gross profit margins.

So the old ways have power again! Gross margins have big power. If a firm has thin margins, it'll probably do best early on in a bull market. Thin-margin firms get punished in bear markets, when investors fear they don't have enough of a cushion to survive. They're usually over-punished, so they're over-rewarded when stocks bounce and thin-margin firms bounce bigger. Later on, in the back half of a bull market, investors get choosier and want firms with more stable earnings growth and more ability to fund growth past any potential upcoming recession.

This is when stocks with fat gross margins shine (Table 5.1). The bigger a firm's margins, the more resources it has to ensure its future. Invest in more research to find the next cutting edge. Market more. Afford more capital expenditures to boost production—expand, upgrade, you name it. All of these make future earnings more reliable, which markets love as a bull market wears on and fear of heights takes hold and new buyers, previously too fearful for stocks, start dipping their toes in the bull market's warming waters. (Note, we didn't quite get to high-GPM supremacy in the 2002-2007 bull market, since FAS 157 walloped it before high-margin firms really shined.)

Gross margins are your secret weapon when talking heads fret over earnings. Most blather on about whether a firm "beats" or "misses" (exceeds or lags consensus earnings estimates), as if what happened last quarter is the be-all, end-all. None look to gross margins for a hint of what the future holds. In Financials stocks, few examine net interest margins—banks' equivalent of gross margins—to see how profitable the core is. They look everywhere else! Fines and legal fees! Trading and investment banking revenue versus retail banking revenue! Loan charge-offs! Asset write-downs! But not the one, simple thing that really sings. They miss the elephant.

When Good News Dresses Up as Bad News

Some elephants get their power because the media decides good things are bad. Few elephants are as bullish as these twisted false fears.

In 2014, stock buybacks became this species of elephant. Buybacks are great. We've known this for ages. It was near-canonical truth! When firms buy up their own stock, they reduce supply. Our high school economics courses taught us falling supply props prices. Buybacks are also smart financial management for the companies, which borrow cheap, buy shares in their ever more profitable firm, and pocket the spread. This is all a boon for investors!

But these days, buybacks are given a bad rap. Some think they're a funny accounting trick to hide weak earnings and sad revenues. Others believe they're a drain, siphoning money from investment, hiring and wages—they boost rent-seeking CEOs and no one else. This is putting social issues ahead of stock market issues. Shrinking supply, other things equal, is great.

Maybe, when you read this, buybacks will be "in" again and some other good thing will be forced to cross-dress as bad. How can you tell if it is truly bad or an elephant? Put on your scientist's hat—or Einstein wig, if that suits you—and test the evidence!

To see how, let's dissect the buyback blowback. First, we can poke at the earnings fake-out theory. Buybacks do boost earnings and revenues per share—they drop the denominator. But they do nothing to the numerators! Total sales and total net income (earnings) don't change when share count falls. They are what they are—functions of costs, competitiveness and global demand. Buyback accounting trickery never enters into it. And where they do change the numbers—the per-share measures—this is good. Boosting earnings per share increases each shareholder's slice of future profits, a basic reason folks buy stocks in the first place!

Next, you'd dissect the hard evidence. The anti-buyback brigade cited a *Harvard Business Review* study of how big US firms spent their money from 2003 through 2012. The study's findings: The 449 firms in the S&P 500 that whole time spent 54% of net income on buybacks and 37% on dividends.[1] Using simple subtraction, several pundits decided that meant firms spent only 9% of earnings on capital expenditures (capex) and wages—ipso, presto, buybacks evil!

Here, you'd ask, what about corporate borrowing? Many buybacks are funded with debt—simple arbitrage, as I mentioned above. Tech giant Apple floated nearly $30 billion in bonds in 2013 and 2014 to fund buybacks and dividends. The interest cost was more than paid for by the savings from the buyback. The return on boosting earnings was an immediate return on amortized costs over 100%. Beat that. Companies also use bonds to finance capex—investing in structures, equipment, product development and R&D. This, too, is smart financial management. It lets firms keep cash reserves flush for a rainy day without impeding growth—just use their strong balance sheets to back a bond. Corporate bond issuance is a big reason why corporate cash balances and business investment grew hand-in-hand during the expansion that began in 2009. Few in the media will point this out, but through Q4 2014, business investment rose 15 straight quarters and sits at all-time highs.[2] A fact! Don't take my word for it—you can look it up online at the US Bureau of Economic Analysis. You'd also see that the R&D component has been clocking new highs since 2010. All true—it just doesn't square with the media's thesis.

Recent history is rife with this kind of elephant. US political gridlock is a big one—we'll get there in Chapter 6. Another is so basically bullish you might not believe anyone hates it today: a steep yield curve.

What-ifs about economic growth are impossible to prove or disprove—there is almost never a counterfactual. As Friedrich Hayek suggested while reluctantly accepting the 1974 Nobel Memorial Prize in Economic Sciences, economic measurement and scientific theories are often quite unscientific. They are, as he put it, "the Pretense of Knowledge." Scientism. A quasi-religious belief in mathematically supported theorems that actually demonstrates overconfidence and bias. Hayek opposed the creation of a Nobel for economics because he thought it would solidify this tendency. For investors, the lesson from Hayek's address is that the good contrarian will never focus on numbers to the exclusion of basic logic.

For example, buyback skeptics point to the growth rate of business investment during this cycle, which happens to be the slowest in modern history. But how can anyone know whether investment would have grown faster or slower amid fewer buybacks? We can't! We can only guess. If you ever wondered why economics is considered a dismal science, this is a big reason why. It accepts the theory of opportunity cost, taught in every economics class, but has no real way to measure it.

We can, however, look at the before and after—how does business investment growth in the buyback age compare to the pre-buyback era? I investigated this in Britain's *Interactive Investor* in September 2014: "There is no evidence buybacks weaken capex. If they did, business investment would be noticeably weaker after 1982, when the SEC gave firms carte blanche to buy back all the stock they wanted. But inflation-adjusted growth rates before and after are fairly similar. Some point to CEOs' compensation packages, arguing paying bonuses in company shares incentivizes execs to boost prices with buybacks, but this isn't true. CEOs must grow earnings and revenues, or they're fired—you can't grow a business if you don't invest."

The Yield Curve Curveball

The yield curve—a graph of one country's interest rates at different maturities—has a long, proud tradition as a leading economic indicator. It shows up in academic literature as early as 1913, in Wesley C. Mitchell's seminal work, *Business Cycles*—his effort to offer "an analytic description of the complicated process by which seasons of business prosperity, crisis, depression and revival come about in the modern world."[3] Using a trove of economic, business and financial market data spanning 1890 through 1911, Mitchell sought patterns and relationships to prove or disprove the theories of his day—and to develop his own about when and why economies boom and bust. This work was the foundation of his later contributions to the efforts of the National Bureau of Economic Research (NBER) to develop the Leading Economic Index (LEI), as we covered in Chapter 3, and it is a classic—academic yet readable and a treasure trove of knowledge. But we'll get to that more in Chapter 8.

In the book, Mitchell spends considerable time on how short- and long-term rates fluctuated over those decades, squaring their gyrations with overall business conditions. In one table, titled "Rates of Interest Yielded by Investments in Bonds and by Short-Term Loans in Seasons of Business Prosperity, Crisis, and Depression, 1890–1911," he breaks down the 21-year period into short segments with characterizations ranging from "Prosperity" to "Severe Depression" and shows the average interest rates at different maturities in each period. Of the 25 windows, two were labeled "approach of crisis." Two more were labeled "minor crisis," each occurring before a "depression." In all four, short-term rates were between one and five percentage points higher than long-term rates. You can see this for yourself—Cornell University's digitized version of the entire book is available online at the Internet Archive (https://archive.org). The magic chart is on page 162.[4]

So we've known for over a century bad things happen when short-term rates exceed long-term rates. Mitchell's commentary didn't quite connect the dots, but Reuben Kessel did in 1965, observing: "During expansions, yield differentials between Treasury bills and nine- to twelve-month governments widen. . . . Converse implications are implied for contractions."[5] By the time former San Francisco Federal Reserve Bank economist Larry Butler published "Recession?—A Market View" in December 1978, it was widely accepted that inverted yield curves (short-term rates higher than long-term rates) were a "classic recessionary" feature.[6] The yield curve gained popularity throughout the 1980s, and by 1989, economists James Stock and Mark Watson were lobbying for its inclusion in the LEI.[7]

The yield curve is a magical place where academic theory and real-world experience intersect. That's why it works! As I mentioned in Chapter 1, yield curves represent banks' profit margins—short-term rates are banks' funding costs, long-term rates are their revenues, and the spread is their gross operating profit margin (net interest margin in industry vernacular). When the yield curve is steeper—long rates are way higher than short rates—lending is more profitable. Banks lend more, the quantity of money rises, and growth magic happens. When the yield curve is flatter, lending is less profitable, and banks lend only to the safest bets—low payout, so low risk. That slows money creation and velocity (how fast money changes hands), usually slowing growth. When the curve inverts—short rates exceed long rates—lending isn't profitable, credit seizes and growth eventually grinds to a halt.

So for decades, almost everyone accepted that steep yield curves are good, flat yield curves are blah and inverted curves are dangerous. Yet in late spring and summer 2013, when long-term rates rose and the flat yield curve steepened, folks freaked out! They forgot about the yield curve! Instead they viewed higher rates as risky, fearing they'd dent demand for loans and tank the money supply. From May 22—the day Ben Bernanke first warned quantitative easing (QE) would end soon—through year end, 10-year Treasury yields rose and the yield curve steepened. Magical! Yet most folks dreaded the rise. Without even realizing it, they hated a huge fundamental driver of faster economic growth. That made the yield curve an elephant!

If you looked past the headlines and just believed in the yield curve in 2013—as I reminded folks in the *Forbes* snippet in the below box—you'd see the elephant. The magical truth that always just worked and everyone forgot. It was still there, still working. Ten-year yields rose a full percentage point between May 22 and year end, steepening the yield curve. The S&P 500 rose 13.1% over the same period.[8]

By October 2013, 10-year yields had jumped more than 70 basis points, and headlines were rife with fears this "tightening" would choke growth. Many called it "taper terror," alluding to the Federal Reserve's plans to "taper" the pace of monthly bond purchases. I'd published my views on QE before, in *Forbes* and elsewhere, but you can't hit a false fear like this hard enough or often enough, so I hit it again in the October 28 issue, with "Betting Against Bernanke":

"Long before folks fretted the demise of 'quantitative easing,' I fretted its existence. It proved the reverse of its image, an antistimulus, and we've done ok not because of it but despite it. With its demise forthcoming, I'm bullish on banks, relative to the market.

"Why? Banking's core business is simple: Take in short-term deposits, make long-term loans. The spread between short- and long-term interest rates pretty well reflects future gross operating profit margins on new loans (effectively cost versus revenue). The bigger the spread, the more profitable future loans will be, all else being equal. All of this is one simply huge elephant in the room.

"Ending so-called QE steepens that spread by definition, since it stops the Federal Reserve's buying of long-term debt (thus lowering future long-term debt prices and pushing rates higher). As the spread rises, so will bank profitability on new loans, and banks' eagerness to lend—along with overall loan revenue—will rise in lockstep."

Where Have You Gone, Milton Friedman?

The yield curve's metamorphosis from rock star to elephant was symptomatic of something else: the ascendancy of demand-side thinking over supply-side.

At the most basic level, there are two ways you can stimulate sales of any good or service: boosting supply or boosting demand. Demand-side economists—think John Maynard Keynes—largely believe directly stimulating demand is best. Supply-side economists—think Milton Friedman—believe making it easier for firms to produce sexy new products boosts supply of awesome things people never knew they wanted, which will attract new demand. Get out of the way, let the market take care of things, and watch the capitalist magic unfold.

Demand-side thinking drove the New Deal and other top-down stimulus efforts—effectively putting faith in governments, not individuals. Supply-side thinking gained popularity as the twentieth century wore on and Friedman and the so-called Chicago School hit the A-list, led by the Mundell-Laffer Hypothesis. Their influence at the Fed carried well into the 1990s and 2000s with Alan Greenspan. Even Ben Bernanke was once a self-proclaimed fan.[9] In Britain and America from the early 1980s on, Eastern Europe after the Iron Curtain fell and Peru from the late 1980s (just to name a few), economic miracles stemmed from supply-side thinking. Which side of the demand/supply fray is a superior ideology has been a raging debate for years in the academic community, and I don't intend to step into the fray. Ideology of all kinds blinds. This is an academics' war, and while it can be great fun to watch the debate (sometimes in the form of rap videos), investors don't get much by choosing sides. Neither can be proven superior and the other discredited for all of time.

Yet supply-side thinking lost street cred after 2008. Pundits and politicians scapegoated deregulation, free markets and other supply-side hallmarks for the crisis. Demand-side ideologues twisted the crisis as evidence of markets' failures—blaming overleveraged banks on the repeal of Glass-Steagall and the housing bubble on Greenspan. The nonstop chatter led many normal folks to lose faith in markets. People pinned their hopes for growth on the government, forgetting the government's crisis mismanagement only made things worse. Many forgot recent history, forgot supply-side thinking's many triumphs, and wanted divine intervention, Washington style.

The same shift happened at the Federal Reserve, but in a very different, disastrous way. For much of the twentieth century, the Fed used supply-side monetary policy—manipulating the yield curve to influence the supply of new loans and, ultimately, money. Back then, the Fed controlled short-term rates, and long-term rates were market-driven. If the Fed wanted to tighten—grow the money supply more slowly to stave off inflation—it would shrink the spread by raising short-term rates, making banks less eager to lend. If it wanted to goose money supply growth and the economy, it would drop short rates, widen the spread—steepen the yield curve—encouraging banks to lend more. And it worked, mostly. The Fed didn't always get it right, of course. As I wrote in my 2006 book, *The Only Three Questions That Count*, the Fed has a long history of dumb decisions, but the theory worked. If it wanted faster growth, it enabled banks to boost the quantity of money—then sat back and trusted capital and capitalism.

Early in the 2008 crisis, though, Bernanke's Fed abandoned supply-side monetary policy. Bernanke forgot his old hero, Milton! QE was 100% aimed at demand-side stimulus! It was disaster to the supply side. It attempted to stimulate demand for loans by keeping long-term rates artificially low so borrowers would find borrowing cheaper and more attractive. Fine in theory, but not in the real world where banks need profits! Lower long-term rates make lenders of all stripes less eager to lend. There is a happy medium that somewhat satisfies both borrower and lender. It's the free market for capital. Bernanke missed it.

When loan growth and economic growth were the weakest in modern history, few connected the dots. Many saw weak growth but figured that without QE, we'd be in the red. Almost no one noticed the Fed had whacked loan supply. Most focused on demand, clinging to academic theory, ignoring the real world.

Think real-world; the supply side is easy to see if you push it from where it is to the extreme of pushing long-term rates down. If long and short rates were both fixed at zero, if you're a banker, you'd never lend a cent! You can't take no risk for no profit! You're running a business, not a charity! You have to stay afloat!

Real-world supply-side thinking also helped you see higher long-term rates would boost supply more than they would hit demand. Even a small uptick in rates meant big profit boosts. The yield spread, measured as 10-year yields minus the effective fed-funds rate, rose

(*continued*)

from 1.73 percentage points at year-end 2012 to 2.97 when 2013 ended.[10] Doing some crude math (2.97 ÷ 1.73 – 1), this is a 71.7% increase in banks' potential profits! A huge incentive.

What about borrowers? Here's a pretend role-play I gave British readers in a November 2013 column in *Interactive Investor*:

> Pretend you're a potential borrower—chairman of the board at a moderately big, publicly traded firm. I'm the chief executive who reports to you. Our price/earnings (P/E) ratio is 14 and our earnings yield—the P/E's inverse—is 7%. We have an investment-grade credit rating, so we can borrow long-term money at 5%, 3% post-tax.
>
> Imagine I ask you to approve a new long-term business plan. The expected return matches our earnings yield, 7%. Does it matter to you, chairman, if our borrowing costs go from 3% to 3.5%? Even 4%? No! Even with the higher rates, your profit margin is big. Your eagerness to borrow isn't hurt much by the small cost increase. If the small hike made the deal look bad, it probably wasn't worth doing at all.

The biggest elephant during QE was the supply side. All it took to see it was a bit of real-world savvy, but real-world was out. Academics, not bankers, controlled the Fed. Demand-side economists ran the International Monetary Fund and the World Bank. Many pundits and academics never considered QE from a banker's or business person's viewpoint. It couldn't occur to them—they lacked real world experience. So they couldn't fathom how lower rates hurt banks way more than they boosted borrowers.

Supply-side thinking will return one day. Almost everything has its day in the sun as well as the rain. Demand-side thinking also has its wisdom, like in the depths of what Keynes called a "liquidity trap" crisis when demand truly does need an artificial boost to get money moving again, largely through a lack of true demand in preference for savings that aren't, in terms of traditional economics, disintermediated. If businesses and consumers aren't spending, capital has to come from somewhere. Governments might spend that capital unwisely, but it eventually gets where it is needed.

While supply-side thinking is in the rain, it is an elephant. If you can look at monetary policy and economic policies from a supply-sider's viewpoint, you'll see what most of the demand-side-focused media misses.

When Elephants Attack

We've chronicled some friendly elephants, but some elephants aren't nice. Risks can be elephants, too! A charging elephant is even scarier than a charging bear.

The risky elephant mirrors the nice elephant. Nice elephants are good things everyone knew, then forgot. Mean elephants are risks everyone knew, then forgot. Think back to those long-term fears we covered in Chapter 4. As long as they're widely discussed, like they are today, markets discount them. But if folks move on and forget their fears, they can become actual risks! Bad elephants! This is the market's version of the boy who cried wolf. After a while, everyone discounted him. When he was finally right, no one paid attention. Same with markets.

For example, debt fears are everywhere today and have been for ages. Between the US Treasury's online tracker and the marquee outside the IRS headquarters, anyone can see America's debt, to the penny, whenever they want. It is out there, well-known and widely discussed. As we covered in Chapter 4, debt isn't a risk today—not in the next 30 months! As long as everyone fears debt, as long as it remains a talk-radio staple, it should stay baked into prices. But if folks stop talking, it could become a risk! What if people forget to fear debt? What if interest rates skyrocket and stay there, debt service costs eat up too much tax revenue, we can't afford it, and no one notices? An unseen debt crisis in the world's largest economy, hiding in plain sight, would be a terrible shock for markets worldwide.

A Brief History of Tragedy

Forgotten history breeds mean elephants, too. Early in this chapter, we saw how old market volatility faded from memory. People didn't just forget old panics, corrections and bear markets—they also forgot how stocks reacted to some deeply negative events!

Here's one you might think I'm terrible to even consider—Presidential assassination. We don't want to think about it, but to beat TGH, you must consider the unconsiderable.

We've had assassinations before. Everyone knows they're possible. We remember the attempt on President Reagan. Many my age can easily recall November 22, 1963. But most folks don't really think it will happen again. America is too civilized. The Secret Service is too good (despite a scandal over some severe 2014 lapses). Intelligence is too good. They've thwarted every attempt and rumored attempt for decades.

An assassination might be improbable, but improbable isn't impossible. No matter how strong your political biases might be, you don't want this to happen. Investors don't. Nor do markets. The security breech alone could shatter confidence. The tragedy would also cause massive uncertainty. We know the Vice President, but only as the veep. Usually a lieutenant with a narrow portfolio of administrative responsibilities and maybe a funny gaffe or two, à la Dan Quayle and Joe Biden. We haven't had to consider how America would change under his leadership—potential changes in economic policy and international relations aren't baked in yet. Nor are folks' feelings and opinions of the veep as a leader. When Presidents are elected, markets get to discover all these things slowly and price them in during the campaign, before the winning candidate ever takes office. In contemporary times, in 2014, no one is thinking of the veep as a potential President in the here and now. It isn't priced in. An assassination would make markets price this in real-time. If they don't like what they see, it could be deeply negative.

The market history here is limited, of course. Only four Presidents have been assassinated, and two assassinations—of Lincoln and Garfield—occurred before we have reliable stock market data. That leaves Kennedy and McKinley.

Markets were resilient when Kennedy was shot in 1963—assassination isn't an automatic bear-market trigger, just a potential one of many. The S&P 500 did lose 2.7% the day of the shooting, November 22.[11] But it jumped 4.5% the next trading day, November 26, and the bull market continued.[12] However, Lyndon Baines Johnson was a well-known political commodity at that point, having held national office since 1937 and having come second to Kennedy in delegates in the 1960 primaries. As Senate Majority Leader, Johnson's calling card was brokering deals to win support. Few expected policy to get wild.

When McKinley was killed in 1901, however, it was a different story. Before he was shot on September 6, the Dow was recovering from a 12% correction, which had bottomed August 6.[13] This recovery reversed September 6, and stocks slid as McKinley's health worsened.[14] He succumbed on September 14, the Dow kept falling, and the correction turned into a bear market.[15] Said otherwise, stocks likely moved fast down in light of a then not-well-known Vice President, Teddy Roosevelt, who carried a radically different agenda, style and peer group of counselors relative to McKinley. This piece of market history has largely faded, giving it elephant status. The Cowles Commission hasn't verified data pre-1926, so most mainstream analysis of market history begins there. But while turn-of-the-century Dow data are limited and imperfect, they provide precedent and illustrate the risk.

When Textbooks Lie

Here's another terrible event everyone knows but most believe can't happen: World War III.

Everyone knows a massive global conflict would be unspeakably horrible—a horrendous loss of life, potentially with weapons of mass destruction leveling entire cities. We've all read the dystopian novels, seen the films. From *1984* and *Brave New World* to *The Hunger Games,* we see how terrible another world war and its aftermath could be.

But that's all fiction! Fiction isn't reality! As a society, we've largely convinced ourselves another world war is impossible. The world economy is too integrated, trade relationships too strong and diplomacy too good. We've evolved. We use sanctions, not bullets, to keep rogue world powers and wanna-be troublemakers in check. America and Europe have nuclear weapons as a deterrent, not for actual use. The Soviet Union died, ending the Cold War, and Russia keeps getting ever more backward.

A World War is a highly improbable event, but again, improbable isn't impossible. Most folks thought the world too civilized and integrated in 1914, but World War I happened anyway. Dow data—again, limited but illustrative—show a 31.8% drop between Archduke Franz Ferdinand's June 28, 1914, assassination and the end of the year.[16] Stocks rose in 1915 and 1916, but the Dow peaked November 21, 1916—just after the Battle of the Somme, and the very day HMHS *Britannic* was sunk by a German mine. Stocks bottomed over a year later, on December 19, 1917, after losing more than 40% as fighting raged across the European theater. And, of course, it was "the war to end all wars." Didn't happen.

Again, these old Dow data are unreliable—always be skeptical! Market data during World War II have been painstakingly verified, and they paint a similar picture. When Germany annexed the Sudetenland in mid-1938, the S&P 500 appeared to be recovering from the bear market that began in 1937. But Hitler's seizure of Czech territory truncated it—his limitless territorial ambitions became clear, forcing markets to price in the likelihood of a long, destructive global conflict. They bounced sideways for months, but when France fell, the bottom fell out.

Back then, everyone thought France was good at war. The French were the experts at trench warfare in the Crimea. The Franco-Prussian War was a hiccup, but they redeemed themselves by fighting the Germans basically to a draw. World War I, another trench success. The Maginot Line's marketing tag was probably "Nothing beats a French trench." (Sloganeers like rhyme.) But when Germany had paratroopers and could sneak tanks through Belgium, that trench did no good. Believe it or not, that was a surprise. German troops maneuvered around the Maginot Line and invaded France on May 10, 1940. Between May 9, 1940—the day before—and April 28, 1942, the S&P 500 fell –38.4%.[17] France's fall was the huge negative surprise no one saw coming.

Market history shows world wars kill bull markets. It is a fact! Yet it gets distorted by many high school history textbooks claiming World War II was bullish! Millions of Americans grow up believing the "guns and butter" economy was the only reason we emerged from the Great Depression. Folks see the bull market beginning in 1942, fully three years before Allied victory, and forget the market's reaction to Hitler's aggression early on. Terrible as we know war is on a human level, textbooks might lull America into complacency.

World War II didn't cause America's upswing. The timeline doesn't even match! Gross domestic product (GDP) resumed growing in 1939, two years before World War II spending started in earnest. The private sector drove growth in 1939 and 1940. Table 5.2 shows annual real GDP growth during this stretch, along with each major category's contribution to growth. In 1939 and 1940, the feds contributed far less than consumers and private investors.

Look closely at 1942 and 1943, and you'll see something interesting. As government spending skyrocketed, private investment tanked and consumer spending wobbled. There are two schools of thought here. One says only the war effort kept America afloat—the "guns and butter" miracle. Another argues massive government spending crowded out the private sector, making life harder for businesses and people. Here, too, demand side versus supply side.

Economists, historians and ideologues have debated this for decades. How should you think about it? Up to you! But using our contrarian brain-training, I think the supply side raises curious points. The demand-side view doesn't explore

Table 5.2 Real GDP Growth and Contributions to Real GDP Growth, 1938–1943

	Annual Percentage Change					
	1938	1939	1940	1941	1942	1943
Gross Domestic Product	-3.3%	8.0%	8.8%	17.7%	18.9%	17.0%
Personal Consumption Expenditures	-1.6%	5.6%	5.2%	7.1%	-2.4%	2.8%
Gross Private Domestic Investment	-31.2%	25.4%	36.2%	22.4%	-44.3%	-37.6%
Government Consumption Expenditures and Gross Investment	7.6%	8.7%	3.6%	68.1%	132.1%	50.0%

	Contributions to Real GDP Growth					
	1938	1939	1940	1941	1942	1943
Personal Consumption Expenditures	-1.15	4.11	3.72	4.9	-1.5	1.52
Gross Private Domestic Investment	-4.13	2.39	3.99	3.13	-6.45	-2.63
Government Consumption Expenditures and Gross Investment	1.09	1.41	0.57	10.31	28.03	19.31
Net Exports of Goods and Services	0.88	0.07	0.52	-0.64	-1.19	-1.16
TOTAL (Real GDP Growth)	**-3.3%**	**8.0%**	**8.8%**	**17.7%**	**18.9%**	**17.0%**

Source: US Bureau of Economic Analysis, as of 10/16/2014. Percentage Change in Real Gross Domestic Product and Contributions to Percentage Change in Real Gross Domestic Product, 1938–1943.

the counterfactual—what would have happened if there weren't a war? What if production weren't diverted from consumer goods to war machines? What if Americans never had to face rationing? How would businesses and people have allocated capital? Would America have grown even faster?

I didn't make any of this up. The philosophy dates at least to French economist Frédéric Bastiat's 1850 essay, *That Which Is Seen and That Which Is Not Seen,* which explored the unseen consequences of government spending. Part I, "The Broken

Window," is a parable about a shopkeeper whose son breaks a window. The shopkeeper is peeved—that window costs six francs to fix! "But on the bright side," say the neighbors, "you'll keep the glazier employed."

The neighbors see the broken window as a positive—stimulus for glassmakers! Their reasoning is easy to buy, because we see the glazier fix the window and get paid. This is the "seen" effect of the broken window.

Looking only at the "seen" is too myopic! So Bastiat explored the "unseen." The six francs spent on the window were six francs the shopkeeper couldn't spend on shoes or books. What if the shoemaker or the bookseller would have put those six francs to better use than the glazier?

"The Broken Window" was a rebuttal to a French politician who claimed burning down the entire city of Paris would boost France's economy because rebuilding would create demand and jobs, but it works most anywhere. You can apply it to World War II spending—and the widely held belief that postwar rebuilding was a massive stimulus for Western Europe. Big natural disasters, too. When you see these arguments, remember Bastiat's conclusion: "Society loses the value of things which are uselessly destroyed . . . To break, to spoil, to waste, is not to encourage national labor; or, more briefly, destruction is not profit."[18] Often true whether physical property or personal opportunities are destroyed. On the other hand, sometimes we demolish buildings, bridges and more to build newer, bigger and better ones on prime real estate, creating greater wealth. It can go both ways.

"The Broken Window" is an elephant, too. It is age-old and widely read. Henry Hazlitt updated it in his classic, *Economics in One Lesson* (Harper & Brothers, 1946). The broken-window fallacy, as it is now known, is a classroom staple. But few think of it when disaster strikes or government programs are launched. Most focus on the seen—few fathom the unseen. Fathom the unseen, and you have contrarian power. We'll see this more in Chapter 6.

It Can't Be an Elephant If ...

Even if something sounds sensible, if everyone is talking about it, it can't be an elephant. Remember, we're looking for the pre–*Grumpy Old Men* Jack Lemmon and Walter Matthau—not Brad Pitt and George Clooney. Unless you're reading this in 2035, and Brad and George are has-been geezers. Then, maybe you do want Brad and George! But you don't want the A-list celebrity.

If Wall Street loves something, no matter how strong the logic, it can't be an elephant. Here's an example: "disruptive technology." This twenty-first-century buzzword refers to innovations that transform (or disrupt) entire industries, displacing old technologies. Think the Internet, PC, cell phone, smartphone, robotics, 3-D printing and hydraulic fracturing. When a new firm comes along with a sexy new technology, pundits pile on the bandwagon, telling investors to get in on the Next Big Thing before it's too late. It is happening right now in 3-D printing—where specialized printers read a three-dimensional design (usually from a CAD program) and form the object by "printing" razor-thin cross-sections in resin or metal, layering them from the bottom up, and fusing them together. Pundits champion the firms manufacturing the printers, assuming the pure-play investment is best. You see similar enthusiasm toward robotics and drone makers.

These aren't elephants! The technology may be great and game-changing, and its creators and makers might make big profits, but pure-play investments often aren't where the real magic is. Too loved, too known. Too faddish. And surely too priced.

The elephant in technology often isn't the tech firms. The real elephant is the creative user who spins the technology into something wild. The toymaker married to the circuit designer who dreams up next year's must-have gizmo for kids. The barista in Cupertino who overhears two Seagate employees discussing their newest, smallest hard drive and dreams up talking coffeemakers that think perky thoughts. The worried mom who rigs a microdrone to keep an eye on her kids while they're walking to school and commercializes it.

These are the real disruptors—the inventive folks using new technology to take on industries. Netflix didn't invent DVDs or streaming. Reed Hastings just figured out how to use them to drive Blockbuster out of business. Uber and Lyft didn't invent smartphones or apps. They spun off those existing technologies to turn taxi service on its head. Steve Jobs didn't invent the mobile phone. He and the Apple engineers just collided cell phones with microprocessors, touchscreens, tempered glass, flash memory, a camera and powerful software. In 3-D printing, the inventive users are the industrial firms using the new technology to slash production costs. Or the medical device firms 3-D printing heart valves. Look past the headline technology, find the inventive users, and you'll find some elephants.

Elephants can live anywhere. As we'll see later on in Chapter 8, many live in old books. Others live in a thorny place we're about to journey to: politics. We're friends now, so it's safe. Ready? Turn to Chapter 6!

Notes

1. "Profits Without Prosperity," William Lazonick, *Harvard Business Review*, September 2014. https://hbr.org/2014/09/profits-without-prosperity (accessed 2/24/2015).
2. US Bureau of Economic Analysis, as of 2/10/2015. US real non-residential fixed investment, 3/31/2011–12/31/2014.
3. *Business Cycles*, Wesley Clair Mitchell (Berkeley: University of California Press, 1913), vii. https://archive.org/stream/cu31924003462680#page/n185/mode/1up (accessed 10/14/2014).
4. *Business Cycles*, Wesley Clair Mitchell (Berkeley: University of California Press, 1913), 162. https://archive.org/stream/cu31924003462680#page/n185/mode/1up (accessed 10/14/2014).
5. "The Cyclical Behavior of the Term Structure of Interest Rates," Reuben A. Kessel. First published as Chapters 1 and 4 of NBER Occasional Paper 91, 1965. Citation comes from *Essays on Interest Rates*, Vol. 2, Jack

M. Guttentag, ed. (UMI, 1971), 384. www.nber.org/chapters/c4003.pdf (accessed 10/14/2014).

6. "Recession?—A Market View," Larry Butler, Federal Reserve Bank of San Francisco *Economic Letter*, December 15, 1978. https://www.fedinprint.org/items/fedfel/y1978idec13.html (accessed 2/24/2015).
7. "New Indexes of Coincident and Leading Economic Indicators," James H. Stock and Mark W. Watson, *NBER Macroeconomics Annual 1989*, Vol. 4, Olivier Jean Blanchard and Stanley Fischer, eds. (Cambridge, MA: MIT Press, 1989). www.nber.org/chapters/c10968.pdf (accessed 10/14/2014).
8. FactSet, as of 10/14/2014. US 10-Year Treasury Yield (Constant Maturity) and S&P 500 Total Return Index, 5/22/2013–12/31/2013.
9. "On Milton Friedman's Ninetieth Birthday," remarks by Governor Ben S. Bernanke at the Conference to Honor Milton Friedman, University of Chicago, Chicago, Illinois, November 8, 2002. Speech published by the United States Federal Reserve. www.federalreserve.gov/boarddocs/Speeches/2002/20021108/default.htm (accessed 10/14/2014).
10. FactSet, as of 10/15/2014. US 10-Year Treasury Yield (Constant Maturity) and Effective Fed-Funds Rate, 12/31/2012–12/31/2013.
11. FactSet, as of 1/14/2015. S&P 500 Price Index, 11/21/1963–11/22/1963.
12. FactSet, as of 1/14/2015. S&P 500 Price Index, 11/25/1963–11/26/1963.
13. FactSet, as of 1/14/2015. Dow Jones Industrial Average, 12/31/1900–12/31/1901.
14. Ibid.
15. Ibid.
16. FactSet, as of 1/14/2015. Dow Jones Industrial Average, 6/27/1914–12/31/1914.
17. FactSet, as of 1/14/2015. S&P 500 Price Index, 5/9/1940–4/28/1942.
18. *That Which Is Seen and That Which Is Not Seen*, Frédéric Bastiat, 1850. Reproduced by Maestro Reprints.

CHAPTER 6

The Chapter You'll Love to Hate

Politics!

There. Are you angry yet?

Nothing makes folks touchy quite like politics. Few humans lack strong political opinions. Partisans love their side, hate the other. Centrists hate extremists of both sides while caring little for ideology. The far left and far right think the center-left and center-right are wishy-washy weaklings. And they're all surely, confidently, right. It's a battle for America's heart and soul, and we aren't supposed to bring it up before dessert.

But we're friends now, so here we go. Politics are charged, but they matter for stocks. Nasty laws and regulations have caused or worsened bear markets. Seemingly tiny rule changes can disrupt entire industries and capital markets. Widespread myths about ideology and partisan rhetoric can give contrarians big opportunities to game the crowd.

We'll cover all of this and more in these pages. Warning, you might not like it. If you lean one way or the other—doesn't matter which way—your instinct will be to hate at least 50% of this chapter. Just human nature! Battling this instinct is step one. Whether liberal or conservative you're far from alone, and your ideology is surely priced always. That's very hard for most people to swallow.

To help spare your sanity, we'll stay away from pure sociopolitical factors. I don't do sociology. That's for someone else. As I mentioned in Chapter 4, it is fine and dandy to think and have opinions about these. They impact everyday life! But they're out of the investing realm. Markets focus narrowly. Stocks don't care who your neighbor Bob marries and whether they replace the champagne toast with ceremonial pot smoking at the reception. Stocks care how rules and regulations impact the flow of capital and resources, profits, foreign trade and the ease and cost of commerce—and whether that's already priced or not and really only over the next approximate 30 months or so. Narrow variables, and easy to isolate if you know what to look for and can train your brain to be objective.

You might already be skeptical. That's ok! I won't cry if you skip to Chapter 7. But I hope you don't, because this chapter has some prime contrarian tricks and powerful elephants in the room. Here's the menu:

- How to clear your brain of bias, one of investing's deadliest traps
- The biggest elephant in the political living room—and not the one on the Republican Party's logo
- When new laws matter … and when they don't
- Why Congress isn't always stocks' biggest political enemy

Step 1: Ditch Your Biases

Presidents, prime ministers, governors, senators, members of Congress, members of parliament, military dictators, fascist thug dictators and commie thug dictators have one thing in common: They're politicians. Experts at self-promotion and marketing. Big-time elected politicians run on focus-group-tested platforms. Dictators survive on manufactured cult of personality. In and out of democracies, political life is one big ad campaign.

There are exceptions, perhaps. Maybe some wanna-be Mr. Smith went to Washington with ideals and values. Life can imitate Frank Capra films. But most high-ranking politicians are megalomaniacs with a high incidence of observed psychopathic traits.

I didn't make that up—several psychological studies show it, including one from the *Journal of Personality and Social Psychology* in 2012.[1] Life imitates *The Onion*, too: "Nation Tunes In to See Which Sociopath More Likable This Time," which skewered the 2012 Presidential debates, wasn't entirely satire.[2]

My point isn't that all politicians are evil. If you like a politician or two, be my guest! Have opinions! Again, societal and political issues are important, interesting and fine to think about. Education, foreign policy, civil liberties and all the rest matter. It is natural and great to have strong opinions in these areas. But markets don't care about ideology. So when you're thinking about markets, turning off your opinions is best. Political bias blinds.

The easiest way to turn off bias, in my experience, is to make "he's just a politician" or "she's just a politician" your mantra. If you find yourself believing Presidential candidate John or Jane Chowderhead will be wonderful or terrible for stocks based on speeches, debates and campaign ads, remind yourself: "Just a politician." They're in marketing mode. Their goal is to pique your emotions. When investing, you want to turn off your emotions.

The more you remember they're all politicians, the easier it is to objectively assess how politics impact stocks. Politics matter! But not in a "Party X is good for stocks and Party Y is bad" kind of way. Or in a "Party Y is good for stocks and Party X is bad" way, lest you think I'm an anti-Y-ist. "Y," you might ask? Because "Y" and "X" are always priced. Stocks care more about actual laws, rules and regulations. Policies' seen and unseen consequences. Get past your opinions, and reality is easier to see.

My Guy Is Best, Your Guy Is Worst and Other Unhelpful Opinions

Investing on opinions is folly, but many folks do it. Talking heads and op-ed pages encourage us. Many state their beliefs as fact, with ideology and cherry-picked factoids as evidence.

Fine for them—they're pundits, not analysts! Their job is to be opinionated and attract eyeballs. But most don't provide usable facts for you, the cool-headed contrarian.

Markets discount this quickly. Political opinions are everywhere! All over TV, your newspaper, the Internet, your office, your neighbor's dinner table—widely discussed and therefore pre-priced. A lot of it conflicts! One paper could call a candidate with big spending plans a welfare state-loving socialist nightmare. Another could call him a pro-growth dream who will turn the underprivileged into employable human capital and bring jobs to our underemployed youth. One cable pundit could call a tax-cutting supply-side reformer the market's knight in shining armor. Another could call him the austerity-obsessed first horseman of the apocalypse.

Same goes for new laws. Take the Affordable Care Act (ACA), or "Obamacare" if you prefer. A Google search for "Obamacare op-ed" returns over a million hits. Over one million published opinions on whether the law is wonderful or a disaster. Some love it. Others loathe it. For hundreds or more different reasons. And they're all just fine opinions.

Opinions are not facts. Facts are solid. Irrefutable. Feelings are squishy, fungible and differ from person to person. For everyone who hates a politician, party or law, someone else loves them. For every person who thinks tax hikes kill consumption, another thinks they're deficit-reduction magic that help fund the solutions we need to help consumers.

Markets reflect all these emotions. The sheer volume of political noise in our media, combined with the fact we have over 146 million registered American voters,[3] makes it impossible for the opinion of "manyone" not to be priced in. However strongly you feel about a President, a candidate, the party controlling Congress or a new law, there is little or nothing in your opinion that someone else doesn't already know. You're unlikely to be "anyone" and likely to be "manyone" in political sociology unless your views are shared by almost no one. Part of a big crowd, fully priced.

Table 6.1 S&P 500 Bear Markets and Presidential Party

Start	President	End	President
9/6/1929	Hoover [R]	6/1/1932	Hoover [R]
3/10/1937	FDR [D]	4/28/1942	FDR [D]
5/30/1946	Truman [D]	6/13/1949	Truman [D]
8/2/1956	Eisenhower [R]	10/22/1957	Eisenhower [R]
12/12/1961	Kennedy [D]	6/26/1962	Kennedy [D]
2/9/1966	Johnson [D]	10/7/1966	Johnson [D]
11/29/1968	Johnson [D]	5/26/1970	Nixon [R]
1/11/1973	Nixon [R]	10/3/1974	Ford [R]
11/28/1980	Carter [D]	8/12/1982	Reagan [R]
8/25/1987	Reagan [R]	12/4/1987	Reagan [R]
7/16/1990	Bush [R]	10/11/1990	Bush [R]
3/24/2000	Clinton [D]	10/9/2002	GW Bush [R]
10/9/2007	GW Bush [R]	3/9/2009	Obama [D]

Source: FactSet, as of 12/2/2014. S&P 500 bear markets, 1929–2014.

Stocks are politically agnostic—they don't care which party is in power. Bear markets begin and end on both parties' watch, as Table 6.1 shows. Neither is inherently good or bad for markets.

Opinions can influence sentiment, but this gets baked in during campaign season. The likelier a candidate appears to win, the more investors vote their feelings and opinions about him or her, and this shows up in prices. If you wake up the day after the election and decide to buy or sell based on how you feel about who won, you're too late.

I wrote about this in my 2010 book, *Debunkery*—I called it the "Perverse Inverse." There, I explained that about two-thirds of American investors lean Republican and see the GOP as pro-business—forgetting they're just politicians. They believe the campaign marketing spin. They also forget Democrats are just politicians, believing all their campaign marketing spin about social fairness and big government. They see Democrats as anti-business wealth redistributors. Two strong opinions! These are usually baked into election-year returns. In election years when the Presidency flips from red to blue, stocks tend to render below-average returns—and fall further if Congress flips, too. When the White House flips to the GOP, stocks average positive, and rise even higher if Congress follows.

But when the new President is in office, stocks U-turn! Stocks are historically up big in Democrats' inauguration years. Even bigger if Congress went blue, too. But they're down in Republicans' first years. Table 6.2 has the numbers, straight from *Debunkery*.

Why? They're all just politicians! The Democrats aren't really so anti-business as feared. Republicans aren't as pro-business as hoped. What was priced in—hopes and fears—in this realm tend to be heartfelt and extreme. These people won a popularity contest to get their job. Their main goal? Staying well-liked for the re-election campaign. Following campaign pledges to a T would alienate almost half the population. The pledges folks love or hate usually get watered down or shelved. All those strong opinions don't matter on a forward-looking basis.

Opinions are feelings about what a politician has done or might do. Stocks can swing on this sentiment in the short term, but you can't time investing decisions around it—too many other variables. Your best bet, when thinking politically, is to look at the will-do. What will actually become law? What is the likeliest impact on commerce, trade, banking and markets?

Table 6.2 Party Changes and S&P 500 Performance

	Election Year	Inauguration Year
Presidency changed from Republican to Democrat	–2.8%	21.8%
Presidency changed from Democrat to Republican	13.2%	–6.6%
Presidency and Congress changed from Democrat to Republican	–8.9%	52.9%
Presidency and Congress changed from Republican to Democrat	25.5%	–3.0%

Source: Global Financial Data, Inc. S&P 500 Total Return, 12/31/1925–12/31/2009.

A Magical Elephant Named Gridlock

Deep political analysis is hard work—identifying unseen consequences and avoiding the broken window fallacy takes imagination and go-it-alone chutzpah. We'll get there later. First, we'll hit the highest, easiest level.

In competitive, developed countries like America, markets hate active legislatures. Stocks know the status quo. They know the rules and how to navigate them. Change requires adaptation. It also creates winners and losers, which markets hate. If Congress can't do anything, they can't screw anything up—a huge relief for stocks.

The more laws Congress passes, the higher the chance they could redraw property rights, rewrite regulation or redistribute wealth, resources and opportunity—all negative. Prospect theory—folks' tendency to feel the pain of loss more than the joy of an equivalent gain—is big in behavioral finance, as we'll see in Chapter 9, but it applies to legislation too. If a new law shifts resources from Group A to Group B, Group A hates it more than Group B loves it. Their net negativity can weigh on stocks. The more active Congress is, the more risk averse markets get. Political risk aversion spills psychologically to market risk aversion.

So to see how politics will impact stocks, first ask: What's the likelihood these greasy politicians pass something radical? Low or high?

This is easy and basic, but few look there. Here, too, feelings get in the way. We have plenty of evidence markets love gridlock. As I showed in my 2006 book, *The Only Three Questions That Count*, years three and four of a President's term have the highest average returns, and gridlock is why. Presidents usually lose power in midterms. They know it, so they front-load big moves into years one and two. Obama did it with the ACA and Dodd-Frank. Bush did it with Sarbanes-Oxley. Clinton did it with tax hikes and attempts at health care reform. Late-term changes like 1999's Gramm-Leach-Bliley are rare.

Markets love gridlock, but people hate it. As people, we hate polarization and bickering do-nothing Congresses. The rancor is annoying. We voted for these clowns so they could fix whatever we think needs fixing, not so they could squabble and sit on their hands. The fewer laws Congress passes, the lower their approval ratings sink. In 2013, Congress passed a record-low 72 measures.[4] That November, Congress's approval rating hit a record-low 9%.[5] They were only nine percentage points more popular than Ebola! But the S&P 500 finished up 32.4%.[6] Voters' broad dissatisfaction with Washington blinds folks—they don't appreciate the fact gridlock blocks new laws potentially spooking stocks. Partisans want their party's proposals to pass. Independent-minded folks want bipartisan compromise and less bickering. Few believe doing nothing is best or even ok—because they too much believe their own ideology. Liberals hate nothing happening because they want what they want. Conservatives too. Non-ideologists too. Only markets like it because when political risk aversion falls, risk aversion falls.

Bipartisan compromise might sound nice. It implies watered-down, middle-of-the-road laws. But history has some big bipartisan stinkers, like Sarbanes-Oxley. The devastating Tariff Act of 1930—Smoot-Hawley—enjoyed broad bipartisan support. So did the Merchant Marine Act of 1920, aka the Jones Act, which bottlenecks US crude oil transportation even today. The Humphrey-Hawkins Act of 1978 was another bipartisan bomb. It created the Fed's dual mandate, tying US monetary policy to the long-ago debunked belief that inflation and unemployment are linked. Bipartisan doesn't mean good. It means popular.

Great as gridlock is, few fathom its market benefits. Gridlock is the elephant in the room! Markets thrive on gridlock, but not because a magic gridlock switch flips in investors' minds. It is more of a non-realization realization that radical new laws aren't passing. The absence of a negative is a positive. Everyone sees gridlock. Most just can't see that doing nothing does a lot for stocks.

The "long-ago debunked belief" about a link between inflation and unemployment is an old model called the Phillips Curve. Its pioneer, AWH Phillips, found an inverse relationship between wages and employment in Britain from 1861 through 1957. He assumed a causal link: High unemployment meant a surplus of workers, letting employers keep wages low. Low unemployment forced firms to hike wages to keep talent. His curve modeled this out, suggesting a given level of unemployment should lead to a given inflation rate.

Milton Friedman challenged this theory in a 1968 speech, "The Role of Monetary Policy."[7] Edmund S. Phelps also took a whack at it in 1967.[8] In a nutshell, they argued Phillips' model ignored money supply—the real driver of inflation (always and everywhere a monetary phenomenon!). Firms, they argued, paid more attention to *real* wages—inflation-adjusted—when deciding how to adjust pay relative to the supply of labor. Inflation was an input to their decisions, not a result.

The 1970s proved Friedman and Phelps right—high unemployment, high inflation. Yet the Phillips curve endures. Academic debates don't die easily.

Where Gridlock Isn't Best

My views on gridlock apply most to competitive developed countries. Think US, UK, Western Europe, Australia and Canada. However you might feel about American economic policy, the backbone of free markets, capitalism and property rights is strong. Is there some room for improvement around the edges? Heck yeah! A simple, short, flatter tax code would be wondrous! Probably won't happen in my lifetime though. Stable money value would be great. Probably won't happen in my lifetime. There is also plenty of red tape to cut. Of course that's just my ideology talking. Oops! Forget I said that if you want. Markets don't care about my ideology any more than yours. Realistically, though, it is very rare for Congress to pass economic-related laws that don't inflict collateral damage. Very rare.

Things are different in uncompetitive nations, young Emerging Markets and many former socialist or Communist states. Most have weak property rights, bloated public sectors, inefficient regulations, high corruption and inequality not of income but of fundamental potential economic opportunity, where the born-poor can't get

(*continued*)

rich as so many do in the West. There, active legislatures with strong pro-growth policies can be good! Opening closed industries to competition, privatizing state-owned albatrosses, welcoming private investment, strengthening property rights, enabling entrepreneurship, freeing trade—all great for markets and long-term growth.

Margaret Thatcher's Britain is a prime example. For most of the mid-twentieth century, Britain dallied with socialism—not as badly as France and most of Continental Europe, but bad enough. By 1979, the state propped miners and manufacturers that couldn't compete globally. Britain's GDP grew in the 1950s, 1960s and 1970s, but its growth lagged America's. Kids, socialism never works—but that's another book. Thatcher became Prime Minister in 1979 and spent the next few years overhauling Britain's economic structure. State-run industries were privatized. Regulations relaxed. The service sector gained room to grow and thrive. The "Big Bang" financial reforms of 1986 modernized capital markets, allowing Britain to compete with—and eventually dominate—the world's biggest financial hubs. The Iron Lady's reforms radically improved Britain's structural backdrop. As privatization and reform escalated from 1985 through the end of the decade, British stocks exploded.

After the Iron Curtain fell, free-market thinking came to the former USSR and its satellites. Vaclav Havel adopted it in Czechoslovakia. Estonia and Latvia followed suit. To them, it was simple! Of course free markets were the way back from bankrupt communist hell! These were big, radical changes—the good kind. There, the status quo was dreadful. Gridlock would have been doom.

Simply finding free-market reforms isn't enough, though—if they're widely known, they're probably priced in. Mexico today is making big free-market progress, busting state-sponsored monopolies in Telecom and Energy, freeing up banking and modernizing labor markets. Great for Mexican people and businesses! But widely discussed. America's next-door neighbor gets too many eyeballs—reforms there are quickly discounted by stocks.

Always ask: How well does the broader market appreciate reforms? Sir John Templeton, arguably the first great global investor, built a career looking at all the countries no one else considered, like postwar Japan. He studied countries everyone ignored and found opportunities few saw. To be like Templeton today, find free-market change in areas no one pays attention to. This used to be Emerging Markets, but now everyone looks there—particularly the biggest ones. It's less likely you can discover un-priced reforms in Brazil, Russia, India, China or South

Korea than in ones fewer study. And fewer focus on smaller Emerging Markets, like Peru and Chile, so opportunities might lurk there. But the biggest opportunities lie further away, in Frontier Markets—Africa, most of the Middle East, Myanmar, Vietnam and the like. Investors aren't used to looking there. Many don't even realize some of these countries have viable, growing economies. Events like Rwanda's 1994 genocide get stuck in our brains. Few fathom how far these nations have come.

Then, too, reform promises alone aren't enough. That's all can-do—markets want will-do. Actions, not words. Remember, they're all politicians! They must prove they aren't just talk and marketing! Stocks pre-price all that. If actual reforms don't meet expectations, you get a sentiment-driven rally that fizzles. This happened in India in 2009. Indian stocks boomed when re-elected Prime Minister Manmohan Singh won a sweeping mandate for free-market reform. He didn't follow through, and boom turned to gloom.

We see it in Japan, too. Japan had a rough go after the 1980s, and its antiquated neo-mercantilist economic structure is why. Huge tariffs block trade. Massive state spending crowds out private investment. The 35% corporate tax rates further discourage. Byzantine labor laws force corporate bloat. Politicians don't let the market deal with poorly governed, unprofitable corporate giants. The behemoth state-owned postal bank basically funds the government. These caused Japan's infamous "lost decade" (going on plural) of deflation and shrinking nominal GDP.

In late 2012, a new Prime Minister promised to fix it. Shinzo Abe. Ok, a sort-of new Prime Minister. Abe is Japan's Grover Cleveland (without the caricature belly and mustache)—he was Prime Minster for a year in 2006/2007. He failed then but promised take two would be different. He swept to power promising a "three arrows" economic revitalization strategy the media called "Abenomics." Arrow one: quantitative easing (uh-oh). Arrow two: fiscal stimulus (uh-oh). Arrow three: deep structural reform (don't think so). Investors ate it up, and Japan outperformed the world as he fired arrows one and two in early 2013.

Over two years in, though, he hasn't fired arrow three. He keeps promising! But his government can't even pass low-hanging fruit like legalizing casinos—too big a gamble for them. He talks vaguely of labor market and immigration reform, corporate tax cuts, free trade and corporate governance incentives, but proposed laws are fuzzy, watered down and phase in too slowly. The more reality disappoints, the more Japan underperforms. It is often said bull markets climb a wall of worry—Abe's Japan is sliding down the slope of lost hope.

(Not) Just a Bill Sittin' on Capitol Hill

Not every fundamentally negative new law mangles markets. Stocks hatc quick, radical change—having to adapt and discover winners and losers real-time. The negative surprise potential is huge. The more time markets have to discover and digest potential negatives (or positives), the more muted the impact tends to be—stocks vet out potential surprises early, sapping their power. They can still hurt or help, but less.

Markets start digesting new laws when the proposal enters public conversation. The initial discussion, draft legislation, multiple rounds of Congressional debate and amendments—and all the media chatter—let markets price the wide-ranging opinions and likely outcomes. Every pundit who discovers a potential winner or loser does stocks a favor, letting them discount the potential fallout. When you know something bad is coming, and you can brace for it, it is easier to deal with than a surprise.

The longer the discovery period, the less jarring the actual law's impact tends to be. Conversely, short discovery periods can bite hard.

Consider stocks' reaction to one of recent history's worst laws: The "Act to protect investors by improving the accuracy and reliability of corporate disclosures made pursuant to the securities laws, and for other purposes," better known as Sarbanes-Oxley or Sarbox. The name sounds great, but it was Congress's overreaction to the Enron accounting scandal. Sarbox tried to improve corporate governance and transparency by doing things like making CEOs criminally liable for accounting and reporting errors. A huge, costly burden on publicly traded companies. Nasty stuff!

Sarbox moved fast. The draft bill was introduced February 14, 2002, after about six weeks of Senate hearings on Enron and other perceived ills of corporate America. House committee debate lasted two months—short by DC standards. The final version hit the full House April 16 and passed April

24. The Senate passed its stricter version July 15. Congress set out to reconcile the two bills July 24 and 25. Most observers thought the softer House version would win the day and become law. Yet largely due to a last-minute sticky situation involving President Bush and personal loans from corporations to board members, he suddenly shifted his support to the Senate version, the law we have today. And, with the WorldCom scandal breaking during the legislative process, most provisions were given more teeth behind closed doors. President Bush signed the law July 30, and it took effect that day. No phase-in—just boom! Let there be rules!

Stocks were already in a bear market, but Sarbox likely made it much worse. Between April 16 and July 25, the S&P 500 fell –25.4%.[9] The bear market lasted another two and a half months. But a bull market began October 9—even though Sarbox was big and bad, cyclical factors overruled it. The existence of big rules doesn't keep stocks from rising. Markets can adapt, and they adapted to Sarbox. The initial shock hurts markets. Then life goes on.

Few fathomed this when Congress passed another sweeping overhaul, the ACA. The ACA isn't as fundamentally negative as Sarbox. Sarbox hamstrung all of corporate America! The ACA was big, but tamer—it created winners and losers in health care, and incrementally raised investment taxes and businesses' costs. But many investors saw it as the devil, half a step from socialism. When it passed in March 2010, folks feared it would sink stocks. Fears resurged repeatedly for years. Yet, as much as folks hated the law, stocks did fine. Why? It was priced!

As I said before, stocks start discounting laws when people start discussing them. ACA entered the national conversation way back in 2008's Presidential campaign. Not as the ACA! But John McCain and Barack Obama both promised big health care reform. After Obama won, markets knew they'd get his version. He outsourced it to Congress, which spent over a year writing, debating, rewriting and neutering the legislation.

It passed on a Sunday, March 21, 2010. Stocks rose the next day. A correction ran from April 15 to July 5, but that had much more to do with fears Greece would collapse and take the euro down with it. Health Care stocks didn't do great in 2010—they underperformed through early 2011—but that's normal when a law radically alters an industry's foundation. Some segments of Health Care, like managed care facilities, had to overhaul their business models. Just normal. Health Care stocks still rose! Just less than the overall market.

ACA fears resurged repeatedly for four years, but stocks fared well. Markets rose amid the early 2012 Supreme Court arguments and in the run-up to the decision. The Court affirmed most of the ACA's constitutionality on June 28, 2012. Stocks marched higher. The 2012 Presidential election was widely seen as a referendum on the ACA, and Obama's victory the law's final affirmation. Stocks fell a bit the two weeks after the election, then turned higher—and Health Care outperformed. In July 2013, when Obama delayed the hotly contested employer mandate for one year, stocks yawned—not what you'd expect if the delay were wildly bullish (or bearish, depending on your viewpoint). When folks found out they couldn't keep their plans, contrary to Obama's promises, their anger didn't sink stocks. Neither did the investment income tax tweaks that took effect in 2013. Markets rose throughout the botched rollout in late 2013 and early 2014. All these negatives were priced. And here is the kicker: From early 2011 on, throughout all the eyeball-grabbing events above, US Health Care stocks beat the S&P 500 (Figure 6.1). And why? Maybe it was because the ACA was much smaller than originally feared—a point still today few have noticed.

During the 2008 Presidential campaign, there were 44.7 million uninsured people, 14.9% of the population.[10] Obama claimed his health care reform plan would insure about 35 million of them. Well, one year in, he overshot. Most sources estimate that the net reduction in the nominal uninsured population from 2013 is between 7 and 10 million, but this

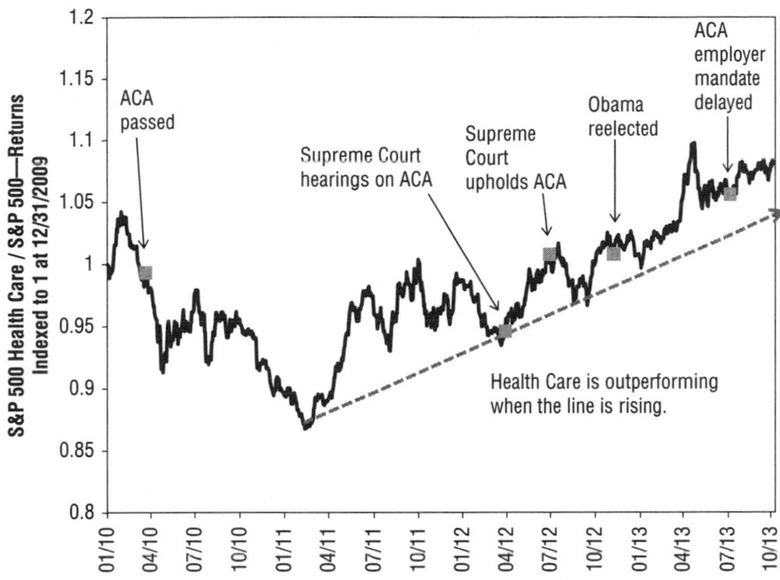

Figure 6.1 S&P 500 Health Care Versus S&P 500

Source: FactSet, as of 10/9/2013. S&P 500 Health Care and S&P 500 Total Returns, 12/31/2009–10/8/2013. Indexed to 1 on 12/31/2009.

is somewhat skewed by population growth. Private and government estimates both show the percentage of uninsured folks in 2014 declining to levels a bit below 2008. Health and Human Services and the Centers for Disease Control and Prevention (CDC) put it at 13.1%; Gallup polls say 13.4%.[11] Either way, that 35 million increase didn't happen.

Why is this important? With the ACA, folks first feared and priced the cost of subsidizing insurance for 35 million folks, and markets couldn't quickly discover the likelihood of sky-high costs. As Nancy Pelosi infamously quipped, Congress had to pass the ACA for anyone (including them) to find out what was in it. Markets initially digested that much bigger outcome, then gradually came to realize the ACA wouldn't work as intended. In the end, it cost about 10% to 15% of what folks initially assumed, for a 10% to 15% increase in the insured population. There are mountains and there are molehills.

In the end, we went through all this rigmarole for a few million folks who weren't insured before but are now—maybe 1.1% of the total US population.[12] If someone had said in 2008 that insurance premiums would rise 4% to cover 1.1% of the population, the world might have looked at it differently. If someone says, we're creating a new program for 35 million people, that's huge! For 3.5 million, it's much smaller. Markets would have known the ACA wouldn't bring down the broader world the way people feared it would. Instead of massive subsidies to cover 10% of the population, we're talking about 1%. For the 99%, the piece of the cost to cover the 1% is much lower. This smaller-than-expected outcome gave markets relief. I think. Maybe I'm wrong.

There was an elephant in the ACA, but it wasn't market-related. In all the hubbub, folks forgot Obama's goal was to take 45 million uninsured down to 10 million. Very few realize that for all the cost, hassle and aggressive marketing, coverage improved just modestly—evidence government programs don't work. That's the elephant. In this day and age, and few fathom this, it is nearly impossible for the government to "do" much. Too much arteriosclerosis.

The ACA's ultimate fecklessness stared us in the face from day one. Think of it this way: Wal-Mart's global empire wasn't built in a day—Sam Walton started small, with one store in Arkansas in 1950. It took decades of trial and error and organic growth to build an efficient, massive marketplace. If it took a genius businessman like Walton decades, how could the government implement the massive infrastructure of the ACA in three years without a hitch? The outcome was always going to be huge up-front cost, clunky rollout and limited benefits.

Markets don't care about this, though. The government has spent inefficiently since about always—no shock factor. And the bill didn't sink us—like we chronicled in Chapter 4, we don't have a debt problem. Not a market risk—just a political problem and more fodder in the big versus small government debate. And one that will likely come back as the liberals who championed the ACA find out there are still over 40 million uninsured folks—the people they wanted to help weren't helped so much. The universal health care debate will return, whether in 10 years, 15 years or whenever. Some other group will cook up some new scheme, saying Obama was too timid and didn't do it right. Maybe they'll try to tax the wealthy to create a Social Security–like trust for 25-year-old meth heads who can't otherwise snort insurance. Who knows—and not in the next 30 months! But it won't end. The king is dead, long live the king.

Once upon a time, earlier in my lifetime and before, America's government accomplished things. It built major road systems, bridges, dams, all kinds of stuff! And it worked! America's highway system is a marvel! So many folks still see that as feasible and fine for good government programs, but nowadays they're harder to do. For all the talk of "shovel-ready" projects, government can't complete as much today. Whereas San Francisco was rebuilt in a flash after the 1906 earthquake, it took years to rebuild the road damage after 1989's temblor. Not because government is too big! But because it has too many pieces, too much complexity.

Think of all the agencies that must approve any new cross-state project. Federal government. State government. Local authorities. The Army Corps of Engineers. The Environmental Protection Agency, which usually requires the Fish and Wildlife Service and sometimes the Department of Forestry to sign off. And all the state and local equivalents. All these different parts of government must have a say (and veto power) before projects can move forward. Near impossible.

For good or ill, the days of top-down governmental decision making are gone. Elected officials rotate out of office, but the agency employees are entrenched. They don't have to agree or do what they're told by the top. This is the system Americans created! Societally, we decided we want it! But it keeps government from accomplishing much. Unless they enter a completely new realm where no existing agencies have a say, the bureaucracy gets in the way. It's a heck of a lot easier to build one commercial office building than for government to build a road spanning two cities, counties and states.

That Which Is Seen and That Which Is Unseen

The ACA had huge unintended consequences, but they weren't as huge as expected and were too minor and too well-known to matter to stocks. The ACA misaligned the incentives to own health insurance. Since the law raised insurance firms' regulatory costs, premiums went up. For many businesses, it was cheaper to pay the fine than comply with the mandate. Many provided health benefits anyway—great for recruiting and retaining workers! But others cut their plans, shunting consumers to the state and national health exchanges. Some folks bought insurance, but others realized there, too, the penalty was cheaper than premiums. With the ban on pre-existing conditions gone, healthy folks could just pay the fine, pay for basic doctor's visits out of pocket, and wait to buy health insurance until they needed something major. Unintended, but not unseen.

What really rankles stocks are the unintended consequences few see—Bastiat's shoemaker missing out on a six-franc sale because the shopkeeper's son broke a window. Downstream unintended consequences that will catch folks by surprise.

These can rear their ugly heads years after the law is passed—this is when "not in the next 30 months" meets "now." Take Sarbox again. As we explored in Chapter 1, 2008's panic happened because hyper-aggressive asset write-downs wiped about $2 trillion from America's banking systems. The mark-to-market accounting rule was the direct culprit—a secondary regulatory change, not Congress's handiwork (perhaps more dangerous, which we'll get to shortly). But you have to wonder, would banks have slashed their balance sheets so ruthlessly if CEOs and CFOs weren't criminally and civilly liable for bogus accounting as defined in Sarbox? Without the threat of jail time, would write-downs have dwarfed the roughly $300 billion in actual loan losses?[13] Consider: In 1990, then Fed Chairman Alan Greenspan wrote a letter to Securities and Exchange Commission (SEC) Commissioner Richard Breeden suggesting that mark-to-market accounting for illiquid bank loans was wrongheaded because bankers could get aggressive with valuing assets with no ready market, based on sheer irrationality. He couldn't know it then, but post-Sarbox, the incentives flipped.

Sarbox played out in a way no one—at least no one publicly documented beforehand—saw coming. Seeing these things takes imagination. It also requires you to go against the grain and move past the chatter—true contrarian stuff. When it comes to laws, the crowd focuses on the immediate seen consequences. Will the ACA whack growth? Will tax hikes hit spending? These are fine questions, but they're often too widely discussed to matter to stocks. The trick is training your brain to imagine what others can't.

Here's an example. Europe's parliament just cracked down on bankers' bonuses. They decided bankers' exorbitant bonuses caused the financial crisis by encouraging risky behavior that brought down the entire system. Wrongheaded, but politicians always need a scapegoat, and bankers are an easy target. No one ever told small children bedtime stories aimed at encouraging them to grow up to be bankers. So they passed a rule capping bonuses at 100% of annual salary—200% if shareholders approve. They believe this will crisis-proof their system because bankers will no longer have a monetary incentive to make risky bets.

This is wrong, obviously—crisis-proof is a fairy tale. Worse, it introduces negatives. Some get plenty of headlines. Britain filed a lawsuit with Europe's top court arguing the cap would hollow out London's banking sector as firms fled the stupid rule, eroding the economy. A tad overstated, perhaps—banks need a European hub, and Britain's competitive advantage is huge—but fair enough. (The court, predictably, is unsympathetic.) Widely discussed, though—the market has probably dealt with it.

There is another high-potential negative, though perhaps years downstream. Bonuses are discretionary compensation—variable costs. Paying big bonuses lets banks keep salaries low, giving them more flexibility to get lean in tough times. But banks aren't so dumb. They need top talent! If they make everyone take pay cuts, talent will flee to other industries. So they'll amp up salaries and pay smaller bonuses, keeping total compensation roughly the same. Here's the problem: Salaries are a fixed cost. The next time trouble hits and revenues dive, bonus-cutting won't get costs in line. Banks will face a choice: Make massive layoffs or take huge losses and fail. This is a fundamental negative for banks somewhere down the line. Not in the next 30 months! Not for current markets. But someday. It is an elephant that will remain patiently, quietly, unseen in our room awaiting crisis-oriented movement.

What's Worse Than a Politician?

Many unseen negatives don't come from Congress. At least not directly. Lawmakers have their faults, but sometimes they realize they're collectively stupid and not experts in business, so they outsource rule-writing when they reform regulations. They did this with the Dodd-Frank Wall Street Reform and Consumer Protection Act of 2010. The law itself was about 2,000 pages deferring action to regulatory bodies—the SEC, Federal Reserve, Federal Deposit Insurance Corporation (FDIC), Office of Thrift Supervision and so on. Some provisions were placeholders for actual rules. Others mandated studies, with loose directions for the regulators to write rules later if they decided it was necessary.

There is an elephant here, and it is a bad one! To many, outsourcing rulemaking sounds sensible. Again, members of Congress aren't bankers. They aren't experts, so of course they can't write rules governing banks without inflicting collateral damage. From that viewpoint, having the regulators do the dirty work sounds logical. Even good!

Here's the problem. Regulators often don't know their own bounds, and often no one really manages or monitors them. Congress technically has oversight, but this usually amounts to snoozing through the occasional testimony. In practice, regulators can be police, judge and jury.

Regulators also operate in the shadows. When Congress makes a law, everything plays out in public. You can read every draft online, at www.govtrack.us. You can watch the debates on C-SPAN. Journalists observe and report on the debates and negotiating. Negatives are discovered and often pre-priced. You don't always get this when regulators write laws! They do much of it behind closed doors. You don't get hundreds of politicians debating a rule publicly in daylight. You get a dozen unelected, unsupervised well-meaners working in secret.

When unchecked regulators write nasty things into laws that can take effect without long public comment, bad things happen fast. The huge recent disaster, covered in Chapter 1, was FAS 157, the mark-to-market accounting rule. We saw a minor example in December 2013, when the feds released the final draft of the Volcker Rule.

The Volcker Rule, part of Dodd-Frank, started as former Fed head Paul Volcker's three-page proposal to ban banks' proprietary trading—trading for their own book, not customers' accounts. Another misdirected effort to prevent a 2008 repeat—proprietary trading didn't cause the crisis. Banks wrote down assets they planned to hold to maturity, not securities in their trading books. (They already marked those assets to market.) According to the Government Accountability Office, the six biggest banks realized just $15.8 billion in trading losses from Q4 2007 to Q4 2008.[11] Peanuts! A prop-trading ban wouldn't have saved Lehman Brothers. But politicians will never see this.

When Congress passed Dodd-Frank, it outsourced the Volcker Rule to the Fed, FDIC, Office of the Comptroller of the Currency (OCC), Commodity Futures Trading Commission (CFTC) and SEC. This alphabet soup released a draft in 2011 for public comment—nice of them—and the public commented.

The regulators went back to work, reviewed the comments and rewrote parts of the law. On December 10, 2013, they released the rewrite, called it a final rule and made it effective in July 2015. No ifs, ands or buts (they said).

Problem was, the final rule contained some nasty nuggets that weren't in the draft. One banned banks from holding collateralized debt obligations (CDOs) backed by trust-preferred securities—TruPS-backed CDOs, in bankerspeak. I'll spare you the boring technical details here, but these were pooled debt securities community banks have long owned without trouble. They (used to) have favorable accounting and regulatory treatment, and they pay nice interest, so banks would buy and hold them to maturity. Under the amended Volcker Rule, however, collecting income meant banks had an ownership interest (rather than passive stakes). No-no time! This forced banks to reclassify TruPS-backed CDOs as "available-for-sale" assets and mark them to market. Uh-oh!

Within two weeks, Zions Bancorporation—a Utah-based regional bank—announced a $387 million write-down on TruPS-backed CDOs, blaming Volcker. The American Bankers Association (ABA) sued the feds, claiming community banks were whacked without cause. The public hates big banks, not so much small banks, so the feds bent. But they haven't patched a similar rule banning banks from owning certain collateralized loan obligations, which the ABA estimates could trigger a $70 billion fire sale. Nowhere big enough to cause a 2008-style write-down spiral, but illustrative.

Not all regulatory wrangling comes from Congressional outsourcing. The Executive branch does damage on its own, too. The Treasury introduced some unseen negatives in 2014 when they cracked down on "inversion" mergers and acquisitions (M&A) deals—where an American company buys a smaller foreign company and moves corporate headquarters there for tax purposes. America has the dubious distinction of being the only major developed country to tax companies' foreign earnings after they've already paid foreign taxes.

Companies pay only if they repatriate earnings, so piling up cash abroad is an obvious solution, but firms want to invest here! Inversions are the solution. By becoming "foreign," companies could bring foreign earnings back to America and invest as they see fit, while reducing tax costs. A win-win. But you won't read that in media.

Inversions became a bogeyman. Politicians hate losing tax dollars! So they spun a shaggy dog story about inversions whacking business investment (ignoring that inversions' primary purpose is to enable investment!). It caught on fast. The Treasury tried to goad Congress into legislating a ban, calling it their patriotic duty, but gridlock got in the way. So the Treasury took action, "reinterpreting" the tax code to make inversions more difficult and to chip at the benefits—they banned some creative transactions that inverted firms would use to transfer earnings back to America. The logic here is inverted (pun intended)—if you say you hate inversions because they kill investment, the solution shouldn't make investment more difficult.

But that isn't the elephant in the room here—most firms don't care about inversions. They care about rules changing. Usually Congress changes the rules, but the Treasury set a precedent by rewriting rules when Congress couldn't! The changes were small and toothless, but they chipped at the law, changing the game. Now firms have to wonder: "If the Treasury can do this, what else can they do? What other rules will they tweak? How the heck do I plan for it? How can I, when I don't know how in the h-e-double-hockey-sticks they'll try to hurt me?"

This uncertainty discourages risk taking. Why make a bold move or start a long-term project with high up-front costs if regulators could change the rules with no warning and pinch your profits? Forget it!

These are small negatives, but illustrative of the unseen surprises the budding contrarian wants to watch for. Train your brain to look for these, and you'll have an easier time spotting the big one—the unseen rule change that could wipe a few trillion off world GDP and kill a bull market.

Why the Government Already Made the Next Crisis Worse

I have one more story for you before we kiss politics good-bye and move to more polite topics. There is one more source of unseen political risk. Risk doesn't come just from laws and rules! Politicians' non-rulemaking actions have consequences, too. Actions send messages—sometimes terrible ones that turn into ticking time bombs. The Obama administration created a big time bomb in the wake of the 2008 crisis—one every savvy investor should know and learn from.

Politicians have one purpose in life: getting elected. Most don't think past "Will this get me votes?" when making decisions. If their voting public thinks a business or industry is a villain, politicians are all too happy to crucify it.

After 2008's panic, people decided banks were villains. Evil rent-seekers that forced loans on naïve folks who didn't qualify, knowingly packaged bad loans into toxic securities, defrauded Fannie Mae and Freddie Mac into buying them, gleefully foreclosed on innocent people when housing crashed, and made off with hundreds of billions in taxpayer money. The public demanded their pound of flesh, and pandering politicians delivered five. They didn't care that the popular narrative was ridiculously false—only votes mattered! From 2010 through August 2014, the government slapped over $125 billion in crisis-related legal fines on the six largest banks. Probably more by the time you read this. Not important by itself (except to them).

JPMorgan Chase and Bank of America account for over $100 billion or 80% of the total. Trouble is, most of the lawsuits and charges weren't really against them. They were against the firms JPMorgan and Bank of America bought during the crisis. Those acquisitions did Washington a favor. If this is how the government "thanks" banks who help by buying failing banks in a crisis, it sends a message: Don't help us again. Pretty amazingly dumb phenomenon.

This cuts against over a century of crisis management tradition. Healthy big banks have long helped during financial crises. They lend to or buy failing banks and guarantee customers' deposits, helping prevent bank runs. When they buy, they assume the liabilities, but they also get the assets (on the cheap) and the customers. This isn't charity—it makes business sense in the long run. But we've done it every crisis (and some in between).

JP Morgan—the man and his bank—rode to the rescue during the Panic of 1893, engineering and guaranteeing the government bonds sold to repatriate gold from foreign investors and replenish reserves. He effectively spent his own money to bail out the US Treasury. He did it again in the Panic of 1907, serving as lender of last resort (that was pre–Federal Reserve). If he determined cash-crunched banks were fundamentally solvent, with solid assets and workable business models, he arranged funding. He cobbled a coalition of strong banks that pooled money to keep struggling ones alive. When brokerage firm Moore and Schley became insolvent after it couldn't repay over $6 million (a lot then) in loans backed by shares of the Tennessee Coal, Iron and Railroad Company (TCI), Morgan arranged for US Steel (which he controlled) to buy the stock and ultimately buy TCI. Moore and Schley was saved. He also bailed out New York City, helping save the New York Stock Exchange.

North Carolina National Bank (NCNB) was the savior during our infamous savings and loan crisis (when more banks and money value of banks failed than in the 2007–2009 recession), buying the failed First Republic Bank in 1988. NCNB bought several other failing lenders in Texas and nationally over the next several years. Never heard of NCNB? Or forgot the name? That's because through a series of mergers it became NationsBank, which bought Bank of America in 1998 and took on the name. For all intents and purposes, today's

Bank of America is the same institution that helped the FDIC time and again in the late 1980s and early 1990s.

Ken Lewis, Bank of America's CEO in 2008, came from NCNB. He was NCNB CEO Hugh McColl Jr.'s right-hand man in 1988, running NCNB Texas National Bank—the entity resulting from the First Republic business. He learned the art of buying failing banks firsthand, and he put it to use in 2008, buying the failing mortgage lender Countrywide and flailing Merrill Lynch. Meanwhile, JPMorgan Chase CEO Jamie Dimon (who was mentored by Citi's earlier takeover maestro, Sandy Weill) went back to his firm's roots, buying the ashes of Bear Stearns at the Fed's behest in March 2008. When Washington Mutual (WaMu) failed in September, JPMorgan Chase bought it as a favor to the FDIC.

Imagine, for a moment, life without these purchases (or Wells Fargo's purchase of Wachovia). Chaos! Markets started panicking when Bear Stearns appeared to go under—they stabilized and rallied when JPMorgan stepped in. The WaMu purchase saved the FDIC from paying on insured deposits—a huge expense, considering WaMu had an estimated $165 billion in deposits when it failed.[15] Bank of America's purchase of Merrill Lynch granted the brokerage house access to the Fed's emergency discount window, keeping it alive and likely sparing huge taxpayer expense. People think the Troubled Asset Relief Program (TARP) was too expensive, but the $423 billion spent through TARP is nothing compared to the cost if the Treasury and FDIC didn't have private sector help.[16]

This is how the system is supposed to work. You want the private sector to handle this stuff. The private sector does it way better than the government ever could. We saw how that worked when the Federal Reserve and Treasury killed Lehman Brothers after finagling the JPMorgan/Bear merger and effectively nationalizing Fannie Mae, Freddie Mac and American International Group (AIG). They arbitrarily picked winners and losers and created sheer panic. If they had to pick the fate of WaMu and Merrill Lynch too? Lord help us.

JPMorgan and Bank of America kept things running, kept customers relatively secure and probably prevented a much deeper panic. The government should have thrown a parade. Instead it turned on the white knights. The feds sued Bank of America for Countrywide's alleged mortgage fraud. They charged and fined JPMorgan for Bear's and WaMu's dirty deeds. All for political gain!

There is a terrible irony here. The banks that threw up their hands in 2008 and said, "Heck no, we won't help!" didn't get hurt much. Goldman Sachs paid just $900 million in fines. Morgan Stanley paid $1.9 billion. Those that didn't step in and help didn't get hurt much. But the good guys got whacked.

By hurting the helpers, the government sent a super-strong message: "Don't help us bail anyone out ever again." The good guys heard it. I'll let Jamie Dimon speak for himself: "Let's get this one exactly right. We were asked to do it. We did it at great risk to ourselves. … Would I have done Bear Stearns again knowing what I know today? It's real close."[17] You can believe Bank of America feels the same. Wells Fargo—lucky to escape with just $9 billion in fines—is watching.

The next time a big bank goes under, the government could find itself isolated. We'll all pay a price for politicians' greed and popularity quest. This is more likely to exacerbate a bear market than cause one. Banks fail primarily in bad times, not good ones! But it is an entirely unnecessary political risk.

Politicians might not be the most dangerous people in America—most aren't deranged axe murders. But they're among investors' worst enemies. The more you know your enemy, the easier it is to beat him.

I've told you these stories and chronicled these risks not to scare you—just to help you know your enemy. Now you know his tricks and weapons, and you're ready for the fight!

Which means we're also ready for far more pleasant topics! What fun is in store? Time to turn to Chapter 7 and find out!

Notes

1. "Fearless Dominance and the US Presidency: Implications of Psychopathic Personality Traits for Successful and Unsuccessful Political Leadership," Scott O. Lilienfeld, Irwin D. Walderman, Kristin Landfield, Ashley L. Watts, Steven Rubenzer and Thomas R. Faschingbauer, *Journal of Personality and Social Psychology*, Vol. 103, No. 3 (September 2012): 489–505. http://psycnet.apa.org/journals/psp/103/3/489/ (accessed 10/21/2014).
2. "Nation Tunes In to See Which Sociopath More Likable This Time," *The Onion*, 12/16/2012. http://www.theonion.com/articles/nation-tunes-in-to-see-which-sociopath-more-likabl,29946/ (accessed 2/24/2015).
3. US Census Bureau, as of 7/6/2014.
4. "Résumé of Congressional Activity—First Session of the One Hundred Thirteenth Congress," Congressional Record—Daily Digest, US House Clerk's Office, February 27, 2014.
5. Gallup, as of 10/21/2014. Congressional Job Approval Ratings, 1974–2014. www.gallup.com/poll/1600/congress-public.aspx (accessed 10/21/2014).
6. FactSet, as of 9/30/2014. S&P 500 Total Return Index, 12/31/2012–12/31/2013.
7. "The Role of Monetary Policy," Milton Friedman, *The American Economic Review*, Vol. 58, No. 1 (March 1968). https://www.aeaweb.org/aer/top20/58.1.1-17.pdf (accessed 10/21/2014).
8. "Phillips Curves, Expectations of Inflation and Optimal Unemployment Over Time," Edmund S. Phelps, *Economica*, New Series, Vol. 34, No. 5 (August 1967): 254–281. www.columbia.edu/~esp2/PhilipsCurvesExpectationsofInflationandOptimalUnemploymentOverTime.pdf (accessed 10/21/2014).
9. FactSet, as of 10/22/2014. S&P 500 Total Return Index, 4/16/2002–7/25/2002.
10. US Census Bureau, as of 12/31/2008.
11. Department of Health and Human Services and Centers for Disease Control, as of 3/31/2014. Gallup-Healthways Well-Being Index, as of 6/30/2014.
12. United States Census Bureau, as of 1/15/2015. Total United States Population, 2013.
13. Testimony of William M. Isaac, Former Chairman, Federal Deposit Insurance Association, before the Subcommittee on Capital Markets, Insurance, and Government Sponsored Enterprises, US House of Representatives Committee on Financial Services, March 12, 2009. www.williamisaac.com/published-works/testimony-before-the-us-house-of-representatives/ (accessed 2/24/2015).
14. "Proprietary Trading: Regulators Will Need More Comprehensive Information to Fully Monitor Compliance With New Restrictions When Implemented," United States Government Accountability Office Report to

Congressional Committees, July 2011. www.gao.gov/assets/330/321006.pdf (accessed 10/22/2014).

15. According to Washington Mutual's regulatory filings, the bank held about $181.9 billion in deposits as of June 30, 2008. The Office of Thrift Supervision estimates customers pulled $16.7 billion in September. *Sources:* Washington Mutual, Inc., Form 10-Q for the quarter ending June 30, 2008. United States Securities and Exchange Commission, www.sec.gov/Archives/edgar/data/933136/000104746908009146/a2187197z10-q.htm (accessed 10/23/2014). "WaMu Is Seized, Sold Off to J.P. Morgan, in Largest Failure in U.S. Banking History," Robin Seidel, David Einrich and Dan Fitzpatrick, *The Wall Street Journal*, 9/26/2008. http://online.wsj.com/articles/SB122238415586576687 (accessed 10/23/2014).
16. "Report on the Troubled Asset Relief Program—April 2014," Congressional Budget Office, April 17, 2014. www.cbo.gov/publication/45260 (accessed 10/23/2014).
17. "JPMorgan's Dimon Hits Back at Government Over Bear Stearns Suit," Sarah N. Lynch and Kim Dixon, *Reuters*, 10/10/2012. http://www.reuters.com/article/2012/10/11/us-jpmorgan-dimon-bearstearns-idUSBRE8991CE20121011 (accessed 2/24/2015).

CHAPTER 7

Put Those Textbooks Away

Does an MBA help you be a better investor? What about a CFA? Are finance professors great investors?

In fields like medicine, engineering and law, education is critical. But investing is a different game. Some of the greatest investors had little or no formal training. And some of the greatest thinkers and theorists were absolutely terrible investors.

I call this the Peter Bernstein Effect. Bernstein, who was a giant in the field of professional investment thinking and ideas and was a great guy, wrote a fascinating book, *Capital Ideas* (John Wiley & Sons, 2005), which traces Wall Street's intellectual evolution. He profiles many of the scholars who contributed to investment theory, like Alfred Cowles, the forefather of the Standard & Poor's (S&P) indexes. William Sharpe, of Sharpe ratio fame. James Tobin, who formalized the then-radical idea of goals-based investing in 1958. Paul Samuelson, the first US Nobel laureate in economics. And many more. Few (if any) of these great thinkers were great investors. Some were infamously terrible! They had lots of can-do—but no done-it.

Investing is something you learn more by doing than by reading. Just like baseball! Done-done it Yogi Berra didn't go to baseball class when he was a kid. He just played street ball. You can go to investing school if you want, and that isn't necessarily bad, but textbook theory by itself won't get you anywhere but back to school—too detached from the real world. Success comes from learning from your mistakes. Understanding your behavioral tendencies so you can overcome your own biggest enemies, your emotions and biases. (More on that in Chapter 9.) Studying the real-world real-time with real money. Sometimes reality will match theory! But it often won't.

Higher learning is good—it teaches critical thinking skills. You might also just like learning theory! Maybe you're a finance nerd! That's fun! But the MBAs, CFAs and professors most successful at investing know they have to move past the curriculum. They let it be a building block, or not, but not a rulebook. They use the critical thinking skills they acquired, while not being a slave to the rules.

Even if you don't have a finance degree, you've probably seen the textbook theory and rules. They've seeped far into media coverage of markets, and many pundits portray them as Gospel. So this is a chapter for CFAs, MBAs, finance degree holders and self-taught folks alike! Whether or not you're a market expert on paper, chances are you'll benefit from knowing:

- Why textbook theory and rules "everyone knows" usually don't work in the real world
- Whether you should believe long-held "rules" about valuations, small-cap stocks and more
- Why Federal Reserve policy doesn't make sense—and might not ever again!

Don't Toss Your Textbooks—But Know Their Limitations!

By definition, finance curriculum is discounted. Many textbooks have been widely read for decades. Everyone who has the same learning and reads the same canon is trained to expect the same outcome. These expectations get baked in fast. Priced in.

Textbooks and classes aren't useless. They teach the basics, and the basics matter! Take finance theory, which dictates that to get any return over time, you must take risk—and the more risk you take (if defined correctly), the higher your long-term expected return. If you know finance theory, you have a weapon against brokerage industry sales spin—like the myth "capital preservation and growth" is a realistic, attainable goal. Finance theory tells us this is hogwash. If you want growth, you must take risk—and if you take risk, you have to accept the risk of loss. That isn't capital preservation! If you want true capital preservation, you'd need an all-cash portfolio or something similar. No risk, and no real growth.

Modern portfolio theory (MPT) is another key building block. MPT grew from the research of Harry Markowitz, whose 1952 paper, "Portfolio Selection," showed that in a diversified portfolio, the overall blend of risk and return (asset allocation) influences returns far more than which individual securities you own.[1] The decision to be in stocks or bonds mostly matters more than which stocks and bonds you ultimately buy. Few like this, but it is basic and statistically valid. Subsequent studies showed asset and sub-asset allocation—countries and sectors—are responsible for most of your returns if you're diversified. Stock picking, analysts' lodestar before Markowitz, is least important.

MPT is a good guide for portfolio construction—it helps whittle down the universe of stocks you have to choose from. As I write, there are over 50,000 publicly traded firms globally. If you try to pick the hottest 40 or 50, you might as well use a dartboard. If you start with asset allocation and then choose how much to own in each major geographic region and sector, you have an easier pool of stocks to pick from. This also helps you avoid other traps, like being too concentrated in one area.

The Efficient Markets Hypothesis is another basic. The theory itself—popularized by Eugene Fama in the 1970s—isn't perfect. The underlying assumption that widely known information is discounted is fine. It's the basis for much of this book! But Fama's hypothesis doesn't always work in the real world—a shortcoming most academic theory shares. While markets are efficient in the long run, in the short term they can be pretty darned irrational. Why? Data isn't all stocks price in. As we saw in Chapters 2 and 6, expectations and opinions get priced in, too! That's how contrarians have opportunities to game the crowd!

It takes independent thinking and real-world savvy to see the Efficient Markets Hypothesis's shortcomings. The theory is important! But using it properly requires more than knowing the theory. You must move past the textbook and into the real world.

There are myriad other useful textbook theories. But finance curriculum also has dozens—if not hundreds—of rules. Remember the "rulebook" from Chapter 1? This is where it comes from. Textbook rules can be right sometimes. If they didn't work ever, they wouldn't be in the books! No one would follow them! But reality does something different more often than not—a big clump of rule-followers is an easy target for The Great Humiliator (TGH). Here, too, beating the books requires street smarts and a critical mind.

Much of the scholarly research in finance comes from the *Financial Analysts Journal*, the official publication of CFA Institute and the brainchild of Helen Slade, a mid-twentieth-century investor and analyst. If Ben Graham is the Father of Security Analysis, Helen Slade is surely the Mother (and Ben's mentor in many ways). As Secretary of the New York Society of Security Analysts, she was also social chair, hosting Wednesday-evening salons for 40 to 50 of the best and brightest. Graham attended regularly, as did Lucien Hooper, a young Malcolm Forbes, and even, occasionally, my father.

Helen called her guests her "tipsters." They'd discuss and debate securities and market ideas for hours over drinks and sandwiches. The *Financial Analysts Journal*, launched in 1945 and edited by Helen until her 1958 death, put the tipsters' parties on paper and took them national. Back then, there was no curriculum. The *Financial Analysts Journal* gathered analysis, theories and opinions in one place, creating the knowledge base for future generations to build off. What is canon now wasn't canon then—then, it helped. The theories were new and not priced.

Helen wasn't just a social patroness. She wrote for major financial publications globally—sometimes under her own name, sometimes under the pseudonym "John Dean." She was also a regular panelist at the National Industrial Conference Board's annual economic forum, forecasting business conditions for the coming year and, according to newspaper accounts, even forecasting the 1949 recession.

There is no way to know, and this is just my opinion, but I suspect security analysis wouldn't be where it is today if Helen hadn't thrown parties for 10 years. Getting everyone in the same room let their ideas collide into new theories and knowledge. The profession would have come along! But likely not at the same rate.

The First Commandment: P/Es Aren't Predictive

Here's an example as old as dirt. Most curriculums claim stocks with high price-to-earnings ratios—P/Es—are "expensive" and therefore risky. Low-P/E stocks and markets are "cheap" and therefore scream, "Buy me!" The more stocks and P/Es rise as a bull market wears on, the more pundits preach that stocks are too pricey and must soon fall.

This might sound sensible in theory. Owning stock means owning future earnings, so of course high P/Es would imply an overvalued market—euphoric investors too far ahead of themselves. However, to borrow a phrase from my 2006 book, *The Only Three Questions That Count*, this is false mythology. Flat untrue!

There is no actual valid statistical evidence that high-P/E markets are any riskier than low-P/E markets in any timeframe people ever really try to game, like one, three or five years. None. You can see this for yourself online at www.multpl.com, which displays Yale economist Robert J. Shiller's robust dataset of historical S&P 500 pricing and P/Es. (More on Shiller in a bit.) The S&P 500's 12-month trailing P/E was above its long-term average when the bull market began in June 1962. P/Es were above average for most of the 1990s bull market. The 2002–2007 bull market started with a P/E over 29—the P/E spent all of that bull market above average! In March 2009, a bull market began when the S&P's trailing P/E was over 100. Anyone following the "high P/Es are risky" rule would have missed big bull market returns.

Low P/Es aren't reliable, either. The 1980–1982 bear market began with a tasty 9.19 P/E. When the 1956–1957 bear market started, the S&P 500 P/E was a benign 13.81, below average. Folks following P/E mythology then got whacked.

The P/E myth also fails the logic test. One, it ignores the denominator! Earnings get whacked in recessions. In recoveries, stocks bounce first—they pre-price rebounding growth and earnings. As a result, P/Es are often high early in bull markets. Two, it assumes past returns predict the future—always and everywhere untrue.

Finally, saying high P/Es mean stocks are overvalued and low P/Es undervalued assumes that stocks have an inherent fair value—and implies the market is wrong whenever the P/E deviates. Think thoughts like that at your mortal soul's peril. Well, in the very short term, maybe that's true sometimes. As Ben Graham said, in the short term, the market is a voting machine; people buy and sell on emotion, and feelings are often irrational. But in the long run, the market is a weighing machine, discounting future fundamentals. Was the market wrong in 1996, 1997, 1998 and 1999, when above-average P/Es shot higher as stocks zoomed alongside the tech boom? Few fathom this today, but tech didn't reach true bubble status until very late 1999 or early 2000, when junky initial public offerings (IPOs) reached fever pitch and most investors were too dot-com drunk to notice they were bidding up firms burning quickly through cash on hand and operating deep in the red. Was the market's 1996 and 1997 price irrational? Beyond an opinion, believing you know with certainty is arrogant and folly.

P/Es can help you see sentiment, but no P/E by itself is inherently too high or too low. P/Es often stay high for years as bull markets mature—normal as sentiment brightens. Some argue the long-term average P/E is fair value, but stocks don't always mean-revert. Sometimes they do. My opinion is that more often than not they don't. Doing so would be much too easy to game for TGH's tastes. The average P/E comes from hundreds of data points high and low. It is a blend of extremes, not a gravitational force.

If you've read my older books, this argument is probably familiar—I've bashed the P/E myth for decades. Meir Statman and I punched it in our 2000 paper for *The Journal of Portfolio Management*, "Cognitive Biases in Market Forecasts." We studied 128 years' worth of P/Es and returns from 1872 through 1999—also from Shiller's dataset—and found no statistically significant relationship between P/Es on January 1 and full-year returns. P/Es are unreliable forecasters.

Here's another fun nugget from that paper:

"Many investors are especially concerned about the short-horizon implications of very high P/E ratios, fearing that they forecast imminent disastrous returns. Yet history offers little support for such fear. For example, P/E ratios over 19 have never been followed by losses greater than 10% during the following year. While high P/E ratios can surely be followed soon by disastrous returns, it is ironic that investors believe such returns are the common feature of stock market history."[2]

Why do they believe it? Media hype and textbooks! Always question the rules.

The CAPEd Crusader Is No Superhero

Shiller and his research partner, John Y. Campbell, rightly acknowledged that recessions skew earnings, but their "solution" seems as useless to forecasting as normal P/Es. They blended years of earnings together, creating a super backward-looking P/E they argued could forecast the next decade's returns. (A fool's errand—does anyone buying stocks really make hard-and-fast 10-year bets?)

Shiller chronicles their early efforts in his 1996 paper, "Price-Earnings Ratios as Forecasters of Returns: The Stock Market Outlook in 1996."[3] There, his P/E compares price to the 30-year moving average of trailing earnings. That isn't a typo—30 years! His logic? Ben Graham and David Dodd's 1934 classic, *Security Analysis,* admonished investors to weigh average earnings over "not less than five years, preferably seven or ten years."[4] If one decade was preferable, surely three decades were golden!

According to Shiller, in January 1996, the 30-year P/E was 29.72—crazy high! His forecast and advice: "It is hard to come away without a feeling that the market is quite likely to decline substantially over the succeeding 10 years; it appears that long run investors should stay out of the market for the next decade."

You read that right, too.

Based on this analysis, Shiller gave a presentation to Alan Greenspan on December 3, 1996, arguing the bull market had reached bubble status. Two days later, Greenspan gave his infamous "irrational exuberance" speech. The bull market lasted another three years, three months and three weeks.

Shiller and Campbell refined their methodology in 1998, chopping their earnings component down to 10 years. This is what the world now knows as the "Shiller P/E" or "Cyclically Adjusted P/E"—CAPE for short. Their forecast then matched Shiller's findings in 1996: The current CAPE suggested "substantial declines in real stock prices, and real stock returns close to zero, over the next ten years."[5]

Though they cautioned that with few other incidences of super-high CAPE, readers should take their conclusion with a grain of salt.

As you'll see in the box on page 181, taken from *The Only Three Questions That Count,* CAPE caught on because it upheld the long-standing myth everyone believed—and appeared to prove it with data! Never mind that the data had to be tortured to death until they fit the hypothesis (in this case, earnings smoothed over 10 years and adjusted for inflation using an antiquated price index).

Even though CAPE was wrong in the 1990s, its popularity endures. Partly that's because it was very right between 1998 and 2008 (even if very wrong from 1996 to 2006 or 1997 to 2007), but a broken clock is right twice a day. And in most 10-year periods since its creation, including the last 10 (2004 to 2014), CAPE has been wrong. Yet pundits regularly cite it when warning stocks look bubbly, and Shiller's 2013 Nobel Prize gives it massive ivory tower credibility.

You can use history and the logic test to disprove it in about 30 seconds, though! You don't even need the heavy statistical analysis Meir Statman and I did in our 2000 paper, where we also poked at CAPE! You can go right to the long-term dataset, also at www.multpl.com, and see plenty of times when bull markets endured while CAPE was high. That's the history test.

As for the logic test? As I mentioned earlier, past performance alone never predicts future returns. True whether we're talking stock prices or the past decade of earnings! Anyone who ever ran a business would get this. CEOs and CFOs don't make long-term business plans by extrapolating the last decade's profits forward. Nor do they assume they'll mean-revert after a decade of high or low profits. Any CFO who tried that would get fired for both laziness and stupidity. They weigh the up-front and ongoing costs of new projects versus the likely revenues. They consider current economic conditions, their expectations for the foreseeable future, interest rates, labor costs and many others. Recent history can help set their expectations for the next recession or other events! But they don't (and shouldn't) assume the past predicts the future. It doesn't, ever. Or at least rarely.

Then, too, Shiller and Campbell never designed CAPE to forecast cyclical turning points. (Though the media should probably get a pass for the frequent misapplication. Shiller himself argued high CAPEs were signals of a looming fall in 2013 and 2014—concluding they showed investors were euphoric again and high valuations wouldn't persist.[6] Only to argue *three weeks* later that folks were irrationally *negative*—not the sort of sentiment generating high valuations.[7]) Initially, CAPE sought to forecast the unknowable, 10-year returns. Ten years is way beyond the next 30 months! Even if CAPE worked and weak 10-year returns followed high CAPE readings, that doesn't mean all 10 years are lousy.

Even history's lousiest decades had great bull market years. The S&P 500 did fall –13% from 1998 through 2008, that 10-year period following Shiller and Campbell's paper.[8] But only because it was bookended by two massive bear markets, and nothing in 1998 could have told you mark-to-market accounting would become reality and wipe out a bull market prematurely in 2007. Moreover, even though stocks finished 10 years down, you wanted to be in during the 2002–2007 bull market. If you're investing for long-term growth, you must participate in bull markets.

Let's assume for a moment CAPE actually did work for a period. It isn't as though Shiller and Campbell kept the tool all to themselves, profiting off it quietly along the way. Two questions: Why not, and is the market efficient or not? You can answer the former for yourself; I will take a stab at the latter—it's pretty efficient but not perfectly so. This is why the price-to-sales ratio I championed in the early 1980s worked for a spell. Until others realized it. Then it largely stopped once it got popular. You can't gain an edge using a tool most of Wall Street is aware of, much less infatuated with.

From *The Only Three Questions That Count*, 2006:

"Campbell and Shiller's bizarrely engineered P/E gave a result consistent with what society always believed—that high P/E means low returns, high risk. And the world loved it.

"In statistics, a calculation is done called an *R-squared* which shows the relative *relatedness* of two variables—how much of one variable's movement is caused by the other. For their study, Campbell and Shiller's regression analysis gave them an R-squared of 0.40.[9] An R-squared of 0.40 implies 40 percent of subsequent stock returns are related to the factor being compared, in this case, their reengineered P/E. Statistically, not a bad finding (although not an overwhelming one). Though not a whopping endorsement of their theory, this finding still supports their hypothesis.

"*Note:* Campbell and Shiller's study, tepid support or not, became wildly popular because it supported the view society had long held [that high-P/E markets are risky and have further to fall]. If you present data violating society's myths, those data won't be met with great popularity. That's nice because when you discover the truth, the world won't be trying to take it away from you in a hurry."

The 0.40 R-squared also means fully 60% of the subsequent returns—half again bigger and more powerful—came from something else. Which is more important for forecasting—a 40% fact or 60%?

Small Beats All?

Another textbook adage says small-cap stocks have the best returns. History appears to show it: From 1926 through 2013, small cap averaged 11.5% annualized, compared to big cap's 10%.[10] Numerous studies claim to prove it, including the landmark paper introducing Eugene Fama and Kenneth French's famous three-factor model.[11] Pundits love it, proclaiming small cap is best forever and ever, amen. Consensus scholarly wisdom (uh-oh) agrees smaller firms are inherently riskier, so their returns are naturally, automatically higher.

History? Check. Logic? Seems like a check. And yet—if small cap is so darned superior, why the heck do people ever own big cap?

A tip: When questions like that pop into your brain, that's your independent-thinking contrarian instinct taking over. Don't ignore it—follow it!

Small cap's long-term average return does beat big cap. No argument there! But averages are made of extremes. Small cap simply has a handful of years, a small minority, where it trounces big cap. It isn't superior. Every category, correctly calculated, has its time in the spotlight. Big cap takes center stage plenty.

The reality: In most years between 1926 and 2013, large cap beat small cap. Small companies usually fly highest during the first third or so of a bull market. Big cap typically leads the rest of the time.

Small cap's long-term "premium" comes from a few gangbusters early bull market runs. Table 7.1 updates a chart I first made way back in 1999 for *Research* magazine. It shows big cap's and small cap's returns in the first year of each of the past 13 S&P 500 bull markets. Right off the bat, you'll see small cap went nuts in 1932 and 1942. What happens if we exclude those years? The annualized averages drop to 9.8% for small cap and 9.4% for big cap. That's a rounding error. Toss small cap's gonzo returns in just four of the biggest early bull runs—the first two years of the raging bulls beginning in 1932, 1942, 1974 and 2002—and the scales tilt mildly toward big cap. Excluding those eight years, average annualized returns dwindle to 7.6% for small cap and 7.9% for big cap. Most of history, big cap slightly beats small cap.

Isolate the bull market first years, and small cap looks phenomenal—annualizing 69.16%, pummeling big cap's 42.9%. But in the other 75 years, big cap wins, annualizing 5.07% to small cap's 3.7%.

Table 7.1 Small-Cap Premium Following Bear Market Bottoms

Bottom	Small Cap	Big Cap
6/1/1932	316.45%	160.58%
4/28/1942	147.29%	61.35%
6/13/1949	35.41%	33.74%
10/22/1957	46.63%	30.04%
6/26/1962	31.12%	31.06%
10/7/1966	74.74%	20.94%
5/26/1970	42.83%	34.84%
10/3/1974	33.04%	25.95%
8/12/1982	73.43%	44.11%
12/4/1987	25.02%	16.61%
10/11/1990	50.39%	33.59%
10/9/2002	61.64%	36.16%
3/9/2009	97.90%	72.29%
Recovery Period Totals	**Small Cap**	**Big Cap**
Cumulative	92,756.61%	10,264.98%
Annualized	69.16%	42.90%
Annualized Premium	**26.25 ppts**	
All Other Periods	**Small Cap**	**Big Cap**
Cumulative	1,423.57%	3,978.15%
Annualized	3.70%	5.07%
Annualized Lag	**-1.37 ppts**	

Source: Morningstar, FactSet and Global Financial Data, Inc., as of 6/2/2014. Small-cap returns are based on the Ibbotson Associated Small Stock Total Return Index from 1/1/1926 to 12/31/1978 (Morningstar) and the Russell 2000 from 1/1/1979 to 12/31/2013 (FactSet). Big-cap returns are based on Global Financial Data's S&P 500 Total Return Index from 1/1/1926 to 12/31/2013.

Which is truly superior? The category that's spectacular every now and then, or the one that does best most of the time? Probably depends on who you are and what you are really going to do.

For most of us, however, the answer is probably neither! Again, no category is inherently superior—this goes for country, region, sector, size, style or any other breakdown the powers that be might cook up. The leaders and laggards trade off often and irregularly. If you're good at timing these, good for you. Great for you! But history is also crystal clear that most investors regardless of intent or background buy these categories high and sell them low, timing it terribly—even when they don't see themselves as timing.

Small caps are simply a leveraged play off the bottom of a bear market. That's it! They get hammered hard in big bear markets, so they over-bounce in the recovery. Sometimes small cap's heyday lasts a few years, sometimes it fizzles fast. If you can time this perfectly every time, you'll win huge—but if you can do that, you don't need to be reading this book.

For most folks, though, small cap's sexy long-term returns are unattainable in the real world. They exist on paper! But to actually get them in your portfolio, you'd have to have bought in 1926 and held ever since. Through the Crash of 1929 and the Depression to get those gonzo gains in 1932 and past the start of World War II's bear market to get to 1942. Through Nixon's price controls, the tech bubble's aftermath, 2008 and all the other gyrations and seismic events along the way. And probably be over 100 years old. Possible! But not terribly likely. And those steel-nerved centenarian marvels surely aren't reading this book. At the bottom of markets, most folks are too fearful to own tiny stocks.

Fancy Formulas and Other Academic Kryptonite

Warning: If you are the sort that glazes over at Greek letters, skip to page 188 and take this away: Fancy math models can't predict long-term returns, and most attempts are the stuff folks dream up to sound impressive at cocktail parties. But if you are the sort that revels in fancy theory and has a thing for mathematic formulas, this section is for you.

Another branch of academic folklore revolves around quantitative forecasting models. These aren't for the casual market student—they're dense and complex, and theoreticians have spent decades debating whether they work.

Intimidated? Don't be! You don't need mathy models. Most have the same drawbacks as P/E ratios and other valuations in general. Models are fine things to know if you're into that sort of thing, but they won't get you far in the real world.

Models are only as good as their inputs, and you only ever have two choices: past results or hypothetical assumptions. Neither predicts the future.

The capital asset pricing model (CAPM) is a popular, age-old model that fails the faulty input test. It sprang up in the early 1960s as a way to compute a stock's expected future returns. Its theoretical underpinning sounds fine—it assumes the more volatile stocks should reward investors with higher potential upside than the broad market as compensation for the excess risk taken. Basic intuition would tell you the same! But your real-world experience would also tell you the stock could fall hard, too.

The standard CAPM equation looks like this:

$$E(R) = R_f + \beta(R_{\text{market}} - R_f)$$

$E(R)$ is the expected return. R_f is the market's "risk-free" rate. ß—beta—measures volatility by comparing a stock's daily price movement to the overall market. R_{market} is the broad market's expected return.

Hey, look, a vomiting squirrel! (Just kidding—that was to cleanse your mental palate in case the Greek was getting you.)

Take these one by one, and it is easy to see the flaws. R_f is usually the current 10-year US Treasury yield—a reasonably rational expectation for the future time value of money. No issues with it as a starting point for a risk/return calculation. But beta is problematic. Beta measures past volatility. This isn't predictive! Past volatility is an iteration of past performance. It doesn't tell you how volatile the stock will be in the future or how much it will return. R_{market} also falls short. Essentially, it's a guess! Many analysts will base their assumptions on the market's earnings and dividend yields, again assuming that the past predicts the future—the earnings yield is simply the P/E's inverse. It does help set reasonable expectations for ultra-long-term average annualized returns, but it doesn't account for growth and productivity. It also doesn't help much in forecasting over any gameable period, rendering it largely useless in this context.

CAPM spun off another textbook model, the equity risk premium (ERP). ERP is what's inside the parentheses in CAPM—an estimate of how much stocks should outperform bonds over a given period.

There are many, many ways of calculating this, but most have the same drawbacks as the CAPM—they're almost always based on arbitrary assumptions and a belief markets revert to the mean, whether that mean is the average earnings yield, dividend yield, earnings growth rate, dividend growth rate, or whatever else one might use here.

I have no qualms concerning the belief that stocks should outperform bonds over long stretches of time (though history shows TGH will whack you there every now and then). But you can't pinpoint the exact amount.

That's the bad news. Here's the good news: You don't need to! Think about why anyone would want to calculate stocks' margin of victory over bonds over the next 10, 20 or 30 years: portfolio construction! There are better, less limited, more mathematically robust ways to find the optimal blend of stocks and bonds to match your long-term goals.

At my firm, we use Monte Carlo simulations—a computer model that simulates thousands of random scenarios based on real, historical results, then aggregates the results to assess the probability of various outcomes. As I explained back in my 2013 book, *Plan Your Prosperity*, the program we use lets us punch in a client's objectives, time horizon and annual cash flow needs, then calculates the probabilities of survival and growth across different asset allocations.

Monte Carlo simulations aren't perfect by a far cry (nothing is in markets), but they're scientifically sound. The popular modern version was created by Stanislaw Ullum in the 1940s while he was working on the Manhattan Project and trying to figure out how thick radiation shielding needed to be to keep the scientists safe. (It worked.)

How do investing Monte Carlo simulations work? Pretend you have 1,068 rubber racquetballs and a spreadsheet showing the S&P 500's monthly total return from 1926 through 2014—returns in every bull market, bear market, correction, "lost decade," feast and famine. Take a permanent marker, write one monthly return on each ball, and throw every last ball into a swimming pool. Then blindfold yourself, grab a net, and pick a ball at random. Take the blindfold off, open your portfolio simulation spreadsheet, and enter the return in Month One. Then throw the ball back, put the blindfold back on, and pick another ball. Repeat this several dozen times until your simulation matches your time horizon, and then compound these returns off your starting portfolio value. This is one sequence of hypothetical returns. Then repeat it about 2,500 times, and calculate the percentage of returns that reach your goals. That tells you, realistically, how likely a 100% stock portfolio is to reach your goals. You can do the same exercise for bonds, too, and test different asset blends (70/30, 60/40, 50/50).

Personally, I recommend skipping the pool and finding an online tool (or getting an Excel whiz kid to make one for you)—faster and far less wet.

Monte Carlo simulations tell you far more than the ERP or any other hypothetical model would. Yes, they use past returns, which aren't predictive, but the sheer hugeness of the data sample lets you game reasonable probabilities—all we're trying to do. We aren't trying to put an exact number on future returns—we know we can't know that (not in the next 30 months!). We're just shooting to find the asset allocation that provides the highest likelihood of reaching a client's goals. A Monte Carlo simulation gives you that. Based on has-done, not guesses.

Just Do It—More Than a Marketing Slogan

Why does academic theory endure even though its conclusions are often wrong? Why is its frequent wrongness usually swept under the rug? This is only a guess, but I suspect it is because we've evolved to a world where people prefer prestige resume items over experience. We've come to value the prestige of an academic resume over grubby business success. In case you haven't had a chance to read a newspaper in the last 50 years, business is bad. And if you did read those newspapers, it appears academics aren't. They're experts! I am, of course, being sarcastic. But ours is a world where Nobel laureates are heroes and CEOs villains.

Perhaps things are different if you're reading this in the future. But as I write, the ivory tower elite hold all major national economic positions and have for decades. When Janet Yellen was appointed Fed head in 2013, pundits lauded her Yale PhD—just as they had lauded Princetonite Ben Bernanke in 2006. Both were deemed wonderful, extremely qualified choices almost entirely for papers they'd written and academic positions they'd held. Theory, resume and controlled studies—all can-do.

Every President since Reagan came from Harvard or Yale. Ditto for eight of nine Supreme Court justices. Only Elena Kagan didn't—she did most of her classes at Yale but they let her have her degree from Columbia, poor girl, since her husband moved there before she finished. She's the exception that proves the rule.

When you're in the real world, though, academic pedigrees don't matter. Markets don't give one darn about where you went to school or if you did, only if you're right. You need smarts and real-life experiences. Want to be a great investor? You don't need to major in it! In the hard sciences, schooling and book learning matter. But investing isn't like biology, chemistry, engineering or computer science. The most successful investors learn by doing.

Most don't intuitively value experience. But think of it this way: Imagine you're going on a safari. Do you want the guide with an elite school PhD in zoology but no field experience who never fired a .30 caliber semiautomatic? Or do you want the guy or gal who grew up on the African savannah, has some scars, has a photo journal with the most amazing close-up shots you've ever seen—but never graduated from college? I'm betting you want the one with savannah savvy. That comes from doing, not studying.

You can apply the same logic to many other trades. Pretend you're general manager of a baseball team, and you're hiring the next coach. Do you pick a guy with a Yale PhD in baseball? No way! You hire the guy who actually played the game! It doesn't matter if he has a GED, high school diploma, some college or a college degree. That isn't important in the dugout! Sure, folks fawned over former A's and Cardinals manager Tony LaRussa with his law degree, but he too is the exception that proves the rule. No one thought that law degree made him a great manager—it was just a fun fact (and yet another example of society's fascination with parchment and sheepskin). The world championship and winning record are what made him great.

For decades the media fawned over recently deceased Joe McNamara, the only major-city chief of police with a PhD (from Harvard, no less). And he was very cop-critical, which they liked more. But there is scant evidence he was better than his peers. But we love PhDs, even where they don't help.

The point is probably clearest in the music world. America's most prestigious universities and performing arts schools offer music theory and composition majors. Anyone can study and learn, in theory, how to be a great composer or songwriter. But can you name any great songwriters with music theory degrees? Brian Wilson didn't have one. None of the Beach Boys did. Wilson and Mike Love wrote their first hit single, "Surfin'," in two hours during a jam session when they were teenagers—before the rest of the group could even play their instruments. As Carl Wilson later recalled: "The group really learned how to play after we made records."[12] They taught themselves and learned through trial and error. Not books.

Mozart was self-taught. So were Son House, Robert Johnson and the other blues greats. Buddy Holly. The Beatles. Mick Jagger. Keith Richards. Jimmy Page. None had degrees in music theory or rock stardom. They just played, just did it. Nor did Irving Berlin, George Gershwin, Victor Herbert, on and on. (Yes, Richard Rodgers and Oscar Hammerstein II had music degrees from Columbia University, but they didn't have PhDs.)

Theory Isn't Reality

It's fine to learn and know investing theory, but investing on theory alone won't get you far. Theory doesn't always work in the real world. Consider economics. Many economic theories are true only if "ceteris paribus" (all else is constant or equal). But in real life, nothing is constant and all else is never equal.

The real world is full of changing variables. Theory doesn't get you far.

The Federal Reserve is Exhibit A. For the first 60 years or so of the Fed's existence, bankers were in charge—real-world people who understood the relationship between the yield curve and the quantity of money. They were in the business of lending for a profit, and they understood incentives. But post-Greenspan, we keep getting pure ivory tower economists (we had some before Greenspan, too, and they weren't so hot either). Smart people with good pedigrees but zero practical experience. They're good on paper, but they're too steeped in theory and models. They don't know all else is never constant or equal in the real world because they never worked in the real world! Their policies don't work because they're based on theory, not reality. Janet Yellen has zippo real-world experience and she is today's central banker norm, not the exception. She is like the PhD boxer who knows all about it with no experience in the ring.

We chronicled one example back in Chapter 5—quantitative easing (QE). QE came straight from demand-side academic theory, assuming that lowering long-term rates would boost demand for loans, which would stimulate lending. Fine theory! But it assumed supply would be constant and thus ignored the variables that influence supply—banks' cost of money and lending revenues. QE ignored profit motive. The Fed never considered whether lowering long-term rates while short-term rates were fixed near zero would make lending less profitable and therefore less attractive for bankers. They never considered whether weak profit potential would discourage banks from lending, crushing credit growth no matter how eager borrowers were. But Ben Bernanke was never a banker. Being a banker is way too grubby for the world's desire for a non-real-world central banker.

Bernanke's ivory tower limitations also showed themselves in 2008. In academia, he made his name as a scholar of the Great Depression. When crisis struck, pundits assured us Bernanke the Depression expert would be a safe pair of hands. But he was the opposite! He skipped over the tried-and-true, real-world-tested crisis management weapons in the Fed's arsenal. Because as a non-real-world expert, he presumed they wouldn't work. As a Depression scholar, he should have known what worked and what didn't work. But he skipped the what-works and went straight for the unconventional. He had grandiose theories to test in practice—a true hammer looking for a nail. In retrospect, this doesn't surprise. Bernanke long admired FDR for a similar approach to fighting the Depression. As he wrote in 1999: "Roosevelt's specific policy actions were, I think, less important than his willingness to be aggressive—in short, to do whatever was necessary to get the country moving again. Many of his policies did not work as intended, but in the end FDR deserves great credit for having the courage to abandon failed paradigms and to do what needed to be done."[13] In other words, don't just do no harm—first do something, anything.

So Bernanke did exactly what he admired in FDR—experimented and showed a willingness to be aggressive, without getting actual results. He skipped battle-tested tricks and launched an alphabet soup of liquidity facilities and, eventually, QE. Despite all that cash supposedly sloshing around the financial system, credit froze, lending zeroed and broad money creation by traditional measures of M2 and M4 didn't happen.

Why? He skipped the oldest trick in the book! The Fed controls two rates—the discount rate, which applies to banks borrowing straight from the Fed, and the fed-funds target rate, which applies when banks lend to each other. For most of its history, when the Fed needed to pump liquidity into the system during a crisis, it would drop the discount rate below the fed-funds rate. That way, banks could borrow cheaply from the Fed, lend at slightly higher rates to each other and pocket the spread. That small safe profit was an incentive for banks to keep money moving. But in 2008, Bernanke's Fed flipped history. They did the opposite! They set the discount rate 25 basis points above the fed-funds rate and kept it there all year. They couldn't understand the harm this did because they lacked simple knowledge of how things work in the real world. Because they were experts.

This isn't because they're bad people. Most just never ran banks or businesses. There were exceptions. Elizabeth Duke, a Federal Open Market Committee (FOMC) Governor during the crisis, had over three decades of banking experience—including over 20 years as an executive—before President Bush appointed her to the Fed in 2007. She voiced real-world concerns from a banker's viewpoint throughout 2008, explaining how planned moves could sap profits and freeze credit. She also questioned and argued against mark-to-market accounting (though not until the December 2008 meeting). The others, though, largely went from academia to central banking. Regional Fed presidents collected anecdotal evidence from banks and businesses in their districts, but they couldn't put themselves in those business owners' or bankers' shoes.

We got more proof in 2014, when Ben Bernanke humbly revealed he couldn't refinance his mortgage—the bank turned him down![14] Even though he was Ben Bernanke, king of the astronomical book deal and six-figure public appearance fee. He took the blame, admitting stricter regulations on mortgage lending made credit too tight. He didn't mention the yield curve, though. He didn't seem to realize the bank was probably making a risk/reward decision. They didn't see him as Ben Bernanke, king of the astronomical book deal and six-figure public appearance fee. To banks, he was Ben Bernanke, newly employed at a nonprofit think tank, no longer earning the stable, predictable salary he hauled in at the Fed. Ben Bernanke, credit risk! Not something banks leap at when profits are slim. But that's real-world stuff, not theory.

If Not School, Where?

How do you learn real-world stuff if you can't learn it in school? Find yourself a mentor! In education, mentoring is the elephant in the room. Find yourself a successful mentor, and you can learn straight from those with will-do and have-done. That beats can-do and might-do every day of the week. George Gershwin had three mentors. That's ok, too. Yogi Berra had street kid mentors.

The animal kingdom figured this out long ago. Mama mountain lions don't send their cubs to mountain lion school where they read books on hunting. Mama just takes them out herself! They watch her a few times, see how she stalks her prey and makes the kill, and then they start doing it. If you ever have the chance to observe this training, you'd see the cubs out front and the mom following at a distance, watching them work. She watches their mistakes, watches them learn by doing, and if they can't get it, she shows them how again. It's remarkable to see.

Animals also pass down innovation. This is how black bears survived as populations grew and their traditional food sources became more scarce. Through trial and error, California black bears figured out tree sap is carby, sugary goodness—fuel! Then they figured out they could climb all the way to the top of a second-growth redwood tree, 120 feet in the air, peel the bark all the way down to the bottom, then lap up all the delicious sap that seeped out. DIY maple syrup for bears! They figured it out on their own and taught their young. Now California's northern second-growth redwood forests are full of tree-climbing, sap-guzzling bears. That's one-on-one training. Today's black bears are a far bigger threat to redwoods than people. They're real-world. Let's not get started on black bears and garbage cans.

Not a nature person like me? Here's the prime sports version: Muhammad Ali. The young Cassius Clay didn't have a research fellowship at Boxing University. He learned in the ring from his coach and mentor, Angelo Dundee. He didn't research and write a dissertation on the physics of floating like a butterfly and stinging like a bee, then defend his thesis in front of Sonny Liston. He just knocked the "Big Bear" out! He black-bear-like innovated the rope-a-dope on his own to knock out formidable George Foreman in the real-world "Rumble in the Jungle" of Zaire. No fancy-pants boxing degrees or certifications. Just practice and one-on-one coaching. That's why he was The Greatest.

All of this translates to investing. Warren Buffett went to Columbia, but he'll tell you he learned most of what he knows from Ben Graham. Valuing companies? Finding good, overlooked buys? All that came from training with the Father of Security Analysis. Graham did it, and he taught Buffett how to do it.

Ben Graham passed on in 1976, but you can still study with him and other late, great mentors. How? They wrote books! Not theory-heavy, sleep-inducing textbooks. I'm talking literature. Readable, relatable. Lots of elephants are hiding in classic investing books, if you know where to look. Want to know where? Time to turn to Chapter 8!

Notes

1. "Portfolio Selection," Harry Markowitz, *The Journal of Finance*, Vol. 7, No. 1 (March 1952): 77–91.
2. "Cognitive Biases in Market Forecasts," Kenneth L. Fisher and Meir Statman, *The Journal of Portfolio Management*, Fall 2000.
3. "Price-Earnings Ratios as Forecasters of Returns: The Stock Market Outlook in 1996," Robert J. Shiller, Yale University. www.econ.yale.edu/~shiller/data/peratio.html (accessed 10/29/2014).
4. *Security Analysis*, Benjamin Graham and David Dodd (New York: McGraw-Hill, 1st ed., 1934), 452.
5. "Valuation Ratios and the Long-Run Stock Market Outlook," John Y. Campbell and Robert J. Shiller, *The Journal of Portfolio Management*, Winter 1998: 11–26. www4.fe.uc.pt/jasa/m_i_2010_2011/valuationratiosandthelongrunstockmarketoutlook.pdf (accessed 10/29/2014).
6. "The Mystery of Lofty Stock Market Elevations," Robert J. Shiller, *The New York Times*, 8/16/2014.

7. "Parallels to 1937," Robert J. Shiller, Project Syndicate, 9/11/2014.
8. FactSet, as of 10/30/2014. S&P 500 Total Return Index, 12/31/1998–12/31/2008.
9. "Valuation Ratios and the Long-Run Stock Market Outlook," John Y. Campbell and Robert J. Shiller, *The Journal of Portfolio Management*, Winter 1998: 11–26.
10. Morningstar, FactSet and Global Financial Data, Inc., as of 6/2/2014.
11. "The Cross-Section of Expected Stock Returns," Eugene F. Fama and Kenneth R. French, *The Journal of Finance*, Vol. 47, No. 2 (June 1992): 427–465. www.bengrahaminvesting.ca/Research/Papers/French/The_Cross-Section_of_Expected_Stock_Returns.pdf (accessed 10/30/2014).
12. *The Beach Boys and the California Myth*, David Leaf (New York: Grosset & Dunlap, 1978).
13. "Japanese Monetary Policy: A Case of Self-Induced Paralysis," Ben S. Bernanke, Princeton University, December 1999. https://www.princeton.edu/~pkrugman/bernanke_paralysis.pdf (accessed 11/3/2014).
14. "You Know It's a Tough Market When Bernanke Can't Refinance," Elizabeth Campbell and Lorraine Woellert, *Bloomberg*, 10/3/2014. http://www.bloomberg.com/news/articles/2014-10-02/you-know-it-s-a-tough-market-when-ben-bernanke-can-t-refinance (accessed 2/24/2015).

CHAPTER 8

Throw Away This Book!

The title of this chapter is about 50% ironic—I'm not really suggesting you should trash this. Or recycle or sell it at the nearest used-book shop. I took the time to write it, after all! And it is really great for propping up the missing rear leg of a tried-and-true, comfy sofa. But this book does have a drawback if you're reading it in 2015: It's new. Few new books contain actionable advice you can use to beat the crowd—too much chatter! Too much attention might make everything in here priced for a while. You might be best off coming back to this one in 10 or 20 years, pulling it out when you junk that peg-legged sofa.

Maybe not, though. One of the reasons I wrote *The Only Three Questions That Count* was to see if my methods would get discounted after I published them for all to see. I wanted to see if they'd still work! As it happens, most of them do, even after two editions and a ride on the *New York Times* bestseller list. So maybe this one has staying power, too. Only time will tell.

While you're waiting, though, there are plenty of other wonderful, useful investing books you can read. Some teach genuine how-to tips. Others show how Wall Street works and where you can be led astray if you aren't careful. Classical works of economic philosophy show the beauty of markets and capitalism, which can help you analyze economic policies today. Some books simply teach you how to think. Not ideologically, of course. History books remind us this time is almost never really different and help put current events—and myopic media gloom—in context.

We'll cover all of these and more in this strange chapter. I like to think of it as an on-paper book club. Of course, it's a one-sided book club, since you'll only get my side of the conversation, but you can always chime in later!

Here's what we'll cover in this fun guide to financial literature:

- Why you shouldn't expect much investing help from trendy new books
- Forgotten classics, brilliant biographies and helpful history
- Modern classics to help you battle the doom-obsessed media

Miley Cyrus, Justin Bieber and Pop Star Economists

New books can't be the elephant in the room. They're what everyone talks about! Their theories, forecasts, opinions and conclusions are usually priced in fast, particularly if popular. Even if their conclusions are correct, they probably aren't actionable for you.

Some new books are instant classics, as we'll see later. But most fall into one of two buckets: current events or long-term forecasts.

Current events books can be interesting, fun reads. But there is usually way too much chatter surrounding the books and their subject matter. The author's beliefs and biases bleed in, too, like mine here, making it hard to separate fact from opinion or even fiction popularly disguised as nonfiction. Some very entertaining, readable books fall into this trap—think reality TV or anything from Michael Lewis. That brand of bestselling financial journalism can be fun to read! But the onus is on the reader to discern fact from fiction, and it isn't easy.

Most books focused on recent trends and events also have very short windows of relevance. They're the Miley Cyrus and Justin Bieber of the book world. (If you're a Boomer and don't know of Miley and Justin, think David Cassidy or Donovan.) Soon they'll be replaced by new fads. Unless these books teach timeless lessons, they won't be useful a year or two out.

> The key to market staying power methodology is to be right but not too popular—like my dieting advice. There are endless dieting books. Some have been huge sellers. I lost over 100 pounds years ago and kept it off with my own magic diet that will never be popular and is analogous to market techniques that won't be discounted. How to lose weight? Never eat anything you like, and you won't overeat, and the pounds ripple off! Almost no one will ever do that. Or buy a book about it.

Many books emerging from 2008's financial crisis fell into that bucket, lacking actionable investment advice. Several seized on investors' generally apocalyptic sentiment to peddle hastily written books forecasting a return to crisis. "Depression" and "doom" remained book title mainstays years afterward. Crisis survival guides dominated, some seemingly straight out of an episode of *Doomsday Preppers*. All made the fundamental mistake of assuming "it's different this time"—the four most dangerous words in investing, as Sir John Templeton famously said. They ignored cyclical factors, even after the market and economy's obvious upturns. Some have been revised multiple times in a vain attempt to find relevance years into the new expansion. Reading these would help you see where sentiment was at that time, but not reality—and you could get sentiment from the titles, so you didn't need to waste time reading. The sheer volume would tell you those views and dismal expectations were priced. That's a great way to be contrarian and game the crowd.

The long-term forecast books usually aren't very useful either. (Not in the next 30 months!) This category encompasses pretty much everything by Harry Dent, who gained popularity using demographic changes to forecast long-term stock returns. You might recall his 1999 prediction that the Dow would hit 35,000 by 2009—or his 2012 prediction for Dow 3,300 by 2022. These claims are sensational and eye-catching, but it should be fairly obvious they aren't of much value for investors.

Other long-term forecast books have more academic rigor but equally little usefulness for investors. Many weren't even written for investors to act on! They're more policy prescriptions dressed up as long-term economic outlooks. The big bestseller of 2014, Thomas Piketty's *Capital in the Twenty-First Century* (Harvard University Press), is a prime example. He argues income inequality is widening, putting economies at great long-term risk, but his aim is to goad governments into punitive taxes on the wealthy and high earners. That also tells you there is some ideological bias at work, a sign the analysis might be more opinion-driven than fact-driven. (Indeed, the data underpinning his thesis suffer the same flaws as the income inequality data we dissected back in Chapter 4.) But even if his conclusion is ultimately correct, it fails the "not in the next 30 months" test.

I'm picking on Piketty's book here because it is the latest example, but it isn't alone in this regard. Carmen Reinhart and Kenneth Rogoff's 2009 treatise from Princeton University Press, *This Time It's Different* (you can hear John Templeton rolling over in his grave), which built off several of their earlier studies on debt and economic crises, was also policy prescription as economic analysis. Its claim (since debunked by economists who found errors in their dataset) that high debt causes slow growth underpinned many of the eurozone's crisis-era austerity policies. Reading this, *Capital in the Twenty-First Century* and other similar books can help you understand the beliefs and philosophies that drive economic policy. If you're into that sort of thing, you'll probably enjoy these! Just remember, they're sociology. And quite possibly biased sociology. Not investment guides.

Classics Are Classic for a Reason

But enough on books that don't help. What *should* you read to find useful, actionable investment tips?

Start with the classics!

You're much likelier to find the elephant in the living room in old books. Classics everyone has read but many or most may think represent the "old ways." They're perhaps discounted as too stale. But markets and people don't really change in vitally important and fundamental ways—the old ways can still matter! Which makes old books full of useful, long-overlooked concepts and methods. Legendary investors were legendary for a reason. The classics let us learn from them directly.

First, a warning, an apology and a suggestion—this list is incomplete. There are dozens of worthy classics, and this short space forces me to exclude some. For a much more complete list, check out *Best Books on the Stock Market: An Analytical Bibliography*, by Sheldon Zerden, published in 1972 by RR Bowker. It highlights over 100 books, mostly must-reads, with a roughly page-long summary on each. It contains wonderful wisdom on market basics, history, investor psychology, contrarian thinking and so much more. Because of its age, it misses the few modern classics, but it really is the baseline bibliography for any investor—perusing it will prompt a long, joyous literary journey. Used copies abound on Amazon and AbeBooks.com, and they're dirt cheap.

The Intelligent Investor, Ben Graham, 1949

This one is mostly historical, but it has plenty of wisdom. Graham's other opus, 1934's *Security Analysis* (written with David Dodd) is often called the investment world's Bible, and it's a gem. But *The Intelligent Investor* is more useful for our purposes and less antiquated—particularly since he updated it in 1973. *Security Analysis* is all about stock picking—engrossing, necessary, but less impactful in a diversified portfolio. *The Intelligent Investor* is more about the market. Mr. Market, to be exact—the stock market in human form, the star of Graham's parable about volatility. Mr. Market's whims—overly enthusiastic one day, panicked the next—show how markets really are irrational "voting machines" in the short term, as Graham famously said. This irrational behavior creates our contrarian opportunities in an otherwise efficient market.

Mr. Market is probably the most famous part of this book, but Graham has plenty of treats for you. His discussion of risk reminds us that short-term volatility and actual risk are different animals. His indictment of Dow Theory shows us how and why the academic formulas we discussed in Chapter 7 are limited and mostly pre-priced. And he reinforces that old truism: There is no such thing as a good stock or a bad stock. Companies can be good or bad! But stocks are stocks. These and the other lessons Graham teaches can help you avoid most common blunders.

If you want to read Graham's *Security Analysis,* focus on the original 1934 version—the original and classic. The early revised editions are fine, too, but more modern revisions have watered Graham's classic to a stew where taste is overpowered by modern academic mish-mash and completely unrecognizable relative to Graham's voice or views.

Common Stocks and Uncommon Profits, Phil Fisher, 1958

Warren Buffett once described his investing philosophy as "85 percent Benjamin Graham and 15 percent Fisher."[1] "Fisher" is Phil Fisher, my father.

Father taught me how to think. This book can do the same for you by showing how *he* thought. He was an outside-the-crowd critical thinker through and through. This was the first investment book to be on the *New York Times* bestseller list. It still sells well today via Amazon.

Most of *Common Stocks and Uncommon Profits* is company-focused. Father thought diversification was overrated, and he wasn't much concerned with gaming market cycles. Read this and absorb it anyway—it's short. You'll finish it in an afternoon. You'll see why stock evaluation should be qualitative, not just quantitative. You'll see, over and over, the importance of knowing you can be wrong and learning from your mistakes—and not letting pride blind you to your own wrongness when it happens. You'll see events of mass psychology drive investors astray, like the apocalyptic sentiment surrounding the 1949 recession. You'll see the dangers of letting emotion influence your decisions—and the virtues of being disciplined and not selling because of historical price trends or the recent past, good or bad.

Many of Father's don'ts for investors are timeless. Don't fall for company marketing spin. Don't buy on past performance or earnings over any period, short or long. Father would have hated Robert Shiller's Cyclically Adjusted P/E (CAPE) ratio—if you don't believe me, see the below box. Another good one: "Don't be afraid of buying on a war scare." And most of all, "Don't follow the crowd." I'll let him speak for himself: "The ability to see through some majority opinions to find what facts are really there is a trait that can bring rich rewards in the field of common stocks. It is not easy to develop, however, for the composite opinion of those with whom we associate is a powerful influence upon the minds of all of us."[2]

As we saw in Chapter 7, Shiller's Cyclically Adjusted P/E ratio compares the current price to the past 10 years of inflation-adjusted earnings, claiming a high CAPE means below-average returns over the next decade and vice versa. Father destroyed this claim decades before Shiller dreamed up CAPE. Here's a snippet from Chapter 9 of *Common Stocks and Uncommon Profits*, under the delightful header, "Don't Forget Your Gilbert and Sullivan":

(continued)

"Similarly, many investors will give heavy weight to the per-share earnings of the past five years in trying to decide whether a stock should be bought. To look at the per-share earnings by themselves and give the earnings of four or five years ago any significance is like trying to get useful work from an engine which is unconnected to any device to which that engine's power is supposed to be applied. Just knowing, by itself, that four or five years ago a company's per-share earnings were either four times or a quarter of this year's earnings has almost no significance in indicating whether a particular stock should be bought or sold. Again, what counts is knowledge of background conditions. An understanding of what probably will happen over the next several years is of overriding importance.

"The investor is constantly being fed a diet of reports and so-called analyses largely centered around these price figures for the past five years. He should keep in mind that it is the next five years' earnings, not those of the past five years, that now matter to him."[3]

Reminiscences of a Stock Operator, Edwin Lefèvre, 1923

This is one of my all-time favorite books. In my 1993 book, *100 Minds That Made the Market*, I said no one should invest money they deem "important" without reading this book first. That's still true, decades later. *Reminiscences* is a fictionalized "autobiography" of Jesse Livermore, which tries to get inside his head and show how he thought. In doing so it shows the utter folly of short-term inning and outing. Everyone can learn from his follies during the Panic of 1901 (more on that later), to name just one example.

Livermore actually wrote his own book, *How to Trade in Stocks*, published in March 1940 by Duell, Sloan & Pearce. It's a fine read but a how-not-to guide. He traded on price movement and accumulated pride—tragically false bravado, as the world learned that November when he died broke, killing himself. The genius trader couldn't hold on to money. He made and lost entire fortunes serially, filing for bankruptcy four times—all chronicled in Richard Smitten's 2001 biography, *Jesse Livermore: World's Greatest Stock Trader* (John Wiley & Sons).

But I'm partial to *Reminiscences.* We see young Livermore hit Wall Street straight out of grammar school, taking notes on stock price movement from day one. Through Livermore's rise from clerk to day-trader to the legendary "Boy Plunger" and king of Wall Street, *Reminiscences* illuminates the highs and lows, and its hero happily shares what he learns along the way. Such pearls of wisdom!

Ironically, the biggest lesson appears early on: "I didn't always win. My plan of trading was sound enough and won oftener than it lost. If I had stuck to it I'd have been right perhaps as often as seven out of ten times. In fact, I always made money when I was sure I was right before I began. What beat me was not having brains enough to stick to my own game—that is, to play the market only when I was satisfied that precedents favored my play. There is a time for all things, but I didn't know it. And that is precisely what beats so many men in Wall Street who are very far from being in the main sucker class. There is the plain fool, who does the wrong thing at all times everywhere, but there is the Wall Street fool, who thinks he must trade all the time. No man can always have adequate reasons for buying and selling stocks daily—or sufficient knowledge to make his play an intelligent play."

Livermore would spend his entire career re-learning this lesson and fighting his destructive instincts. Winning with stocks, blowing it all on land schemes, winning it back, losing, lather, rinse, repeat. In the end, his suicide note said it all: "I am tired of fighting."[4] *Reminiscences* captures a happier Livermore, breezily sharing his triumphs and blunders, occasionally bragging but always teaching. Let him teach you.

Contrarian Investment Strategy: The Psychology of Stock-Market Success, David Dreman, 1980

Another old favorite and hugely impactful on me, personally. In some ways, it shows its age. It's grounded in late-1970s sentiment, when folks were grappling with "stagflation" and other woes. Much of the commentary on valuations is now widely known and widely used—not much use if you're trying to be un-crowdlike. But those are small drawbacks in an otherwise excellent discussion of investing groupthink and the futility of following the crowd. Some parts are sort of a prequel for this book, like the chapter showing how professional forecasters' poor track record dates all the way to the 1960s (and probably before). Other parts show how technical analysts and fundamentalists form their own (usually wrong) crowds—just like we discussed in Chapter 1—by using the same models, theories and assumptions. Dreman shows outright the danger of crowd-chasing by chronicling investors' behavior in old euphoric episodes like the Mississippi Scheme and 1962 bull market peak. Overall, this book shows contrarian thinking in action—and in doing so, teaches a thought process you can apply to problems and situations today.

David, of course, wrote a regular column in *Forbes*, starting shortly before I did. It was called "The Contrarian," and for decades he and I alternated appearances in every other issue. He still writes in *Forbes*, but rarely now, and I fondly miss our counterpoint but often parallel arguments. *Forbes*, of course, has always been a great source of contrarian inputs.

Where Are the Customers' Yachts? Fred Schwed, 1940

This is another short, sweet classic you'll breeze through in an afternoon—150 pages with big print. In some regards, it too shows its age. It assumes stocks entered a permabull market after the Depression, and it was written before the Investment Advisers Act of 1940 separated investment sales from service. But it drives home some very old, true basics in simple language anyone can relate to. Short parables show us past performance never predicts future returns. For every buyer there is a seller. Anyone claiming to predict ultra-short-term returns is just guessing.

Schwed's classic also shows behavioral errors, like the danger of assuming the trend is your friend—otherwise known as momentum investing. He also reminds us anti–Wall Street sentiment and banker bashing have existed forever and are often a behavioral error—regret shunning. When The Great Humiliator (TGH) gets us, we'd much rather blame someone else than admit the market won or we made a mistake. This robs us of a chance to learn and is a dangerous trap.

Customers' Man, Boyden Sparkes, 1931

This strange little curiosity is more about the structure of Wall Street than investing—just as important for market participants to understand. *Customers' Man* is fiction, a parable written after the 1929 Crash to prepare brokers (then called "customers' men") for new regulations—the Securities Act of 1933, Securities Exchange Act of 1934 and Investment Advisers Act of 1940. The hero was a musician who went to Wall Street to make enough money to earn his sweetheart's hand in marriage—an honorable fellow who was disgusted by the conflicts of interest in his trade and his colleagues' unscrupulous behavior. The tale shows why rules separating investment sales from service were vital. This line has blurred in recent decades to investors' detriment. Politicians, regulators and investors could all use a refresher on why letting sales and service seep together is dangerous and invites conflicts of interest.

Philosophy and Econ 101

Switching gears now is painful, because I've omitted some gems from that last section. Sorry! There are only so many pages in this book, and pure investment books aren't the only source of library wisdom. What about politics? Economics? We've already seen how both intersect with markets, driving both boom and bust. Literary classics can help us here, too.

That Which Is Seen and That Which Is Not Seen, Frédéric Bastiat, 1850

We explored Bastiat's broken-window fallacy in Chapter 5—this is where it came from. *That Which Is Seen* is a 12-part essay warning nineteenth-century French politicians of the danger of intervening in free markets. As part of the French Liberal school, Bastiat believed prosperity comes from free people and free commerce, and government meddling was the road to ruin. The French ignored it. Modern France is often proof Bastiat was right.

That Which Is Seen is a short and sweet lesson on the law of unintended consequences. On normal paper, it's about 40 pages. It's also free—you can find it at Bastiat.org and other places. As you'd expect of text translated from mid-nineteenth-century French to English, the language is a bit stilted, but the logic is simple and clear, and the topics are timeless. For example: Should countries keep huge militaries to boost employment? Do high taxes and public investment spur growth? Would the fine arts die without government support? Is public infrastructure spending really stimulus or efficient? Will automated manufacturing displace workers and be society's downfall? Would governments allocate credit better than banks?

Our politicians and populace still struggle with these. They probably will always and all ways. Understanding how Bastiat thinks and why will help you weigh the risks whenever Congress tries to "fix" something.

The Wealth of Nations, Adam Smith, 1776

The year 1776 was a banner year for humanity. America declared independence. Adam Smith declared capitalism. You can decide which means more for American freedom and prosperity. But don't decide until you read *The Wealth of Nations*, published in the year of our great country's birth.

When the good Scot made his *Inquiry Into the Nature and Causes of the Wealth of Nations* (the full title), Britain was nearing its boiling point. The Colonies had just declared King George a tyrant, and Brits were awakening to the notion of individualism after centuries of living under nearly all-powerful mercantilistic monarchs. Smith took center stage in what we now call the Enlightenment with a simple, radical idea: If allowed to, the self-interests of every human being will collide and create wealth and progress for all of society, guided by the "invisible hand" of the market—competition and a self-driven quest for wealth and profits. Self-interested sellers will never stop creating newer, better goods, services and technology as they constantly one-up each other, while self-interested buyers will pick and choose the best, reject the rest, demand bargains and pull prices down to their natural level. Everyone wins.

The Wealth of Nations drives this home again and again in 1,000 pages. Adam Smith showed how self-determination drove prosperity in the Colonies—and how the Crown's out-of-sight, out-of-mind de facto *laissez-faire* allowed the Colonies to flourish. (King George got greedy and went for a bigger slice of the pie after they got rich.) He showed how big government and high taxes can sap the life from economies. He showed how specialization and division of labor can drive productivity through the roof—he didn't live to see the industrial revolution's heyday, but he sure imagined it. He showed how fiat money could work as long as people had confidence in the bankers—no gold standard required.

Adam Smith knew his audience, too. He wrote for the masses. This is the most readable 1,000-page tome on economic philosophy on the planet. It won't put you to sleep. It will make you wiser and help you understand why free economies do best—and why markets hate true socialist creeping.

How Capitalism Will Save Us, Steve Forbes and Elizabeth Ames, 2009

One of the greatest titles and subtitles ever: "Why Free People and Free Markets Are the Best Answer in Today's Economy." Says it all! In Chapter 5, I mentioned that capitalism (i.e., supply-side thinking) fell from fashion after 2008's crisis—Forbes uses clear logic and simple economics to remind us why free markets are morally right and with volatility can be counted on still—and almost regardless of what we confront—to raise living standards for all who have them, just as they have for centuries in America and Britain.

Though this isn't an investing how-to book, anyone who has ever owned a stock or plans to own a stock should read it. Understand free markets, and you'll fathom how and why companies and individuals continue creating, driving growth and rendering rewards to shareholders many times over—making once-scarce goods abundant and improving quality of life for all in the process. And all of that happening without benefit of any grand master plan but human self-interest run amok. Understand the unseen force of capitalism, and you'll gain faith in markets' ability to overcome all issues—economic and sociological—the media frets continually. That faith helps us all invest better by providing a valuable long-term perspective the media generally won't cover.

A New Radical's Guide to Economic Reality, Angus Black, 1970

Angus Black is the pseudonym of Roger Leroy Miller, whom I encountered when I was a student at Humboldt State—and who changed my life. I'd taken most (if not all) of Humboldt's Economics classes, and I'd done very well, but I still didn't quite get the big picture. It was as if I'd taken a car apart, studied all the parts, had a great understanding of each and the theory of how they all fit together, but I couldn't get the dynamics of how they could all work real-time to make the car go.

Then Miller gives a talk at my school, promoting this slender, lively free-market manifesto. I'm in the audience, and in walks this young University of Chicago–trained economist with long flowing hair and black boots—radical! If you aren't familiar with Humboldt, it's way up in rural, forested Northern California—pot–smoking liberal hippie heaven then and now. Miller stood up and said, "If you have liberal views, and you think liberal policies work for all these causes you care about, this book will show you the truth." Back then, I'm a 19-year-old liberal thinking, "Boy, my professors are gonna rip this guy apart." And I'm delighted for it! But when Q&A time comes, they all ask timid questions—he knows his stuff better than they do, and they know it, and they don't want him ripping them apart in public.

That's when the wheels in my brain gained traction—in 45 minutes, I knew how the whole car worked, and I became a libertarian. Miller had proved—with facts, theory and common sense—that more government was usually the problem, not the solution. Free choice and free markets could accomplish more than politicians and radical regulations ever could. When I got home, my new wife, Sherrilyn, was stunned—even startled and alarmed—at how much I'd changed. The arguments in Miller's book changed my views on almost everything as a young man. They turned me into someone who understood how neoclassical economics worked and how the entire academic discipline would work. But most important, I learned to apply, with limitations, the neoclassical model to forecasting—of economics and markets.

The book can do the same for you. It's a great way to learn the basics of neoclassical economics in a jiff. Full disclosure (and only so you're free to choose fully informed!), it really is radical—occasionally obscene and politically incorrect. It uses language most readers will find offensive and that I certainly do not endorse. But these are a relic of his time and audience, and may explain why the book has become so unknown. I overlook all of it and hope you will, too. The substance is necessary and timeless.

Business Barometers Used in the Accumulation of Money, Roger W. Babson, 1905–1930

The date range isn't an error—Babson updated his text dozens of times over the years. You can't go wrong with any of them and needn't read them all, as the core doesn't change much. You can find reprints easily, and some editions have been digitized and are available freely online. A Google search will turn them up in half a second.

The *Business Barometer* series is one of the original works on fundamental economic analysis for long-term investors. Babson knew short-term timing would get you nowhere, but longer cycles—bull markets and bear markets, or "periods of decline" and "periods of prosperity"—were possible to identify and forecast. His *Business Barometers* sought to teach us how.

Every edition started with a short chapter called "Two Classes of Statistics," which drew an uncrossable line between "comparative statistics" like earnings and revenues, and "fundamental statistics," which showed underlying economic conditions. Comparative statistics are useful, he explained, but not inherently predictive. He argued investors should and could forecast cycles based on fundamental conditions—a revolutionary concept back then. Some of his preferred metrics, like railroad earnings, are antiquated but have viable descendants, like air freight traffic and intermodal land freight volumes—statistics have evolved. Others, like broad money supply, are timeless. (Although the specific ways to measure the quantity of money evolve as we create ever more "near money," like credit cards, that Babson couldn't have envisioned.)

Babson called *Business Barometers* an applied economics textbook for investors, but that makes it sound dry. It isn't dry! It doesn't even read like a textbook. Dry textbooks don't have parables showing why buying stock on a broker's hot tip is fruitless. This heavy economic analysis comes with plenty of palate cleansers.

Business Cycles, Wesley Clair Mitchell, 1913

I mentioned Mitchell's magnum opus back in Chapter 5. I love it so much, I'm giving it a cameo here, too—it's that good! In my mind, simply, Mitchell was a god of economics, statistics, cycles and forecasting.

When Mitchell wrote *Business Cycles* in 1913, most assumed booms and busts just happened. Kind of like weather. Few fathomed they could be part of an actual cycle, created by the occasional excesses naturally accompanying capitalism. Few fathomed busts were the invisible hand's way of self-correcting these excesses, keeping us all on the capitalist road to heaven if we let it. (Politicians never seem to want to let it.)

Mitchell fathomed it, and *Business Cycles* is his theory and proof. No grandstanding—just the scientific method. He gathered a treasure trove of data and observed, analyzed, tested and deduced. Always entertaining, never dry, he walks us all through an entire economic cycle, explaining the how and why at every step. We see businesses overextend, overestimating potential profits, and getting squeezed when they can't control costs. We see credit costs rise as banks—the market—get wary. Then panic when firms can't pay the piper. We see credit freeze as panic climaxes, and we see the need for liquidity—enter the Federal Reserve that same year. And then we see prices reset, business improve, and an expansion begin anew.

Business Cycles will show you how Wall Street and Main Street are intertwined—never one versus the other, always working in tandem. It is as vital today as it was a century ago. After it you might try his 1927 publication for the National Bureau of Economic Research, *Business Cycles: The Problem and Its Setting*, another tour de force book for those who want to root deeply into the origins of global forecasting.

How to Lie With Statistics, Darrell Huff, 1954

As Mark Twain claims Benjamin Disraeli said, "There are three kinds of lies: lies, damned lies, and statistics." Huff's delightful read shows us how and why that's true. Complete with fun illustrations!

It's a short read, and I won't belabor this blurb—don't need to. The title speaks for itself. Huff shows how statistical analysis is easily skewed to yield a desired outcome, support a certain bias, or perform whatever evil little task the author desires. Anyone can make numbers lie.

Why read it? Think about all the wild claims about the economy, markets, and policies that are underpinned with data! A lot of it is bogus, as we saw with Piketty and Saez. It's easy to test and pick apart if you know how, and Huff teaches you how. You can't think outside the crowd without this book in your brain. I consider it mandatory for anyone considering himself or herself educated—even if you studied statistics extensively in school, as I did. I learned a lot when I got to Huff. But the best part is you don't need the classes to squeeze the juice out of Huff. It's squeezy.

How to Learn From the Legends

Not every legendary investor wrote a book. Many were too busy just doing! Luckily for us, biographers did the job for them. We can read their life stories, see them in action and learn from their successes, failures and experience.

The Rothschilds, *Frederic Morton, 1961*

According to financial folklore, it was Nathan Mayer Rothschild who first said: "The time to buy is when there's blood in the streets." Some historians claim that's apocryphal, and maybe it is. Read *The Rothschilds* anyway. Even if Nathan didn't utter that famous line, he sure lived it.

As the title suggests, this is the 200-year saga of Nathan and the entire House of Rothschild, starting with patriarch Mayer Rothschild in the Jewish ghetto of 1760s Frankfurt. It's blessedly short, at about 300 pages.

The House of Rothschild was the world's first modern private bank. It was also effectively the world's central bank, funding governments and wars as well as industry. All the Rothschilds played their part, but Nathan was the leader and gifted speculator. He made a killing during the Napoleonic Wars, literally buying when there was blood in the streets. He bailed out the Bank of England in 1826, a precursor to JP Morgan in 1893. He pioneered international credit, introducing a paper system to spare borrowers the hassle of moving physical collateral as proof of deposit.

You'll learn plenty from their story. One of the most timeless lessons comes early on, when we witness the family's escapades during the Napoleonic Wars. Nathan's speculating then is legendary, but also key was the family smuggling business. Shady? Heck yeah! But they knew, from the start, that war doesn't stop commerce and normal life. People still want to eat and shop, and the Rothschilds made sure they could. Remember that the next time you hear war is a surefire economic downer. And if you care to know how important this book is to me, after reading it, I named my second son after Nathan Rothschild—for a fact.

The House of Morgan: An American Banking Dynasty and the Rise of Modern Finance, Ron Chernow, 1990

This is the story of a bank—JP Morgan—but also the story of a man. Legendary financier John Pierpont Morgan, without whom modern banking and capital markets might not exist as we know them. Heck, America might not exist as we know it, considering it was Morgan who personally bailed out Uncle Sam in the Panic of 1893. They don't make 'em like Morgan anymore: flinty tough, visionary, multifaceted, cut-throat yet kind. He was one of a kind.

At over 800 pages, this isn't for the faint of heart. But it is an absorbing history of America's financial system and four generations of Morgans. The House of Morgan was America's later equivalent of the House of Rothschild, right down to emergency government funding. You'll witness Morgan (the man) wheel and deal to end the Panics of 1893 and 1907. You'll be a fly on the wall at the secret Jekyll Island getaway and congressional hearings that eventually gave rise to the Fed. You'll see how banker bashing from Ferdinand Pecora and other politicians during the

Great Depression led to Glass-Steagall and the separation of retail and investment banking. Across 150 years of the Morgans' history, you'll see everything markets saw, and it's a rip-roaring tale.

James J. Hill and the Opening of the Northwest, Albro Martin, 1991

The Rothschilds and Morgans were key players in my book, *100 Minds That Made the Market.* Our next three characters were, too—starting with the great Northwestern titan, James J. Hill.

Roger Babson called James J. Hill "a great student of fundamental statistics."[5] The nineteenth-century railroad baron was a great thinker, business leader and investor, too. He was also a classic up-by-the-bootstraps self-made titan, spurring growth and industry throughout the Northwest as he built his railroad empire—without land grants, eminent domain, political favors or a dime of government assistance. Living proof the private sector spurs development far better than the government could dream of.

Hill went to Wall Street late in life, so the bulk of this book chronicles his empire building. But even his business decisions carry wisdom for investors—his analysis of economic conditions and focus on profits translate directly to security analysis today. His Wall Street adventures are where things really start cooking, though. When Hill hit the Street, he became greed personified (as in: Greed is good), cornering the competition in an effort to turn his Great Northern railroad into a transcontinental empire. And he showed a strong contrarian streak. He snapped up the Northern Pacific line after it failed in the Panic of 1893. His bid for the Chicago, Burlington and Quincy line drove rival Ed Harriman mad with jealousy, sowing the seeds of the Panic of 1901. Through Great Northern, he spent $4 million for land containing iron ore deposits in Minnesota's Mesabi range in 1898 and sat on it for eight years before contracting US Steel to mine it. Observers scratched their heads, but that $4 million became $425 million by 1906—a huge win for Hill's shareholders. That group included his employees, after he finagled a way for them to buy shares at half price—an early pioneer of employee stock options, innovation at its finest.

Hill's exploits also contributed to the evolution of securities law and antitrust rules. This book gives a fine overview, but it might leave you wanting more of the drama. Fear not—I have another treat for you later in this chapter.

Dark Genius of Wall Street: The Misunderstood Life of Jay Gould, King of the Robber Barons, Edward J. Renehan Jr., 2005

First, though, if it's drama you want, Jay Gould is your man. Universally hated, Gould made the rest of the Gilded Age's "robber barons" look like kittens. Unless you were related to him, he was a nasty guy. He was also one of our most creative, innovative financiers. I've always kind of liked him for his chutzpah, and it's clear Renehan likes him, too. That's a compliment—this is a zippy, engrossing tale of a true outsider contrarian.

I don't recommend imitating every move Gould ever made. Manipulating a company's financial figures to run its price up will land you in jail. But his inimitable skill and discipline ring true today. He was hated because he was ruthless, and that forced him outside the crowd. He probably wanted to be there anyway—circumstance and instinct made him a contrarian.

The more successful Gould became, the more society derided him. The New York of the Vanderbilts and Astors couldn't abide this new-money man who gained fame and fortune through speculating. He got rich the wrong way, they said! He didn't deserve it! A *New York Times* profile from 1892 pegged his fortune at $70 million (roughly $1.2 billion today), then seethed at his selfish tactics—he didn't create prosperity like the Astors or Vanderbilts, said the *Times*. He was a leech and borderline criminal, in their view.[6]

The irony? Gould was no leech! He drove prices down to buy companies on the cheap, but he didn't raid and ruin. He raided and ran the companies, usually improving them. That creates prosperity, folks. He pioneered what private equity firms do all the time today (without the fees).

You'll get all that and more from this tale. Including a panic! Specifically, the Panic of 1869, which Gould caused. He tried to corner gold and came darned close. He also tried to coerce his crony's brother-in-law, President Grant, to prop up the price. Grant declined, releasing 5% of the Treasury's gold reserves, which sent the price reeling. Speculators were crushed! But not Gould—he had an inside tip from Grant's wife and sold high. (Like I said, you shouldn't imitate everything he did.) There are many other delights, but I won't spoil them for you.

Hetty Green: A Woman Who Loved Money, Boyden Sparkes and Samuel Taylor Moore, 1930

Newer biographies of the "Witch of Wall Street" have made the rounds, but none capture her market savvy and methods quite like this volume—they spend too much time on her oddball quirks and tabloid gossip, not enough on her buys and sells. Hetty hated gossip. This book, published 14 years after her death, is a straightforward account of her life and mad genius.

Hetty shattered the glass ceiling in Wall Street's nineteenth-century old boys' club—the only female bigwig in the age of Gould, Hill and Morgan. She outfoxed the speculators, bailed out New York City at least twice and (legend has it) pulled a gun on rival railroad tycoon Collis Huntington when he threatened to throw her son in jail during their battle for Texas railroads. She hated losing money and chucked her husband after he fizzled her funds on a bad bank deal. Sentimentality? To Hetty that was for the weak. Enjoying wealth through consumer items or services was for the profligate. To save money and avoid taxes, she lived a vagrant's life, shuffling her children from room to rented room in Brooklyn and low-rent Manhattan quarters.

Her frugality bordered on insanity, but her refusal to spend allowed her wealth to compound many, many times over. She turned a $6 million inheritance into $100 million by the time she died, just by targeting 6% a year and letting it compound. She loved buying bonds and mortgages, and if the mortgage defaulted, she kept the house. And she never missed a chance to buy stocks cheap—particularly railroad stocks. After she got caught long in the Panic of 1873, her strategy was simple: "I buy when things are low and no one wants them. I keep them, just as I keep a considerable number of diamonds on hand, until they go up and people are anxious to buy. That is the general secret of business success. I never speculate. ... Such stocks as belong to me were purchased simply as an investment, never on a margin."[7]

Hetty played the market's sentiment lifecycle like a piano. She always bought at the depth of panics and had a knack for getting out near the top. She sold out of Knickerbocker Trust in 1907 because the men working there were "too good-looking." Must be euphoria! Then she turned around and lent her winnings to distressed banks and financiers—a quieter, humbler JP Morgan—but always judiciously and never usuriously (and ever the Quaker). Hetty knew how to weigh risk and didn't shoot for the stars. Get to know this marvelous lady, and learn from her disciplined, crowd-beating ways and love of compound growth. You needn't adopt her miserly ways to learn and benefit from her life.

Templeton's Way With Money, Jonathan Davis and Alasdair Nairn, 2012

Sir John Templeton wrote, but mostly about his faith, science and personal philosophy. This gem and other biographies fill the void, showing the rise and tactics of the greatest-ever mutual fund manager.

As I mentioned in Chapter 6, Templeton pioneered global investing. He was the first! He put some money in Japan shortly after World War II, when most foreigners were scared off by Japan's capital controls. But not Sir John! He studied the country and its culture, learned how its economy and political system worked and made his play. He was one of the first to eye South Korea in the early 1980s, when it was still heavily restricted after the fall of Park Chung-hee's military dictatorship. You'll learn plenty from these and all his global adventures.

You'll also get your Sir Johnisms. Most know Templeton's legendary quote: "Bull markets are born on pessimism, grow on skepticism, mature on optimism and die on euphoria." This book has a treasure trove of such wisdom. Here's a teaser: "If you want to produce the best results in twenty or thirty years, you have to be flexible. A flexible viewpoint is a matter of avoiding a peculiar trait of human nature, which is to buy the things that you wish you had bought in the past, or to continue to buy the things that did well for you in the past."

And you'll see how he lived another Sir Johnism: "Never follow the crowd." He loved buying in times of "maximum pessimism." He shunned headlines and thought for himself, exploring facts. He bought at the depths of our savings and loan crisis—when everyone screamed, "Sell!"—by scrutinizing bank balance sheets one by one. His picks went down a bit more after he bought in, but he accepted that timing bottoms (and tops) with precision is impossible. His thesis remained intact, so he hung on—the right decision! You can learn a lot from his tactics and mindset in this and many other situations. I met him a few times, and he was a marvelous human—farsighted, humble, brave, frugal, business-savvy and flexible.

As I blurbed on the book's back cover, this is a great book about one of the greats. Investors young and old, amateur and professional will benefit hugely from reading and soaking this in. You shouldn't make another trade until you do.

Catching Lightning in a Bottle, Winthrop H. Smith Jr., 2013

This is the biography of a company—a complete history of Merrill Lynch, capturing the firm's many innovations. Merrill was the king of investment banking and brokerage firsts in the twentieth century, driven by Charlie Merrill's goal of bringing Wall Street to Main Street. (Wesley Mitchell would approve.) The first to use investor education as a promotional tool, bettering the investment world and empowering normal people. The first to recognize the existence of an army of female investors—and court them. The first big brokerage to court small retail investors—mom and pop—and not just Big Money. The first to use computers. The first brokerage to issue an annual report. The first to offer cash accounts—complete with check writing and credit cards—so clients could sweep trading proceeds into money market funds in-house, sparing them the hassle of a bank transfer. Merrill became the first one-stop financial services shop. (Alas, it was the second to go public. Can't win 'em all!)

Merrill Lynch's history is really the history of American financial services. The subtitle, "How Merrill Lynch Revolutionized the Financial World," isn't an understatement. Merrill took Wall Street by storm back when Helen Slade was throwing dinner parties. Everything Merrill did first is standard today, and Win Smith was there through all of it. The author's father, the first Winthrop H. Smith, was Charlie Merrill's office gopher straight out of college, in 1916. By 1940 he was in charge. Win Jr. grew up hearing his dad's stories and signed on in 1974. He stayed for 28 years, most of them as an executive. No one can tell the tale better.

I recommend this book with one grain of salt: The latter parts are a bit trite in their heavy-handedness against Stan O'Neal, whom he rightly sees as tarnishing the legacy and driving the bank's decline in the run-up to 2008. That's true, relatively contemporary and covered very widely elsewhere, hence not unique. It's the book's first two-thirds that make it a phenomenal, informative read.

Beware the Autobiography

You'll notice one category is missing here: autobiographies! Namely, economic policy makers' memoirs. Fed members, Treasury Secretaries, Presidential advisors. They nearly always sign book deals as soon as they're unemployed. Some few are great writers, with truly entertaining tales to tell! (Though most use ghosts.) But they won't offer you much as an investor.

With few exceptions, these individuals won't tell you the truth, the whole truth and nothing but the truth. They tell you what they want you to believe. Writing memoirs is more about burnishing their legacy than telling you what actually happened—true whether they're reflecting on their whole career or a short window, like an economic crisis. You might learn their rationale and thought process for doing certain things, but that's about it.

Memoirs are words—actions speak louder and tell you more. You'll find much more of use—and more truth—in the actual historical records from their time in power. Like transcripts of Fed meetings.

It is a blessing and a curse that the Fed releases transcripts of every meeting and conference call five years after the fact. A blessing because we finally may learn the whole truth and see what they knew, when they knew it, and when they blew smoke at us. A curse because five years can be a long time. Time matters. If the transcripts from 2008's meetings were released between then and 2012, Janet Yellen might not be Fed head as this book comes out! The transcripts came out just weeks after the Senate confirmed her. If Senators and the public had the transcripts well before they grilled her, they likely would have asked much harder questions, weighed her actions instead of her resume and can-do. They might have asked why she made dismissive jokes about struggling dentists and country clubs when the financial system was going to hell in a handbasket. Why she didn't have a clue after it had fallen off the cliff in the fall of 2008. They might have even asked why she voted against cutting interest rates the day after Lehman died.

The 2008 Fed transcripts are over 1,000 pages long but full of goodies. They also blatantly contradict the memoirs of former Treasury Secretaries Hank Paulson and Tim Geithner. Transcripts show Paulson and Geithner told some big Lehman whoppers. Paulson claimed UK regulators wouldn't let Barclays buy Lehman the way JPMorgan Chase bought Bear Stearns. Maybe true! But transcripts show the Treasury and Fed made a conscious decision to deny potential funding to help out. Even though they had helped JPMorgan buy Bear under near-identical circumstances. Then they all slapped each other on the back for a job well done. Government folk almost always think they did a swell job. Hard to ever find otherwise. This also directly contradicts Geithner's book. He says he would have supported a Barclays bid. If that's so, why didn't he? Why didn't he speak up during the day-after glad-handing? Why didn't he verbally disagree with all the Fed members who claimed Lehman's bankruptcy was a victory?

You don't have to take my word for this! You can read it all for yourself at the Fed's website. You'll see the Fed Governors and regional presidents congratulate each other for forcing Lehman under. You'll also see Bernanke display more concern about the "marketing" language in that meeting's policy statement than the banking system. You'll see, clearly, none of them thought driving Lehman bankrupt did harm. That's telling! It tells you regulators are often clueless, screw up and cause problems bigger than the ones they're trying to solve. Powerful knowledge! But knowledge you'll near-never get from whitewashed, airbrushed memoirs.

Those Who Forget History . . .

Aren't just doomed to repeat it. Knowing history helps put today's volatility in perspective. History books bring back all the old panics and volatility we're conditioned to forget.

History also guards you from media hype. Most financial journalists in 2008 were too young to understand the crisis was a classic bank panic—endemic in the nineteenth and early twentieth centuries. Not so unusual, just long forgotten. To them, it was unprecedented and by definition apocalyptic. Most didn't know the history of panics, so they didn't know how quickly recovery happens! Their sentiment guided mass sentiment, creating prime contrarian opportunities. Blood in the streets!

The more you know the old corrections, bear markets, crashes and bank runs, the more you know there is little new under the sun. There is less unknown to frighten you. Markets have pretty much seen it all before, lived it and come out the other end higher and stronger.

There are too many wonderful financial history books to name here. There is at least one for every major economic event in history, so I apologize for whittling this list to five. Think of it as the sampler platter—there are plenty more goodies where these came from.

Extraordinary Popular Delusions and the Madness of Crowds, Charles Mackay, 1841

By 1841, the history of financial bubbles already spanned centuries. Mackay captures them here, albeit in stodgy prose—the Mississippi Scheme, South Sea Bubble, Dutch Tulipmania and many other pre-industrial precursors to the modern bubbles we all know and love to hate.

Why bother? Bubbles are near-universally misunderstood. Pundits always see them where they don't exist and miss them when they do exist. We're regularly told bull markets are bubbles, almost from their start. Rising bond, gold, silver, real estate, you name it—all were wrongly deemed bubbles in the last two decades. True bubbles are rare and usually missed.

Bubbles are events of mass psychology. When we're in one, nearly everyone gets caught up in it (hopefully not you, after reading this book!). Even the smartest people in the world! Sir Isaac Newton lost a fortune in the South Sea Bubble. He looked smart at first, getting in early and out after nearly doubling his money, but then he saw his pals make fabulous gains. He got swept up, got greedy, got jealous, and went nearly all-in near the peak. And rode it all the way down, losing £20,000—over $3 million in today's dollars. It nearly bankrupted him.[8] Legend has it he remarked: "I can calculate the movement of the stars, but not the madness of people."[9]

In real bubbles, sensible people chuck reason to the wind to explain why *this time it's different.* Supply and demand no longer matter. Profits don't matter as long as your sexy dot-com initial public offering (IPO) gets clicks. The few who do identify the bubble are mocked in all corners.

This is what Mackay's work shows us—the psychology and mind traps folks fall into as bubbles inflate. The phenomena he describes easily translate to the 1929 Crash, 1980s gold bubble and 1999–2000 tech bubble. The setting is different, but the story never changes. The media tells us it's different this time, but as I wrote when summarizing Mackay's book in *Forbes* in 1985, "Despite what the media says, nothing really important has changed in the financial markets in centuries."[10] Still true! Still routinely forgotten. And still this book is the classic bubble book.

A Monetary History of the United States, 1867–1960 or The Great Contraction, Milton Friedman and Anna Jacobson Schwartz, 1963

This is one of the greatest, most comprehensive and important economic history texts ever. If its size intimidates you, start with *The Great Contraction*, the book version of their long chapter on the Great Depression. It shows, painstakingly, how ill-advised Fed policy drove the downturn. It will suck you in fast, and you won't even mind Friedman and Schwartz's tendency to write extensively in the footnotes.

If *The Great Contraction* is required reading for anyone who wants to understand the Depression, the mother ship is vital for anyone who wants to understand America. It spans a century from the post–Civil War Greenback Era to the steady, even money supply growth of the late 1940s and 1950s. Every shock, panic, boom, bank run, recession, depression and expansion in between—all from a monetarist standpoint. But it isn't all charts and tables. Friedman and Schwartz also tell the stories of banks, bankers, policies, politicians, debt and so much more.

You'll meet colorful personalities like William Jennings Bryan, champion of the Free Silver movement and, believe it or not, the lion in L. Frank Baum's original monetary allegory disguised as children's book, *The Wizard of Oz*—all detailed in my 2006 book, *The Only Three Questions That Count.* You'll go inside the Fed during its early days and meet the men who shaped it. You'll see why the New Deal isn't all it was hyped up to be. When you're done, you'll wish Friedman and Schwartz had published a second edition before they passed on. A chapter on Nixon's price controls would have been dynamite.

Growth and Welfare in the American Past, Douglass North, 1966

This book is an intellectual cousin of *Monetary History* and about 650 pages shorter. But no less informative! Using what was then new statistical information about America's economy from Colonial times on, North re-examines popular perceptions about the past and investigates whether data back the claims. For instance: Did the British really hold us back after 1763? Was the railroad really responsible for dynamite growth in the first half of the nineteenth century? Did the Gilded Age's allegedly evil "robber barons" exploit workers with unlivable wages and unspeakable working conditions as the industrial revolution took flight? In the process, he shows how our market economy, technological savvy, competitive drive and strong education (in the classroom and on the job) collided to produce centuries of growth and better standards of living.

While the history here is great, most useful for our purposes is the historical mythbusting. Why? I'll let North speak for himself: "Many of the major issues that confront the economic historian concern the real or alleged improvement or deterioration in the income position of a segment of society. The standard of life of the worker during the industrial revolution, the discontent of the farmer in the late nineteenth century, or the antipoverty campaign in modern times are a small sample of such issues. Accurate quantitative data are necessary to measure the actual change in income status of any group, and economic analysis will provide an explanation." True today! The specifics are different, but we're still bombarded with claims about how, why and for whom the economy is growing. North's approach and thought process still apply and will remain relevant as long as capital markets exist. He wanted to find the disconnect between historical perception and reality. Just what we've explored how to do in this book!

Harriman vs. Hill: Wall Street's Great Railroad War, Larry Haeg, 2013

We met James J. Hill a few pages ago. He's back here, in this story of the Panic of 1901, an event his biography spends but one chapter on.

The Panic of 1901 was basically collateral damage in a grudge match between Hill and his archrival, Ed Harriman—railroad barons driven by jealousy and greed. Each sought to make his line a transcontinental empire—Harriman with the Union Pacific, Hill with the Great Northern and Northern Pacific—and they competed fiercely to take over regional lines. Hill won the battle for Chicago, Burlington and Quincy, snatching it right under Harriman's nose. Harriman retaliated by trying a hostile takeover of the Northern Pacific. Through Kuhn, Loeb, he sought to buy $90 million in Northern Pacific shares. Hill caught wind and bought furiously to thwart him. Within days, they'd near-cornered the stock, driven the price from $110 per share to over $1,000, lifting the other railroads and most of the market with them. Panic set in as short-sellers were squeezed left and right. Brokerage houses imploded when they couldn't cover. Stocks reeled—the New York Stock Exchange's first crash and stocks' then-biggest decline on record. They bounced fast, too.

The story doesn't end there. After jointly cornering the Northern Pacific, Hill and Harriman were stuck with each other. They formed a joint holding company, Northern Securities, effectively merging their lines (still hating each other). Teddy Roosevelt hated it, and the federal government sued under the Sherman Antitrust Act. Northern Securities lost but appealed all the way to the Supreme Court. It lost there, too, but Justice Oliver Wendell Holmes Jr. dissented, passionately defending property ownership as a moral right. His dissent curbed Roosevelt's corporate meddling and rings through US property rights and antitrust law to this day.

The above is an unpardonably brief synopsis of a tale of market mayhem, intrigue and capitalist triumph. Do yourself a favor. Read it.

The Jacksonian Economy, Peter Tremin, 1969

Pop quiz: What happened when our seventh President destroyed the central bank, pushed hard money and paid off all our national debt?

The way many pundits talk today, you'd be forgiven for thinking prosperity reigned and heaven came to Earth! But reality was near-opposite. The western land sales and fiscal havoc that followed led directly to the Panic of 1837 and a six-year depression, the longest and arguably worst ever. It's hard to find a good history that tells it like it was. Biographies of Jackson focus on the man and the legend of Old Hickory, largely ignoring the economic havoc he created. The legendary *Diary of Philip Hone 1828–1851* doesn't give broad perspective or terribly accurate economics, but it is a drilling attack on Jackson and his lunacy. North and Friedman and Schwartz pay reference to the events objectively, but briefly. And I encourage you to read Hone for his colorfully acrid vision.

But Tremin's book is probably your best bet if you want an objective, detailed accounting of that period. It plays fair, hitting both sides of the argument and largely letting the reader decide. Personally, I think the facts speak for themselves.

Classics in the Twenty-First Century

There aren't many investing books written today that will be classics in 20 years. You might get two a decade. At the risk of making a long-term forecast, here are two candidates—essential reading today.

The Rational Optimist, Matt Ridley, 2010

This is a "history" book that really isn't a history book. Ridley walks us through the rise of human civilization, showing how mankind's capitalist creativity solved problem after problem, shortage after shortage, launching countless new industries and technologies along the way. He tells stories with facts and empirical evidence, showing how scarcity-obsessed Malthusian pessimists were wrong again and again.

Like I said, though, this isn't a history book. It's a retort to our doomy gloomy myopic media. Ridley uses history to show why pundits' apocalyptic forecasts are almost surely wrong—optimism for the future is rational! Throughout human history, wherever capitalism and free markets flourished, ideas collided in marvelous ways, bursting forth with unimaginable (to most) and creative for-profit solutions to shortages, diseases and other potential nightmares—often before they even became problems! The human race when even semi-liberated is remarkable at adapting to and overcoming whatever seemingly dire circumstances befall it. Just as the shale boom twisted the knife in Peak Oil, colliding ideas will solve quandaries we can't fathom today. As Plato said so long ago, necessity is the mother of invention.

This book is an antidote to the morose media hyperbole bombarding us daily. It will keep you sane and giddy over our long-term prospects—and for stocks—after all, a share of stock is a share in magical capitalist innovation. As a bonus, you'll also see why free trade and globalization are so vital to the future. Ideas come together when people do. The more interconnected the world is, the more we exchange ideas as well as goods and services, and the more magic happens. Protectionist pundits can't fathom this. They see the world as a fixed pie, and globalization as a jobs-killing menace. Ridley shows you exactly why this is hogwash.

Senseless Panic, William M. Isaac, 2010

From the first sentence, it's clear this is the rare published history of the 2008 global financial crisis that takes a non-mainstream view: "The financial panic of 2008 and the ensuing deep recession did not have to happen, and I am appalled by the enormous financial, human, and political cost of it all."[11]

Many believe the panic was a natural consequence of a housing bubble, deregulation, overeager banks and financial excess gone wrong. That's the poppycock the media has melted into our mythology ever since. Nonsense. Isaac, who helmed the Federal Deposit Insurance Corporation (FDIC) during the early-1980s savings and loan crisis, was perhaps uniquely equipped to spot the real culprit—mark-to-market accounting. Isaac was one of the first to argue publicly for repealing the mark-to-market regulation in September 2008. If the Securities and Exchange Commission (SEC) and Financial Accounting Standards Board (FASB) hadn't taken more than half a year to listen to him, life might have gotten better much faster than it did.

Isaac builds his case against mark-to-market accounting by walking us through the 1980s bank troubles and showing how regulators' overreaction led directly to the 2008 panic. We see a raft of supposed reforms in the 1990s and 2000s, all aimed at preventing a repeat of the 1989–1992 savings and loan crisis, but instead laying the groundwork for something much worse. Isaac shows how the SEC and FASB incorrectly decided weak accounting standards drove the 1980s' problems and misapplied the "solution" of FAS 157, the mark-to-market accounting rule. He shows how "Prompt Corrective Action" provisions, which forced harsh penalties on banks whose capital falls below the minimum, gave banks huge incentives to unload shaky assets at the first sign of trouble. And he shows how these factors collided horribly into the vicious cycle of asset write-downs and fire sales that culminated in the panic of September 2008. We see, with facts and numbers, how $300 billion in likely loan losses spiraled into $1.8 trillion of largely unnecessary non-market-oriented write-downs, leeching liquidity. When it all snowballed, we see how the Treasury's interference with the Fed politicized crisis management behind closed doors, leading to the arbitrary, devastating events of September. We still don't know why the Fed and Treasury picked certain winners and losers. We just know all hell broke loose when they did.

This book is a fact-driven, searing indictment of mark-to-market accounting and crisis mismanagement. Isaac's viewpoint is rare and right, and it shows in spades how regulators needlessly create risk—just as we chronicled in Chapter 6. Understanding how this created crisis in 2008 won't just help you understand the seminal financial event of my adult lifetime. It'll also help you know what to look for next time.

We've come to the end of our book club now. Is your library list a mile long? I hope so! But make sure you've left room, as there is one literary topic we haven't hit yet: behavioral finance. One of my favorites! Ready? Flip to Chapter 9!

Notes

1. *The Warren Buffett Way*, Robert G. Hagstrom (New York: John Wiley & Sons, 1994), mass market ed., 1997, 27.
2. *Common Stocks and Uncommon Profits*, Philip A. Fisher (New York: Harper & Brothers, 1958), rev. ed., 2003.
3. *Common Stocks and Uncommon Profits*, Philip A. Fisher (New York: Harper & Brothers, 1958), rev. ed., 2003.
4. "Jesse Livermore Ends Life in Hotel," *The New York Times*, November 29, 1940.
5. *Business Barometers Used in the Accumulation of Money*, 6th ed., Roger W. Babson (Boston: Babson's Statistical Organization, 1913), 23.
6. "Jay Gould," *The New York Times*, December 3, 1892.
7. "Seventy Years Rest Lightly on Mrs. Hetty Green," *The New York Times*, November 5, 1905.
8. "Even a Genius Can Get Suckered," Thomas Levenson, CNNPolitics.com, July 29, 2009. www.cnn.com/2009/POLITICS/07/29/levenson.finance.regulation/ (accessed 11/12/2014).
9. *Observations, Anecdotes, and Characters of Books and Men*, Reverend Joseph Spence (London: Walter Scott, 1820), 71.
10. "Gifts of the Gurus," Kenneth L. Fisher, *Forbes*, June 3, 1985.
11. *Senseless Panic*, William M. Isaac with Philip C. Meyer (Hoboken, NJ: John Wiley & Sons, 2010), xv.

CHAPTER 9

When Miley Cyrus Meets Ben Graham: Misadventures in Behavioral Finance

We've spent the past eight chapters honing our brains. Can you feel your head oozing outlying thoughts yet?

If so, don't get too excited. All the smarts in the world are often no match for our biggest enemy—ourselves. The emotions and biases that drive us to make the wrong moves at the wrong times.

There is an entire field devoted to this. Behavioral finance, one of my favorite areas of market research. Behavioral finance, correctly applied, is all about finding ways our brains and feelings trick us into making the wrong moves most of the time. Its goal is to help us all control the emotional impulses and biases that bring bad investment decisions. Behavioral finance is our weapon against our inner Jesse Livermore.

At least, that's what behavioral finance is supposed to be about. In recent years, the field has shifted from "how to control yourself" to "how to beat the market." "Behavioral finance funds" claim to gain an edge by identifying and exploiting mass behavioral errors, and they charge a premium for their supposed specialization. More power to them for trying to game the crowd, but this isn't behavioral finance! Behavioral finance is supposed to be about identifying your own cognitive errors and fighting the urge to repeat them, not exploiting others' mental goofs. Assuming others are stupid is usually arrogant, sometimes simply stupid, and usually not the best basis for a bet.

Newfangled behavioral finance gimmicks might sound helpful, but gimmicks never helped anyone invest better. Self-control might not sound sexy, but real behavioral finance will do a heck of a lot more for you than behavioral fads.

In this chapter, we'll see:

- Who stole behavioral finance, and what they're doing with it
- Where behavioral finance can give you a tactical advantage ... and where it can't
- How to use behavioral finance the way it was meant to be used

Where It All Began

Researchers have studied investor psychology for decades, but behavioral finance didn't really turn mainstream until 2002, when Daniel Kahneman won the Nobel Memorial Prize in Economic Sciences for his seminal 1979 paper (co-authored with psychologist Amos Tversky), "Prospect Theory: An Analysis of Decision Under Risk."[1]

The two psychologists set out to challenge the long-held assumption people are rational in making decisions—choosing only after coolly weighing potential outcomes—known as "utility theory." To do this, they posed a series of hypothetical questions to folks from Israel, Sweden and America. The questions asked people to select from a few options balancing certainty, probability and risk.

The respondents were asked to select between various options: one a relatively high-probability event with a high payoff—a 50% chance to win $1,000—versus a sure payoff of a lower amount, $450. To put these figures in perspective, the Israeli version amounted to winning one-third of the median Israeli citizen's annual income. Big!

Then they turned this around: Instead of winning the funds, folks were asked about losing. To paraphrase, would folks prefer a 90% chance of losing $1,000, or would they opt for a surefire $900 loss?

According to utility theory, rational people would pick the sure gain of $450 and the smaller sure loss—losing only $900 is better than losing $1,000!

But Kahneman and Tversky's results showed people aren't rational when it comes to loss! The majority did select the surefire $450 in the first scenario, consistent with utility theory. But in scenario two, most selected option A, the 90% risk of full loss. The pain of losing is so powerful folks were willing to risk a highly probable total loss in exchange for the slightest possibility they wouldn't lose anything. Conversely, the joy of winning wasn't enough to take a chance of walking away empty-handed. Hence the psychology behind why it is wrong—but feels so right—when you hear the age-old saying, "Rule number one: Don't lose money. Rule number two: Don't forget rule number one." It implies riskless profit, or perfect knowledge—both impossible—but it feels so right.

Prospect theory amounts to investors feeling the pain of loss about two and a half times as much as they appreciate an equivalent gain, also known as "myopic loss aversion." The loss is more painful, so it *feels* more real.

This disconnect is at the heart of most behavioral errors. The desire to avoid further losses after a downswing leads folks to sell low—stopping the bleeding feels better than hanging on and waiting for a potential rebound regardless of a high likelihood. Prospect theory explains why folks react suddenly and irrationally to volatility by selling, even though patiently holding may be the better move long-term. We're all wired to put more effort into avoiding losses than into making gains. Others piled on, building on Kahneman and Tversky's findings to explain the psychology behind all sorts of repeatedly bad decisions, all to help investors battle their inherent self-destructive tendencies. A field was born.

The Beginnings of Behavioral Finance's Drift

For the first decade or so, behavioral finance wasn't supposed to be about beating the market—but about controlling your instincts and avoiding massive screw-ups. A different mentality soon crept in. Those who disagreed with Eugene Fama's theory that beating the market was impossible because markets were too efficient found "proof" in behavioral finance's repeated demonstration of investors' irrational behavior. If Fama claimed markets were perfectly rational, but behavioralists showed investors were inherently irrational, then markets must be beatable![2]

The research soon started evolving to investigate how behavioral errors impacted asset prices—and from there morphed into attempts to predict irrational behavior with models and incorporate those models into market forecasting. This mentality went mainstream during the last decade, as a series of best-selling books peddling behavioral finance gimmickry over self-control became wildly popular. Beat-the-market behavioralists seized on it anew. Out went controlling your emotions. In came the effort to "exploit behavior bias"—identify and predict when and how mass psychology would distort pricing, and then game the opportunity.

None of this helps you. Even where their theories are right—markets *are* irrational in the short term—the methods don't give you an edge. For starters, they suffer from the same new-look drawbacks we saw in Chapter 8—the best-seller function, or the Miley Cyrus effect. The concepts are too widely used not to be pre-priced. *Note:* You can't really find anyone who has done really well as an investor deploying behavioral finance.

When Academics Met Capitalism and Marketing

The twisting of behavioral finance isn't just an academic or literary curiosity. There are also several "behavioral finance funds" that put it into practice. You can buy them! (That isn't a recommendation!) Their individual methods differ, but in general, most try to find evidence of pricing anomalies caused by mass behavioral errors and game them.

Some look for herding—investors chasing each other into certain hot stocks or sectors, driving prices far above what fundamentals warrant or where they would be if markets were truly efficient. Some look for anchoring—investors' tendency to repeatedly base decisions on certain (usually irrelevant) data. This might include folks who assume new highs are self-reinforcing and any drop is thus a buying opportunity. Other funds try to spot widespread over- or under-reaction to certain information, like surprise changes in earnings—another iteration of anchoring (see the next page's box for more on this).

Bizarrely, many of these funds use quantitative models to spot these errors. Philosophically, it just seems funny to use algorithms to spot something fundamentally qualitative. The assumptions in these models also seem suspect, as many rely on some of the antiquated, flawed formulas we discussed in Chapter 7, like the capital asset pricing model or the assumption that price-to-earnings (P/E) ratios and other valuations should always revert to the mean. There also isn't much evidence any of this works—multiple studies have shown these funds don't offer investors any material advantage, in terms of performance or timing. One from the *Journal of Investing* found they resembled and performed more or less like value funds—but cost a lot more.[3]

Yes, behavioral finance funds charge a premium for this niche specialty. "Behavioral finance" is marketing spin now and way cool! On the one hand, you have to tip your hat. People figured out there is a market among investors for psychology-based analysis that tries to beat the crowd. Demand is high, the supply of practitioners is limited, so the market bears higher fees—people perceive value and are willing to pay. Fine! But behavioral finance was never meant to be a marketing tool—again, it's a self-control tool. These funds aren't doing real behavioral finance. They aren't doing anything to help investors control their brains or emotional impulses. Behavioral errors could very well drive folks to buy or sell these funds!

Some of these funds might be fine products and do well over time. If so, great! But the "behavioral finance" label is largely marketing.

> "Anchoring," as it pertains to earnings surprises, is a form of regret shunning widely deployed by almost anyone and almost uniformly by professional analysts. They make their living forecasting companies' earnings—"surprises" happen when the analysts are wrong. Humans hate being wrong. We're hardwired to accumulate pride and shun regret! So analysts ignore the new information—just a fluke. They convince themselves there was nothing wrong with their forecasting models, and earnings will eventually revert to the mean. They'll anchor themselves to existing models with old inputs, not accounting for the more recent changes, not looking for potential new, forward-looking drivers. It might take a year or more of consistent surprises before they'll change course. Like I said in Chapter 2: Pros are wronger stronger and longer.

Behavioral Finance and Tactical Positioning

Behavioral finance can give you an edge in portfolio positioning—which sectors, countries, styles and sizes you emphasize, and even whether or not to own stocks. But not in the way many newfangled behavioralists argue.

For instance, some claim behavioralism shows value investing is inherently superior to all other tactics—hence why those "behavioral finance" funds walk, talk and perform like value funds. They claim misbehavior (greed/fear) causes prices to diverge from the firms' actual value. Which makes these funds value funds! The behavioralism-boosts-value crowd says their managers can identify these mass cognitive errors, creating ripe contrarian opportunities. Therefore, we should all channel our inner Ben Graham, buy low-valuation stocks, shun growth stocks and wait for the magic.

History, of course, shows this theory is flawed. Value does great sometimes but not all the time—no one style is best for all time! Leadership flips and flops. Figure 9.1 shows the spread between monthly returns of the Russell 3000 growth and value indexes—broad, capitalization-weighted benchmarks. Columns on the top half represent months where growth led, bottom half where value led. See how noisy it is? They flip-flop! Since these indexes were born in January 1979, value beat growth in 50.7% of months. A coin flip!

But that's too noisy and tells you nothing. Longer-term trends matter more and are gameable! View growth and value's annual returns, and you'll see each has periods of relatively sustained leadership. Figure 9.2 shows annual returns for both since 1979. Growth led in 16 of these 36 years.

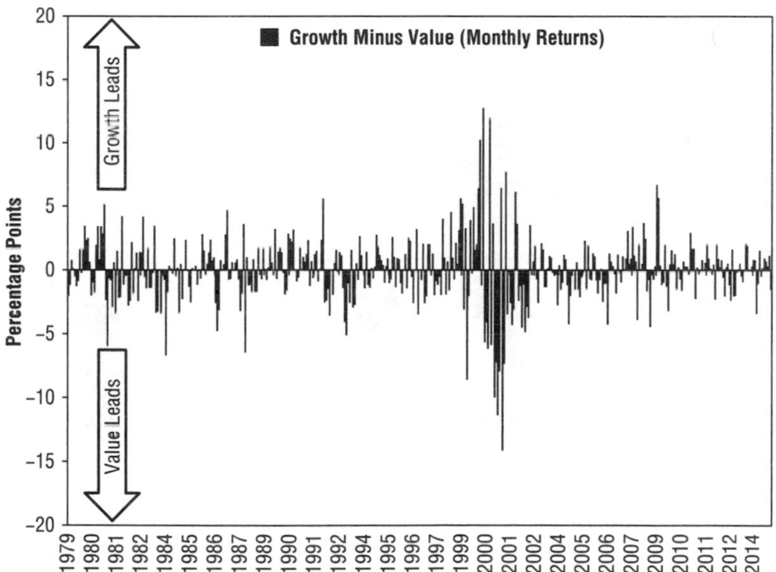

Figure 9.1 Growth Versus Value, Monthly Returns

Source: FactSet, as of 1/5/2015. Russell 3000 Growth and Russell 3000 Value Total Return Indexes, 12/31/1978–12/31/2014.

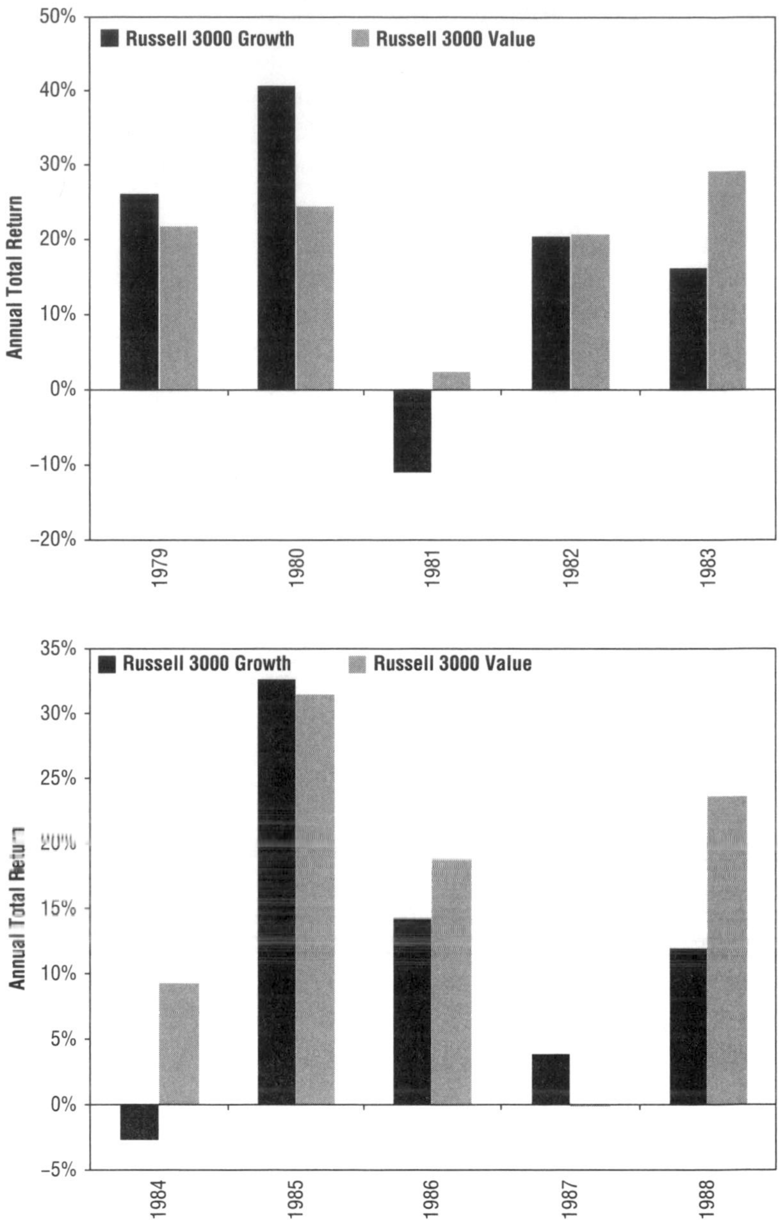

Figure 9.2 Growth Versus Value, Annual Returns

Source: FactSet, as of 1/5/2015. Russell 3000 Growth and Russell 3000 Value Total Return Indexes, 12/31/1978–12/31/2014.

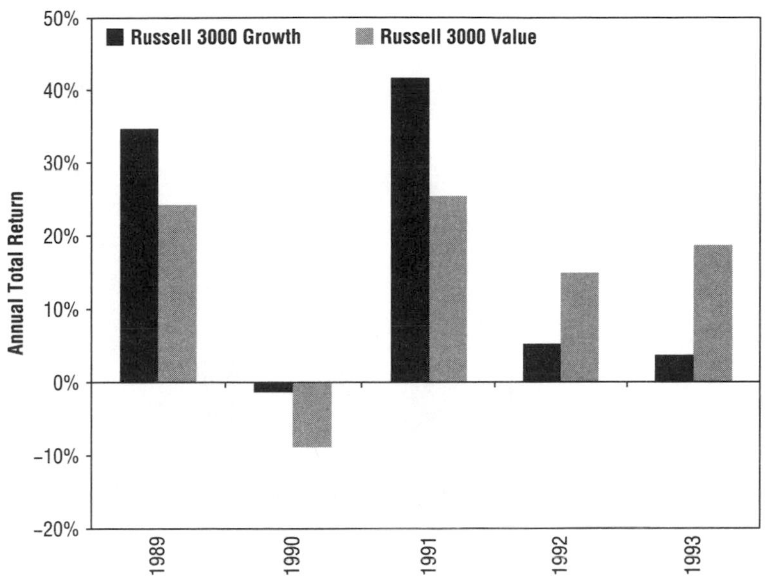

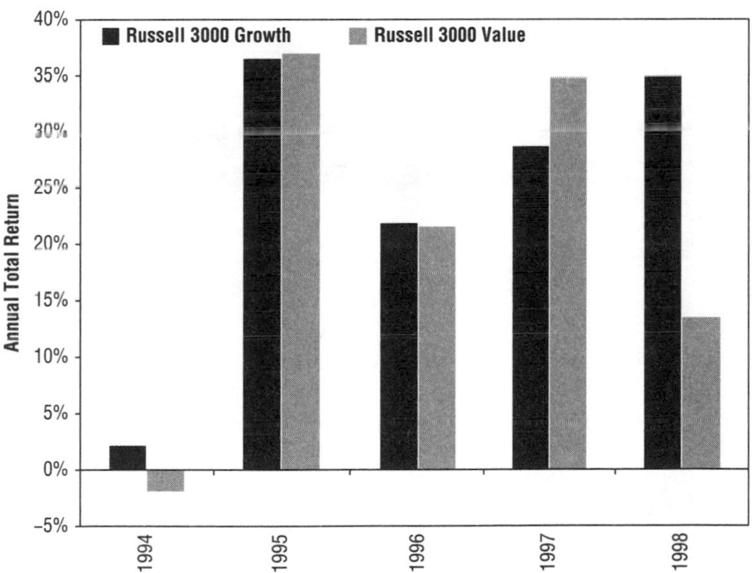

Figure 9.2 ***(Continued)***

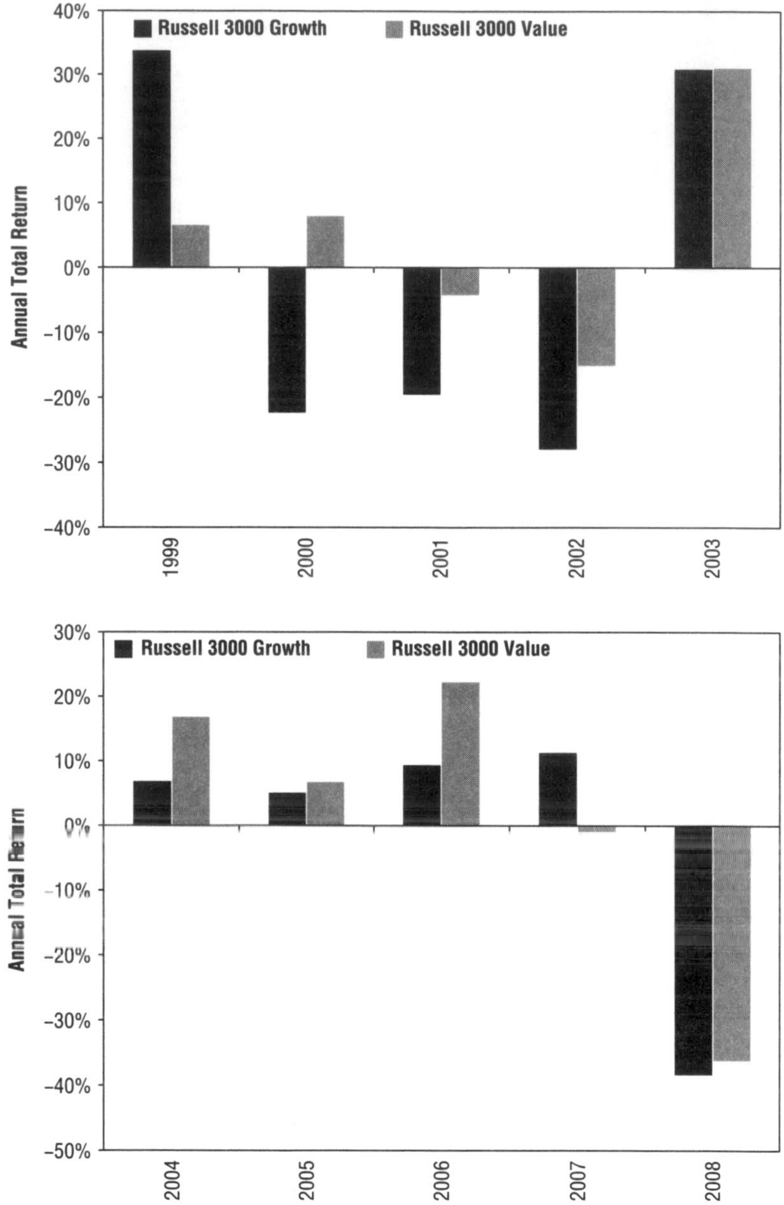

Figure 9.2 ***(Continued)***

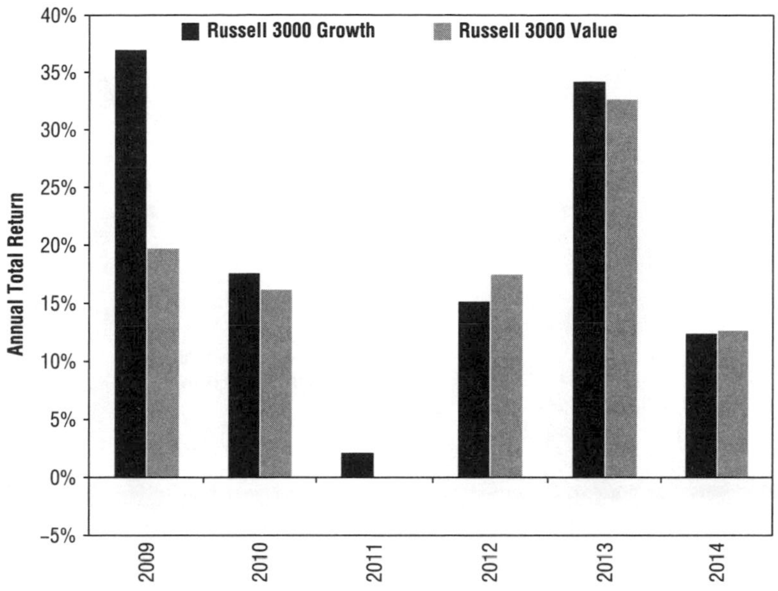

Figure 9.2 (*Continued*)

So when the heck does value take the lead? Probably when you don't want to own it! Let's view value a different way. Figure 9.3 is a series of line graphs showing value's returns relative to growth during the last four full bear-bull market cycles. When the line is rising, value is beating growth. Not necessarily rising in absolute terms! But beating.

Look when value leads. Often during a bear market, when everyone's running scared. Value usually keeps the baton for the bull's first third or half, when most folks remain gun-shy from bear-market terror. Then growth takes over and usually runs through the end of the bull market. The 2002–2007 bull market is an exception—value led until the last 14 months—but growth's abbreviated leadership has more to do with the fact that the bull market was killed early when the mark-to-market accounting rule, FAS 157, took effect (as we covered back in Chapter 1).

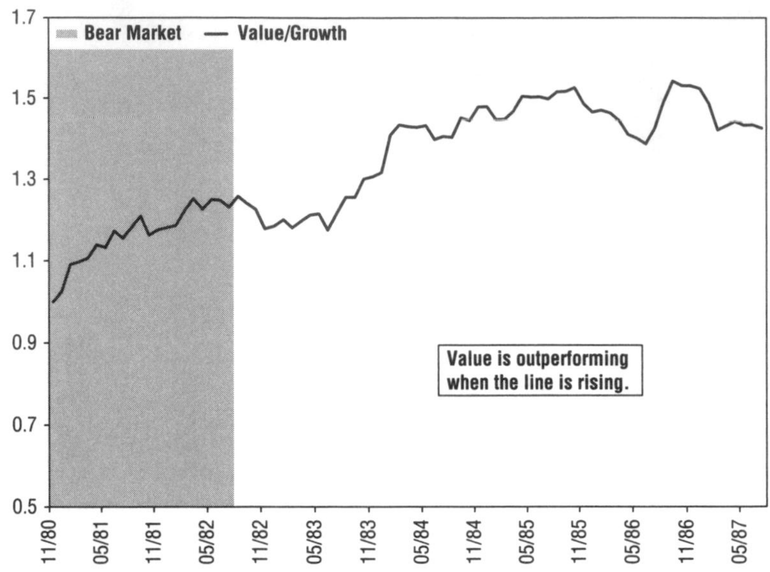

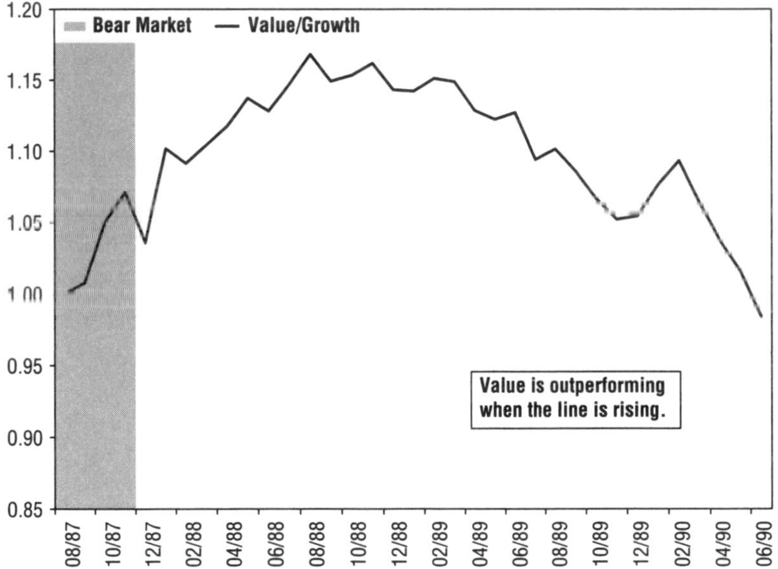

Figure 9.3 Value's Relative Returns in the Last Four Cycles

Source: FactSet, as of 12/12/2014. Russell 3000 Growth and Russell 3000 Value Total Return Indexes, 11/28/1980–10/9/2007. Due to data availability, returns through February 2000 are monthly, daily thereafter.

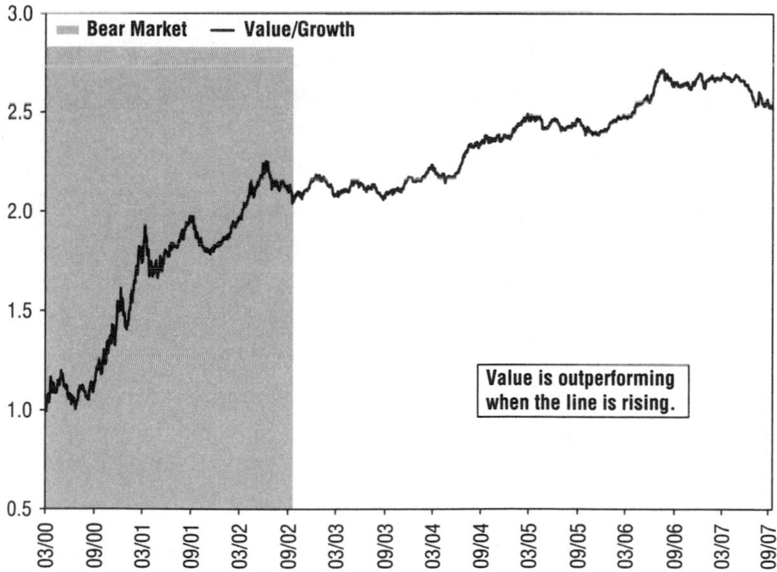

Figure 9.3 ***(Continued)***

Behavioral finance can help you identify this tipping point. It usually comes around the time value gets popular. The higher value flies, the more folks notice. Recency bias—assuming what's hot stays hot—makes them forget leadership's history of flipping. Greed breeds heat chasing. Pundits start pumping the "next big value play," convinced finding the right undervalued firms is the ticket to late bull market success. When this starts happening, that's when it's time to start turning toward growth. It's unloved, unwanted, ignored—the same traits the perma-value crowd believes propel value forever and always. Many are simply too caught up in their own biases to see better opportunities elsewhere.

You might not catch it perfectly—this isn't a precise timing tool. Those don't exist (and if they did, they'd quickly get popular and priced and would stop working). As I wrote early on, even legends are wrong about 30% of the time—wrong about leadership rotations as well as the market's broad direction. But precision isn't necessary. You can still do great over time if you're early to a style rotation. The key is staying disciplined and ignoring all the other nagging behavioral errors that will try to trick you into reversing course. Not stubborn for stubborn's sake, but self-controlled. We'll get there in a few pages.

Value stocks are a behavioral darling and do have their time. But sometimes, buying cheap stocks itself becomes popular, and buying low-valuation stocks doesn't work. That last sentence probably made Ben Graham roll over in his grave, but it's true. High-P/E stocks have their day in the sun, too.

Ironically, the one-style-is-best behavioralists commit a big behavioral error: They let bias drive decision making. A better application of behavioral finance would entail identifying bias, turning it off, and being open to unfathomable facts.

This sentiment tipping point is the thing for the contrarian to be aware of. The trick is identifying it.

Recency Bias and Sentiment

Spotting a leadership shift starts with a simple question: Is this sector/country/style too popular/unpopular?

To figure this out, ask a slightly different question: Why is it popular/unpopular? Is the reasoning rational and consistent with the facts? Or does the crowd suffer from recency bias?

Recency bias—extrapolating the recent past forward—usually leads to folly. Recency bias drove folks to believe tech stocks would zoom in 2000. Recency bias made folks fear stocks would go to zero in March 2009. Figures 9.4 and 9.5 show how this works. Many investors' brains fooled them into believing stocks would follow the dotted lines straight up in 2000 or straight down in 2009. That bias blinded them to the very likely reality, where stocks took a jagged path in the opposite direction. It kept them from thinking about whether

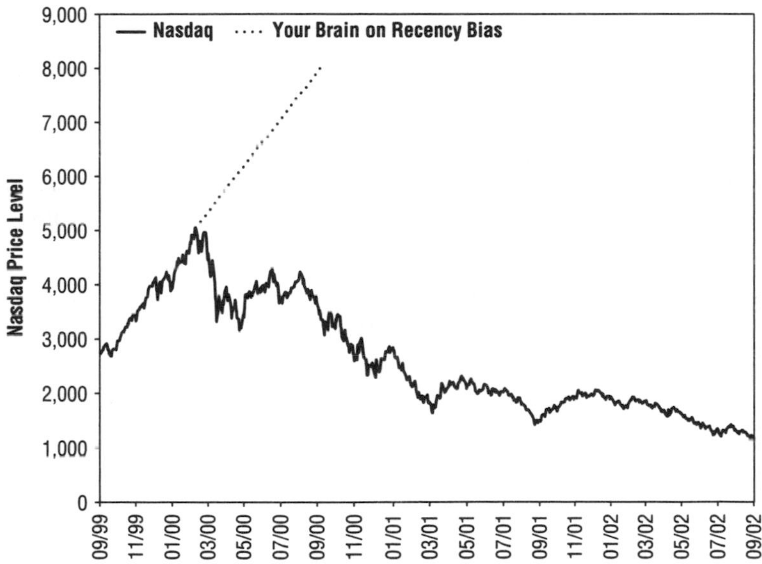

Figure 9.4 Recency Bias in 2000

Source: FactSet, as of 1/31/2014. Nasdaq Price Level, 9/30/1999–9/30/2002. The hypothetical line is an extrapolation of the average daily rise from 9/30/1999 to 3/10/2000.

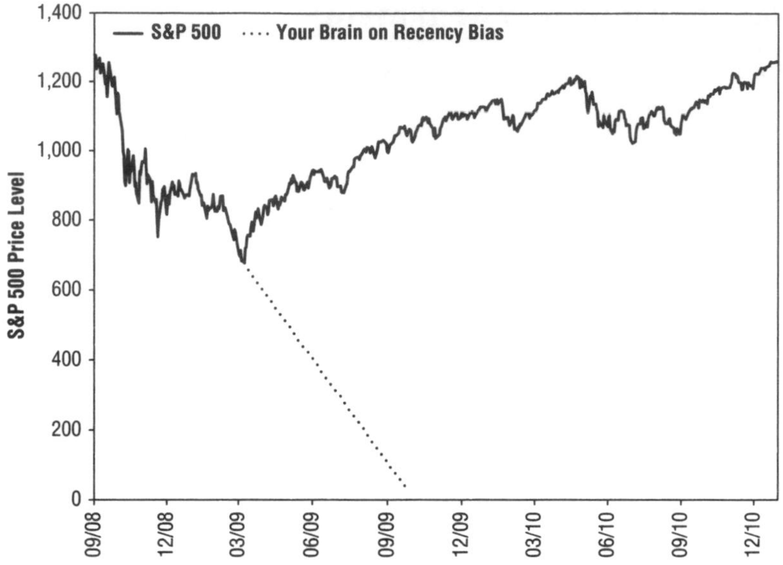

Figure 9.5 Recency Bias in 2009

Source: FactSet, as of 1/31/2014. S&P 500 Price Level, 9/30/2008–12/31/2010. The hypothetical line is an extrapolation of the average daily decline from 9/30/2008 to 3/9/2009.

sentiment was right or wrong. In 2000, that was a sign it was nearing the time to get out of the market. In March 2009, it was a sign staying in after the 2008 pounding was wisest.

Now, let's apply recency bias to style selection. Back in Chapter 7, we explored the myth that small cap is best always and forever. This myth went viral during the bull market that began in 2009, gaining traction as small beat big in 2010, 2011, 2012 and 2013. By early 2014, the media was abuzz with tips on hot, speculative small-cap stocks for the bull market's second half. We know from our historical analysis in Chapter 7 that small isn't superior—it just bounces high early in bull markets, and those few good years pull up the average. This is easy to see and calculate, but recency bias kept most folks from fathoming this.

Most simply extrapolated recent returns forward, assuming small cap (the Russell 2000) would follow the dotted line in

Figure 9.6. Small cap was hugely popular! But the recency bias epidemic suggested small cap was popular for the wrong reasons and therefore too popular. Sure enough, small cap went choppy sideways! And as Figure 9.7 shows, big led big-time. There were identifiable, fundamental reasons big outperformed. But recency bias fooled folks into thinking the trend was their friend, preventing them from considering whether big would take the reins.

True confession: My firm's research indicated small cap was too popular way back in 2012, and we rotated out of small and into the biggest stocks. The bull market seemed to be entering its second half, sentiment was becoming more optimistic, and retail investors scared out of stocks after 2008 were starting to wade back in. They're far likelier to bid up big names they know than speculate on small firms they don't

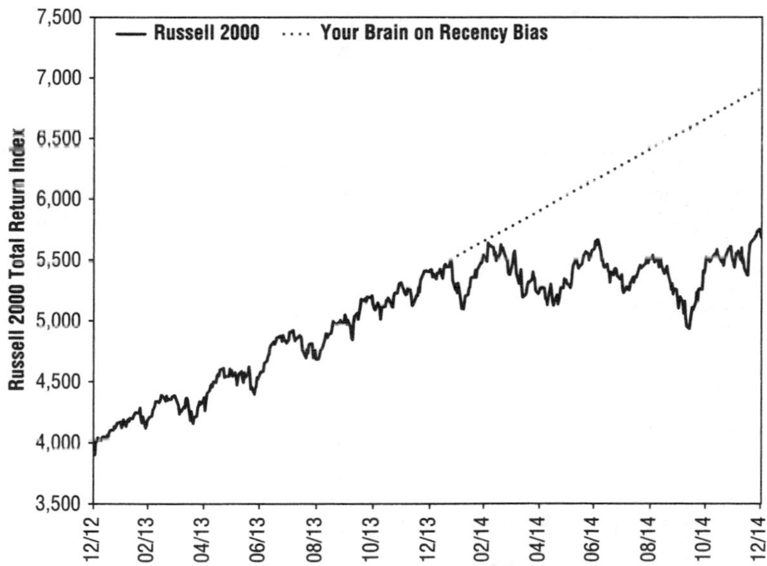

Figure 9.6 Recency Bias and Small Cap in 2014

Source: FactSet, as of 1/5/2015. Russell 2000 Total Return Index, 12/31/2012–12/31/2014. The hypothetical line is an extrapolation of the average daily rise from 12/31/2012 to 1/22/2014.

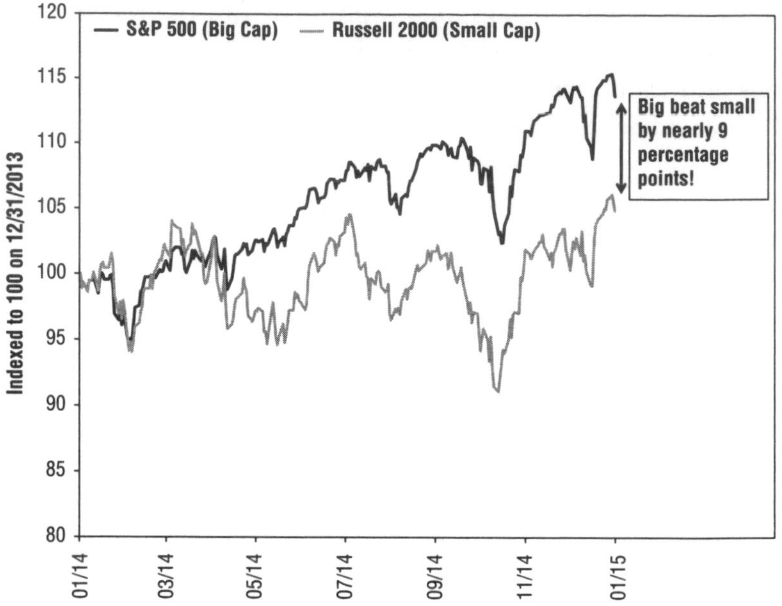

Figure 9.7 Small Cap and Big Cap in 2014
Source: FactSet, as of 1/5/2015. S&P 500 and Russell 2000 Total Return Indexes, 12/31/2013–12/31/2014.

know. In hindsight, we were about 18 months early—The Great Humiliator (TGH) makes everyone look wrong at times, sometimes for long stretches. Get used to it and over it. When that happens, the key is staying disciplined and searching for evidence your rationale was wrong. If it was, correct your course. If it wasn't, just be patient—TGH will try to tempt you to react and flip back into what's hot right then. Often the ticket to buying high and selling low.

How to Gain a Tactical Advantage With Behavioral Finance

You can use recency bias and other cognitive errors to identify opportunities and risks in different countries, sectors, styles and sizes. Or to gauge whether certain stocks are too hot or too battered. Fundamental drivers matter, too, but you don't need behavioralism to weigh those—just the economic and political analysis elsewhere in this book. The behavioral angle is more about determining whether sentiment broadly appreciates the economic and political fundamentals. Or, more simply, are folks too dour or too sunny on a given category?

Now, none of what follows is necessarily about beating the market. It's more about avoiding common, identifiable mistakes made at times by the vast majority of investors. Not being taken in by recent trends. Training your brain to see excesses and overlooked opportunities clearly.

What does a too-popular sector look like? Tech in 2000 and Energy in 1980 are well-known examples that led to big bear markets. Here's a more subtle example: Materials, and specifically Metals & Mining, after 2010.

From September 2000 through year-end 2010, the MSCI World Metals & Mining Index went on a tear, outperforming the MSCI World Index by 455 percentage points.[4] It underperformed from there, lagging the world by over 60 percentage points through mid-2013. Most investors, accustomed to the industry going gangbusters as markets rose, assumed the lag was an anomaly and Metals & Mining would soon bounce high. Popular! Too popular. History and key fundamentals argued against a lasting turnaround in relative performance any time soon.

What were overly enthused metalheads missing? The industry tends to be cyclical—big booms, big busts. Long periods of rising metals prices and industry stocks followed by extended declines. (See Figure 9.8.) This pattern has fundamental causality. Commodity cycles usually start with surging demand after relatively constrained supply growth, causing prices to surge. Producers respond to price incentives by goosing production until it inevitably overshoots demand. Metals & Mining is especially vulnerable given its capital-intensive nature, price-sensitive revenues and the multi-decade life of its assets, making production difficult to stop and start as conditions change. When

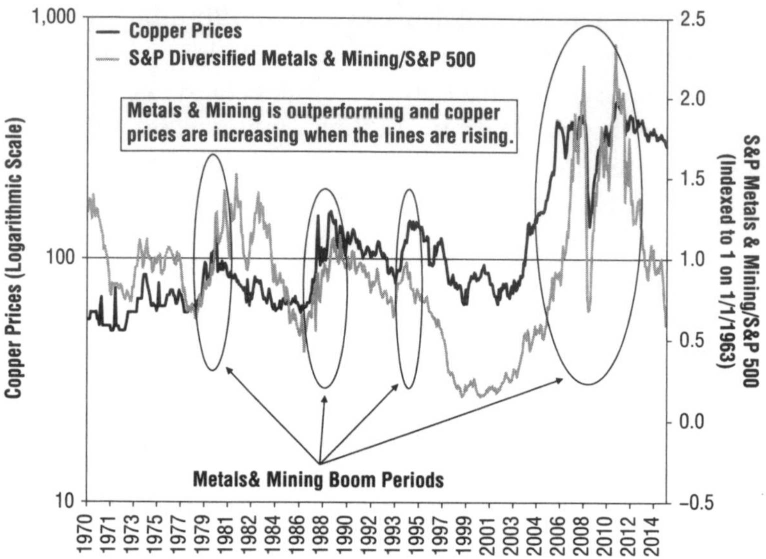

Figure 9.8 Metals & Mining Relative Performance Versus Copper Prices

Source: Global Financial Data, as of 1/7/2015. Copper electrolyte wire prices in US cents per pound, 1970-2014. S&P Diversified Metals & Mining price returns divided by the S&P 500 price returns (indexed to 1 at 1/31/1963), 1970-2014.

prices fall, revenues plummet, combining with high fixed costs to whack earnings (ultimately setting the stage for the next cycle as the industry promises never to overbuild again, constraining supply all over again).

That's what we've seen in Metals & Mining since 2010. Booming prices last decade drove surging investment in new mines, and supply grew significantly as years of major capital expenditure programs came to fruition. Prices have fallen across the board, as shown in Figure 9.9, and Metals & Mining stocks have lagged badly along with all commodity-oriented stocks (Figure 9.10). Energy tends to trade in tandem with Materials for the same fundamental boom-and-bust reasons. In this cycle, the shale boom massively boosted supply, pulling down prices, revenues and earnings.

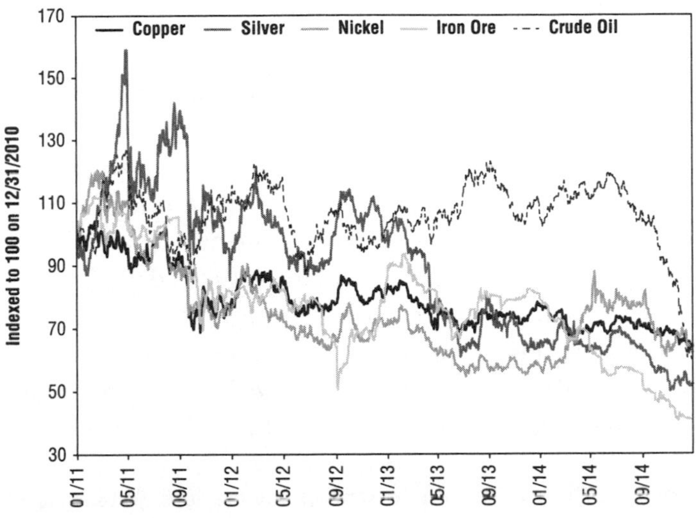

Figure 9.9 Select Commodity Prices

Source: FactSet, as of 1/5/2015. Benchmark commodity prices, 12/31/2010–12/31/2014. Indexed to 100 at 12/31/2010.

Figure 9.10 Energy and Materials Relative Performance

Source: FactSet, as of 1/5/2015. MSCI World Materials Index divided by the MSCI World Index and MSCI World Energy Index divided by the MSCI World Index (indexed to 1 at 12/31/2010) through 12/31/2014. Returns are inclusive of net dividends.

That's what too popular looks like. What does too unpopular look like? Financials in 2012.

When sectors lead bear markets down as Tech did in 2000 and Financials did in 2008, investors typically punish them long after the bear market ends—call it fighting the last war. They're overly scared of a repeat and therefore hypersensitive to every potential negative in the sector, no matter how small. This negativity can be a powerful drag on sector returns early in the next bull market. Eventually it reaches a tipping point. Too unpopular—folks ignore evidence of fundamental improvement.

So it was with Financials in 2012—particularly US Financials. Before then, skepticism was justified. Regulators globally were whacking the sector with new rules, creating a dreary overhang of uncertainty. Legal overhang weighed on returns, too, as crisis-related lawsuits and misdeeds like the Libor scandal forced firms to provision for potentially huge legal fines, eating at earnings. Rising capital requirements forced banks to crimp lending and hoard cash, weighing on loan growth. Quantitative easing (QE) flattened the yield curve spread, dampening profitability.

But by mid-2012, things were starting to improve. Most new rules were written. Dodd-Frank placeholders were slowly being clarified, with final rules eased significantly from earlier drafts. Regulators had strongly telegraphed their plans for implementing the new global capital standards known as Basel III, allowing banks to plan. All bad but not as bad as earlier feared—a bullish improvement. Economic and capital markets activity was picking up in the US and globally, creating new growth opportunities for investment banks and diversified financial services firms.

Investors still broadly hated Financials, but the sector gained steam, trouncing the broader market for the next year-plus (Figure 9.11). Sentiment eventually caught on, weighing on relative returns from July 2013 through mid-August 2014, then flipped again—making US Financials again too unpopular, teeing up another pop.

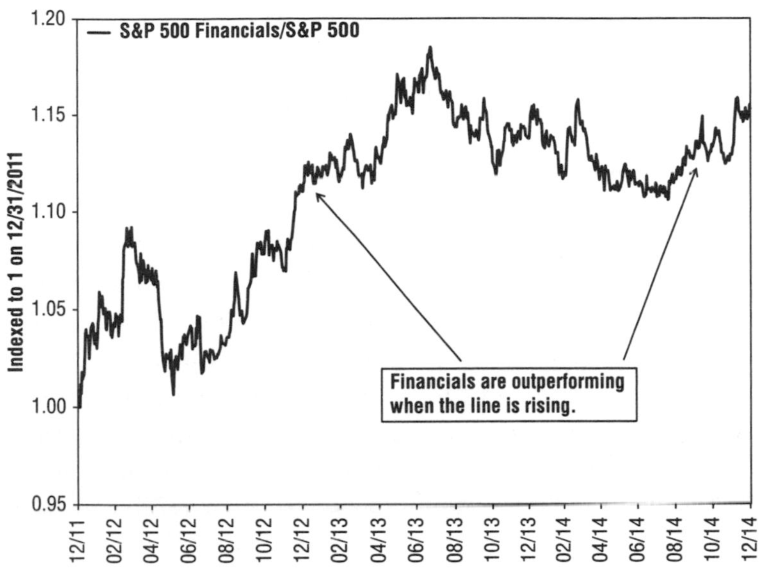

Figure 9.11 US Financials Relative Performance

Source: FactSet, as of 1/5/2015. S&P 500 Financials Total Return Index divided by the S&P 500 Total Return Index (indexed to 1 at 12/31/2011) through 12/31/2014.

In both examples, mass sentiment was too focused on the recent past—that's how you could know potential opportunities to game the crowd lurked. Folks thought Materials would do great because it had done great. Many believed Financials would disappoint because it had disappointed. When folks broadly look backward, not forward, that's your clue to shun trendy thinking and seek forward-looking, fundamental evidence the crowd is wrong.

A Section for Stock Pickers

You can use the same thought process for stock selection. Sector, country, size and style decisions are generally step one, but contrarian behavioral thinking can help you choose stocks to fill out those weightings. It isn't the only way! Company-specific factors like growth potential, balance sheet health, gross margins, global reach, management, customer and vendor relationships, pricing power and many others matter, and you can do great picking companies in your preferred sectors that score high there. This nifty trick—identifying a turnaround scenario—is just one way to pick stocks with a contrarian viewpoint.

I first shared this method way back in 1984 in my first book, *Super Stocks.* It involves finding a young, fast-growing company that, for whatever reason, Wall Street hates. Maybe it hit a rough patch, where management bungled a product cycle or just plain messed up, and investors are punishing it. It's hated universally, but if management can right the ship, it will have amazing potential. Especially if you get in before the herd figures this out.

As *Super Stocks* explained, few companies have permagangbusters earnings growth. Most will hit a speed bump at high speed, creating temporary crisis—a screw-up that whacks earnings. Totally normal! High-quality firms usually bounce back fast, but the crowd, led by the punditry, forgets this.

You can see it in how sell-side analysts react to the early success and the speed bump. When the company dazzles early on, analysts get seduced by seemingly brilliant growth, becoming euphoric about the firm's future and promising it deserves sky high valuations. As the masses bid the price to the stratosphere, pundits rationalize it, hyping the "can't-miss" technology and claiming it opens whole new horizons. But then, when something goes bad, they turn on it, punishing the stock and crucifying the company verbally. Pundits will claim the technology was really weak all along, or management hoodwinked them, or, or, or.

Neither the hype nor the gripe is right. Wall Street's own too-high expectations drove that rapid rise as analysts rationalized recency bias. Their overwrought disappointment compounded the massive fall. The excuse-making is blatant regret shunning—a cognitive error our brains use to feel better after losses (an innate emotional response to myopic loss aversion). By the time the price bottoms, expectations are way too dour. Most expect no future, no rebound, not fathoming that the firm isn't as weak as they think.

Understanding Wall Street's behavioral errors can help you not get caught up in the euphoria or the bloodbath that follows, positioning you to seize the opportunity after that roller coaster ride. It starts early on, as the herd gets carried away by a firm's initial growth, believing it will carry forward indefinitely—and forgetting how product cycles typically work. The cycle starts with the initial idea, then continues with research, engineering and development, and the initial test run—a high-cost phase. Then the marketing, cranking costs higher. But then orders trickle in, and soon sales volumes rise and turn the project from money-drainer to profit-maker. Profits shoot up, and things look great, sparking Wall Street's enthusiasm and claims of can't-miss potential. Yet this burst is always temporary. Products mature, competitors steal the thunder, and sales taper off. The product cycle is always an arc, but Wall Street assumes it's a vector. They extrapolate that initial gangbusters growth far, far into the future. Recency bias!

Some companies keep the party going, planning ahead to identify and develop new products. As one product lifecycle tapers off, others take its place, and sales keep growing. But management teams at young companies are usually pretty green. They learn on the job. They make mistakes. Perhaps they don't anticipate their product losing steam so quickly, or the pipeline is bare. Maybe they planned right but didn't execute, taking longer than anticipated to develop and release the Next Big Thing. Or perhaps their product had a bug. All can be fixed—none are signs of a bad company. They're just temporary setbacks. Normal!

But they still knock profits hard, even rendering losses as costs rise. Chances are costs were already high when the setback occurred. Firms usually ramp up marketing and production in anticipation of higher sales ahead—the proverbial "spending money to make money." These costs are tough to rein in quickly if the near-term outlook dims. Fixing the problem also takes money—troubleshooting, making customers whole if necessary, goosing marketing to rebuild reputations and improving production processes aren't cheap. Management might also have to write off assets if inventory must be scrapped or the production equipment is problematic.

If the firm turns around successfully, these losses are temporary. Once the problem is fixed, revenues grow again, profits return, and in time the dip is a blip. The naysayers who sold out on the way down, assuming permanent damage, miss out.

Most are too shortsighted to see this is normal evolution. They *should* be introspective, figure out where their brains led them astray, become more aware of their own biases, and learn from mistakes. Instead, the regret-shunning crowd stays bitter, overlooking rebound potential. This is the time to buy—exactly when no one else will want to.

On its face, the company will look terrible. Earnings will be down, perhaps even negative. The rebuilding process will probably look like chaos. Employees or managers will resign or get fired. To stanch the bleeding, management will lower overhead as much as possible. Misguided and unproductive developmental programs might get scrapped. Whole product lines could bite the dust. For a true turnaround company, all this is generally good—it means management is getting lean and mean and trying to focus on its core competency. To the outside world, however, it probably looks like they're floundering.

Once this phase passes, early signs of recovery emerge—new product announcements, a pick-up in new orders for existing products. Yet pundits will remain skeptical—we're hardwired to fight the last war. Analysts will talk down the recovery, claiming management is blowing smoke and trashing the company's long-term growth prospects by going for broke—they're still mad at the company for fooling them into hyping it on the way up. They choose to see management as inept, perhaps even deceitful, and therefore far too optimistic. You'll hear them refer to the nascent recovery as an anomaly or a "dead cat bounce." These are all signs a company is too unpopular.

Simply picking pummeled companies the financial community hates won't guarantee you pick a winner. Some companies never recover. They close or spend years clinging on through successive bankruptcies and periodic losses. Management never figures out how to right the ship and return to the glory days of phenomenal growth. That's where fundamental analysis comes in. Behavioral finance can help you find potential opportunities! But it's only half the battle. Once you have the opportunity set, it's time to weigh the company's actual potential. Do managers have a growthy mindset, seeing problems as potential opportunities to improve? Do they have a competitive advantage? Happy employees? Stringent financial controls and a willingness to cut costs when necessary? Do they understand changes in their own market and demonstrate the ability to capitalize with new products and services? The more you can answer "yes," the better the potential.

In *Super Stocks*, I told the story of two companies—Texas Instruments and Transitron—to show how some fail and some succeed after a setback.

When transistors were in their infancy, Texas Instruments and Transitron were Wall Street darlings. Both were "can't-miss." Both had sky-high valuations and cult-like followings.

Then, both suffered setbacks and got hammered hard. Both had good products. Both were key players in a soon-burgeoning market. Only one survived.

Texas Instruments identified its problems, fixed them, evolved and went on to decades of success—a true turnaround. Transitron didn't. For over two decades, it struggled with repeated losses, flirted with bankruptcy and buried itself under a massive pile of debt. Management couldn't take advantage of the nascent technology boom. Transistors and their offspring, integrated circuits, enjoyed truly phenomenal growth. But Transitron couldn't compete.

(*continued*)

Management couldn't replicate its early success in transistor and semiconductor development. At the dawn of the PC era, Transitron shuttered its semiconductor operations, concentrating instead in cables, connectors and circuit boards. Microprocessors became the lifeblood of high technology, but in 1986 Transitron died.

Behavioralism can help you spot the potential opportunities after a setback. Fundamental analysis will help you know your Texas Instruments type companies from your Transitrons.

How to Know Good Strategies From Bad

When someone tells you Strategy X works, maybe it does. Maybe it doesn't. It could be great! Or it could be the person's own biases talking, not so great. How can you know?

Ask: Are there people in the investing world who have succeeded at doing that ever? People have been successful as growth stock investors. There are absolutely legendary value stock investors, like Ben Graham. Even though certain strategies don't always work all the time, as we saw earlier, they have their time and place. John Templeton and others made great careers (and money) being global investors. Some excel as Emerging Markets investors.

The more people have proven success with a given strategy, the more feasible you can know that strategy is. It's a matter of done-it versus maybe can do. On the flip side, if few or no folks have ever been successful at a certain strategy, it's probably much harder to execute. For instance, some claim spotting peaks and short-selling is a winning tactic. Yet only one person—Jim Chanos—comes to mind as repeatedly successful at this. That doesn't make it impossible! Just extraordinarily difficult. Investing successfully is about the probable, not the possible. Over time, stocks rise far more often than not, with 72.7% of years since 1928 positive.[5] A pure short-selling strategy would be on the wrong side of the market more than two-thirds of the time. So to make shorting profitable you have to be extra-super-duper right. And that's extra-super-duper tough to do.

This principle applies to passive investing, too. Passive investing—owning a broad market index fund forever and ever—is perfectly valid! If you can do it, great! (And if that's you, what are you reading this book for?) But who has actually demonstrated success doing this? Owning one or two index funds for 10, 20 or 30 years, with no inning and outing, no hopping from domestic to foreign and back again? Even some of the field's founders and leading lights have advocated flipping countries or sectors. These are active decisions, not passive, and they lead to a slippery slope.

Passive investing isn't merely buying passive products. It requires no active decision making after that, at all. No attempts to navigate trends or cycles. Just setting and forgetting. Precious few investors have the discipline for this. Most make the same behavioral flubs as everyone else—they just happen to buy and sell passive products such as exchange-traded funds (ETFs) or index funds instead of individual stocks or actively managed funds. Trading passive funds is active, not passive.

This is a rough gauge, but you can see it in daily ETF fund flows. While these capture only one side of a trade, they can be a rough approximation for supposedly passive investors' behavior, and they often show widespread reaction to short-term swings. Figure 9.12 shows one example—equity ETF flows during the September–October 2014 pullback, with the S&P 500's daily price level overlaid. Note how the selling continued after markets began bouncing—a classic desire to stop the bleeding. Myopic loss aversion in action. We're all susceptible, whether "active" or "passive."

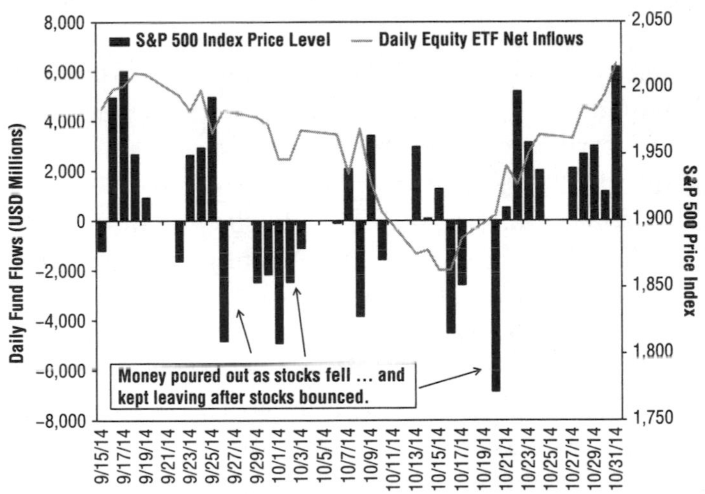

Figure 9.12 "Passive" Investing?

Source: ETF.com and FactSet, as of 12/15/2014. S&P 500 Price Index and Daily ETF net inflows, 9/15/2014–10/31/2014.

Know When to Say When

This book has spent much time on when to stay in stocks. But there is a time to be out. If—and only if—a bear market is forming and stocks look likeliest to fall more than 20% over a long stretch, getting out is wise. Unlike corrections (sharp sudden drops of –10% to –20%), bear markets have fundamental causes and last long enough to game. They're deep and long enough that you needn't time them perfectly. Nor should you try—you can't identify a bear market until after it starts. Being out of the market is the biggest risk a growth-seeking investor can take—the opportunity cost if you're wrong is crippling. Missed returns you never get back. Bear markets usually start slowly enough that if you wait a few months to be as sure as possible, you probably give up only a few percentage points.

Bear markets begin one of two ways. Either bull markets run out of steam after climbing all the way up the wall of worry, fizzling amid euphoria at the end of their natural life, or they get walloped early by a big bad thing no one sees coming. The wall or the wallop! The bear market beginning in 2000 as the dot-com bubble burst started at the euphoric wall-of-worry top. The 2007–2009 bear market started with the mark-to-market-accounting wallop.

Wallops are rare. World War II, as we saw back in Chapter 5, was a wallop, too. Not just any potential unseen risk can wallop a bull into a bear. It must be big! As I write, the world economy is about $75 trillion and counting. Assuming 2% growth a year and 2% inflation, it would take at least $2 trillion of surprising badness to render recession and truncate a bull market. Small negatives won't cut it. Then, too, if everyone sees it, it's likely priced and thus lacks bear-market power. The unseen huge negatives are the triggers.

Since we just saw the wallop, most of the fearful folks seem to be on wallop watch. But euphoria-bred bear markets are far more common. They're also somewhat easier to spot than the wallop, as the euphoria is highly visible and a strong clue the end is nigh—by definition more seeable than a largely unseen negative coming out of nowhere. Provided you know what euphoria looks like, that is, and have the discipline to avoid getting suckered by it! Behavioral finance helps here, too.

Euphoria isn't synonymous with positivity. Recall, from Chapter 8, Sir John Templeton's wall of worry depiction: "Bull markets are born on pessimism, grow on skepticism, mature on optimism and die on euphoria." Most bull markets have a long stretch where folks are just rationally cheerful, seeing good news and rightfully fathoming bright outlooks. Sensible optimism! Euphoria is different. Irrational. Optimism based on far-fetched predictions for the near future, usually based on the very recent past, with "it's different this time" proclamations. A dizzy haze preventing folks from seeing signs things are about to go south.

Euphoria was everywhere in 2000, starting with *BusinessWeek*'s January 2000 cover story, "The New Economy," which predicted Tech's stratospheric run would spread to other sectors. Professional forecasters, after being mostly pessimistic in 1996, 1997, 1998 and 1999, had capitulated—most foresaw double-digit returns. The yield curve inverted, yet few noticed and no one feared it. The Conference Board Leading Economic Index was falling, also unnoticed. Powerful signs the party was about to end and no one was prepared. Even after the S&P 500 started slowly rolling over in March, most continued piling into dot-com initial public offerings (IPOs), greedy for "the next Dell." Most thought the slow decline was a buying opportunity—stocks couldn't sink in the new economy! Classic recency bias. They assumed the recent past would carry forward indefinitely, just like Figure 9.4 a few pages ago. Too euphoric and greedy to see or even look for the negatives. (See the next box for a snapshot of those overlooked bad things.)

Seeing this right requires self-control—knowing what excess and real irrational exuberance look like so you can check yourself before you're swept away, and having the discipline to be skeptical when everyone else is clamoring to buy.

From *The Only Three Questions That Count*, 2006:

"When something is really a bubble, it's not usually called a bubble, and people don't fear it. In the years 1997, 1998 and 1999, there was no rational press coverage of Tech as a bubble. None. Tony Perkins wrote a book in late 1999 describing Internet stocks as a bubble, but it got little notice. My [March 2000] *Forbes* column calling Tech a bubble was one of the first appearances of that word in national print associated with Tech.

"And what I saw in early 2000 was eerily similar to what I had witnessed and later measured without having actually forecasted it in the Energy sector in 1980—a real bubble with the potential to start a rippling, fierce, sector-led bear market.

"Think back to 1980 and how unstoppable the Energy sector seemed. Thanks to 1970s global central bank monetary mismanagement, inflation was soaring and commodities booming. OPEC was powerful while the Iran-Iraq War was raging. Oil was $33 a barrel, and the consensus was forecasting $100 a barrel in four years. No one was calling for oil prices to fall. Just so, in early 2000, the consensus foresaw Internet users tripling globally in four years, and most folks were heralding 'The New Economy,' saying things like: Earnings don't matter. It's a new paradigm. It's clicks, not bricks! You remember.

"There were abundant Energy-to-Tech parallels—in March 2000, the 30 largest US companies represented 49% of the US stock market's value—and half of those were Tech stocks.[6] Rewind to 1980, and the 30 largest US stocks made up a third of the US market's value, and half of those were Energy. The relative valuation multiples compared to the whole market for Energy in 1980 were similar to those for Tech in 2000. Too many parallels—all unnoticed seemingly by anyone—so I could fathom an outcome not dissimilar to 1980's."

Getting Back to Self-Control

The original application of behavioral finance has become a fundamentally contrarian viewpoint and overlooked elephant in the room: using behavioral finance to discover and control the emotional impulses and biases that render bad investment decisions. Your biggest enemy is yourself, and behavioral finance is your defense.

We spent eight chapters learning how to game the crowd, but it won't do you any good if you can't control yourself. Seeing what you envision as errors in others is easy! Seeing errors in yourself is harder. If you can't see where your own impulses and beliefs go wrong, you have a blind spot that can prevent you from seeing the crowd right, too.

Recency bias is just one behavioral trap to know and avoid. There are many others! I chronicled several back in *The Only Three Questions That Count.* Question Three, "What the heck is my brain doing to blindside me now?" was all about diagnosing your own behavioral errors and learning how to beat them. Don't worry, though—I won't make you leave the comfort of your couch to learn. Or your train, subway car, bed, airplane or wherever. I'll give you a quick primer on some of the biggies right here!

Let's start with *confirmation bias*—the instinct to gravitate to information and viewpoints that reinforce our preconceived notions and shut out everything that contradicts them.

Confirmation bias is human nature, and it's everywhere. Remember our discussion of global warming way back in Chapter 4? Folks on both sides of the debate exhibit confirmation bias regularly, clinging to research supporting their views and shunning papers that don't. Economists fall prey all the time—confirmation bias featured for decades in the supply side versus demand side debate, which we touched on in Chapter 5. This is a deep-seated instinct, part of our broader tendency to accumulate pride. It's human nature to like being right! Confirmation bias just feels good.

Fatty food, many drugs and alcohol also make us feel good—but they're bad for us! Confirmation bias is, too. It props up market myths and reinforces bad decision making. Remember back in Chapter 1, when I said we'll all be wrong at times, but acknowledging and learning from wrongness can make us better? Confirmation bias prevents you from doing this. If you latch onto information that supports your views and ignore everything else, you'll never know when you're wrong! You'll rob yourself of the chance to learn and course-correct. You'll make the same mistakes repeatedly.

Confirmation bias is why seasonal myths like "Sell in May" and "So goes January" persist. Folks latch onto the numbers that back them up and ignore the counterpoints—which happen to outweigh the supporting data. Confirmation bias also gave us "Don't fight the Fed," the adage saying rate cuts are good for stocks and rate hikes are bad. Easily debunked when you consider central banks usually cut rates during bear markets and hike during bulls! But mythmakers ignore that and twist data to support their claims—lying with statistics! Always bad.

How do you fight confirmation bias? Try monitoring your emotional response to articles. If certain information makes you feel good, ask yourself why: Is it because it supports your views? Do you have the urge to pat yourself on the back? If you find yourself wanting to dismiss certain information, ask why, too. Is it because it goes against your theories and forecasts? Does it make you feel like you might be wrong? If so, don't run away. Embrace it, keep an open mind, and think rationally.

Next up? *Overconfidence*. You've heard the old proverb, "Pride goes before a fall." Same with overconfidence, which is quite simply our tendency to believe we are far better investors than we really are. Overconfidence results from chronic pride accumulation—believing every right decision is proof of our superior skill, and ignoring the possibility that maybe we just got lucky!

The trouble with overconfidence? It makes us forget we can be wrong or reduces our sense of the likelihood of wrongness. Forget that, and you lose a key fail-safe. You forget to manage risk. This can lead to downright terrible decisions, like going hog-wild for hotshot IPOs, speculating on penny stocks or playing super-volatile, narrow categories for the chance of sky-high returns. Overconfident investors forget the stock market isn't a get-rich scheme.

Overconfidence also messes with our ability to sell. Part of being wrong at least 30% of the time—which, again, would put you with legends—means getting some stock picks wrong. Everyone picks stinkers, and I've certainly had my fair share (to see me eat humble pie, pop over to the next box). If you know you can be wrong, you look critically at the picks that don't work out, find where you went wrong, and—if it makes sense—get out of the dog and into a better opportunity. If you're overconfident, though, this is next to impossible. Selling would mean admitting the decision to buy was wrong. Overconfident investors aren't open to that possibility! They get sucked into believing the stock is just in a rough patch, misbehaving for a bit. They hang on for ages, waiting for it to cooperate and prove they were correct all along (and a genius for waiting). Sometimes, the stock plays along, reinforcing that overconfidence. It happens! But often it doesn't.

If it's just one or two stocks and you're diversified, maybe it isn't a big deal. But if you're overconfident about entire sectors, countries or the market itself, the opportunity cost adds up.

Thankfully, this too is fightable. Just ask yourself: "What if I'm wrong?" Write it on a Post-it, and stick it on your computer screen. Set a recurring calendar alert in your smartphone. If certain stocks or the market don't move like you expect them to, don't dismiss it. Go into research mode, try to figure out rational reasons for that movement (or lack thereof), and then weigh whether you need to make a change. Maybe you will rationally conclude that you're right and whatever is making you look wrong is a temporary, sentiment-driven anomaly! But you might not. Being open to that possibility will put you far ahead of most. And when you're wrong, I promise you're in good company.

It is both a blessing and a curse that my *Forbes* columns provide a public written record of all my market calls and many scores of stock picks. Blessing because it gives a transparent track record to check—I don't believe in hypotheticals and unsupported claims, and neither should you. But if I let pride do the talking, it's a curse, because when I'm wrong, it's like letting the entire world see my bad report card. We actually do report cards annually in *Forbes*, usually in the January or February column. What we got right, what we got wrong, and the occasional whoopsadaisy mea culpa. Here is one such snippet, from my February 27, 2012, column, "Hit the Refresh Button." I share it with you so we can all get in the spirit of admitting wrongness! It's good for the mind and soul.

"In 2011 my 63 investment recommendations lagged the S&P 500 for the fourth time in the 16 years *Forbes* has done a formal accounting of columnists' picks. Equal amounts invested in each of my 2011 stocks would have caused you a 6% loss. That same money put into the S&P 500 would have broken even. Many of my recommendations were of foreign stocks, and they had a lousy year. My worst pick was Aixtron, a German semiconductor company I recommended in July. That stock nose-dived 63%. My best stock was Bristol-Myers Squibb, up 44% since late February 2011. I recommend you hold on to all of my 2011 picks for 2012."

Regret shunning—blaming everything under the sun but ourselves when we're wrong—enables overconfidence. Like confirmation bias, it is an innate, wholly human instinct. Regret shunning is how we deal with the magnified pain of losses—they hurt a whole lot less if we can rationalize the pain away. Adding wrongness to loss adds insult to injury. We never want to feel that bad! So we look for scapegoats to make us feel a bit better. This is how we're able to keep coming back for more after we're wrong.

What does regret shunning look like in practice? Pretend you buy a stock and it promptly plummets. If you find yourself thinking any of the following, you're regret shunning:

"That tipster on CNBC was clueless." "The CEO must have been cooking the books before I bought it." "I'm never listening to my wife's/husband's/neighbor's/co-worker's/barista's stock tips again." You get the drift. All shift responsibility onto a third party, easing you from the partial or full burden of regretting a bad decision.

It's similar when the whole market moves against you. Pretend it's October 2002, the bottom of the dot-com bubble implosion, and you stayed in stocks the whole time. Regret shunning would have looked like this: "Those loons on CNBC said it was a new economy that could never go down. They led us all astray!" "Those sell-side analysts pumping crappy dot-com stocks should go to jail for recommending companies they didn't believe in." "How dare those tech company CEOs tell us clicks are the new profits. They should have been honest about their untenable business plans! Liars!" Or maybe: "Those evil accounting firms should have known Enron and Tyco were cooking the books. How can anyone invest if Arthur Andersen is letting Ken Lay defraud the world?" And when in doubt, there is the timeless, one-size-fits-all approach to regret shunning: "The evil bankers did it." (This is responsible for just about every piece of post-crisis financial regulation ever.)

As I said in *The Only Three Questions That Count,* the real ticket to long-term success is embracing regret and wrongness. Don't shun it—hold on to it! Learn! Figure out where you went wrong, and think how to do it better next time! We did this at my firm after 2008. We realized we went wrong in underestimating how secondary regulatory changes like the mark-to-market accounting rule can make small problems snowball. So our Research department beefed up regulatory and legislative monitoring, scanning every rule globally for potential unintended consequences. These poor guys read every page of Dodd-Frank, similar European Union regulations, global bank capital standards, you name it. All in the name of learning, applying, improving.

So, if something goes wrong, and you find yourself shifting blame to someone else, ask yourself: "Is that fair? Or do I need to be like Michael Jackson and start with the man in the mirror?"

There are many more errors I could include here, but I'll leave you with just one more: *order preference*. In the movie *Airplane II*, there is a scene where William Shatner is trying to keep a lunar space station from descending into sheer chaos as a runaway shuttle approaches at breakneck speed (don't ask—just watch it). One officer approaches him with a disturbing development: "Sir, these lights keep blinking out of sequence, sir. What should we do about it, sir?" Shatner commands: "Get them to blink in sequence." Order preference is our innate need for the lights to blink in sequence.

In investing, that means we want every stock we own to be up. When we fire up our account online, we want an entire column of green arrows and unrealized gains—no red, no losses. This leads us to ignore the whole, over-focus on the parts, and do some dumb things to keep our stocks pristine and green. Like selling something just because it's down, continually chasing your tail in a fruitless attempt to pick only winners. Shunning diversification and over-concentrating in what's hot. These and other similar pitfalls increase risk and, very often, detract from returns.

To fight it, keep perspective: Even when the entire market is up, some stocks will do horribly. But a few stinkers don't bring down the average—as true in a diversified portfolio as it is in the S&P 500. To use a hackneyed truism, the whole is greater than the sum of the parts. If your whole portfolio isn't performing as you expect, take a good hard look! But if the whole is doing fine, it doesn't matter if a few stocks and companies are in the red—you probably have some astronomical winners that cancel them out. Don't overthink either extreme—no pride accumulation! Just focus on the totality.

Want more? There is a lot of good behavioral finance literature out there. Daniel Kahneman—the godfather of behavioral finance—channeled decades of research into his masterwork, *Thinking Fast and Slow* (Farrar, Straus & Giroux, 2011). It's long but not academic, a must-read if you want to understand investor psychology. If you want a short, fun read, then go with Bennett Goodspeed's *The Tao Jones Averages*—a classic from 1984 (Penguin). Kathryn Schulz's *Being Wrong* (Ecco/HarperCollins, 2010) isn't explicitly about behavioral finance, but you'll learn all about how and why your brain tricks you—and how to learn from wrongness. A timeless lesson!

But don't run out to the bookstore just yet—we aren't quite done here! We have one more subject to run through. What is it? Flip to the last chapter to find out!

Notes

1. "Prospect Theory: An Analysis of Decision Under Risk," Daniel Kahneman and Amos Tversky, *Econometrica*, Vol. 47, No. 2 (March 1979): 263–292.
2. "Is Behavioral Finance a Growth Industry?" *Knowledge@Wharton*, Wharton/University of Pennsylvania, October 10, 2001. http://knowledge.wharton.upenn.edu/article/is-behavioral-finance-a-growth-industry/ (accessed 11/18/2014).
3. "Behavioral Finance: Are the Disciples Profiting From the Doctrine?" Colby Wright, Prithviraj Banerjee and Vaneesha Boney, *Journal of Investing*, Vol. 17, No. 4 (Winter 2008): 82–90.
4. FactSet, as of 12/15/2014. MSCI World Metals & Mining minus MSCI World, returns with net dividends, 9/30/2000–12/31/2010.
5. FactSet, as of 11/15/2014. S&P 500 Total Return Index, 1/1/1928–12/31/2013.
6. Standard & Poor's Research Insight, top 30 stocks by market capitalization of the S&P 500 Index.

CHAPTER 10

The Negative Myopic Media

Investing is full of challenges. Overcoming emotion. Battling your urges to chase heat and flee in fear. And a biggie—defending your brain and soul from the overwhelming 24/7 noise machine that is modern media.

Humans aren't wired for this. We're patterned after our stone-age ancestors. Our brains never evolved to filter scores of competing opinions from faraway people we don't know—our distant ancestors never had to! They knew everyone, knew who to trust—broadly true of society up to your grandparents' or great-grandparents' time. Today, few have roots in the community they call home. Some do! You might! But most migrated from somewhere for school, a job, a spouse or pure wanderlust. Most migrated more than once. America's internal migrations keep accelerating as the Boomers retire, and the Millennials are the most mobile generation ever. But all that is recent by evolutional standards. From the dawn of civilization through most of the nineteenth century, life was simpler and smaller. People were born, lived and died in one community. Migration was rare and is relatively new. Each person's reputation was set in stone and known to all.

The same was broadly true of the media for most of the twentieth century. In my father's prime, when I was a boy and young adult, there were three TV networks, one national newspaper and your local paper. Most big cities had a morning and afternoon paper that may have been read in suburbs along with a local town paper. The financial world had four trusted magazines: *Forbes*, *Fortune*, *BusinessWeek* and *Barron's*. The barrier to getting a story printed was higher. Just a few key editors and gatekeepers.

This started changing in the 1980s, when cable TV went mainstream and Ted Turner gave the world 24-hour news. News morphed to entertainment as channels competed for viewers, eventually giving way to today's sexpot anchors spouting sensational stories. Out went objectivity and trusted, gray-suited newsmen like Edward R. Murrow and Walter Cronkite; in came opinions, bias and flash. Then came the Internet, which upended journalism and roiled print media. As websites stole readers and advertisers at vastly lower ad rates, traditional print outlets laid off veteran reporters and editors, which impacts the accuracy and perspective of reporting. The salty old dogs who lived history are gone, replaced by cheaper, younger writers. The old knowledge base evaporated. Even if you're reading a major financial publication, the article was likely written by a cub reporter. You can see it in how they frame events—everything is huge and unprecedented to them, because they haven't lived through history. Many spout antiquated school-taught economic theories as fact, not knowing reality debunked them long ago.

To top it off, we have the blogosphere—where experience isn't required and editorial standards don't exist. Any 12-year old can start a blog and flood the Internet with their uninformed opinions. Some catch on. Writers hide behind aliases, freeing themselves from the burden of personal accountability. Few bother fact-checking, vetting sources or verifying claims. It's a new world in this regard. A new frontier, not always safe.

Through it all, however, one thing hasn't changed: This new media still understands the age-old truth, bad news sells best. William Randolph Hearst and Joseph Pulitzer capitalized on this in the 1890s, one-upping each other with sensational bad-news hyperbole. Readers ate it up, and yellow journalism was born. Doom and gloom were here to stay—the more sensational, the better. In a 1989 *New York* magazine article entitled "Grins, Gore, and Videotape—The Trouble With Local TV News," journalist Eric Pooley observed: "The thoughtful report is buried because sensational stories must launch the broadcast. If it bleeds, it leads."[1] A slogan was born to fit the emerging era!

Front-page financial news might not be physically gory, but it's often a figurative bloodbath. Falling stocks and dismal data get top billing. Blame myopic loss aversion. Journalists and publishers know intuitively that we feel loss harder than we enjoy gains because the loss has shock value; therefore we fear loss more than we feel excitement about the future. No one would watch a newscast or read a paper covering all that's good and right with the world—we want to know the bad, the risks, and prepare. Pollyanna doesn't sell papers—fear does! Media outlets aren't charities trying to inform us objectively out of the goodness of their hearts. Theirs is a for-profit business. They profit by playing into and reinforcing our instinctual, primitive, evolution-based fears.

In this brief concluding chapter, we'll cover some key points to help you battle the media's constant sensory assault:

- How to use the media's negativity to your advantage
- What our ever more sensationalist media might mean for markets long-term
- Why the future is far brighter than the doom-obsessed pundits suggest

How to Use the News

Because media is strongly motivated to sell fear, don't expect headlines to perfectly reflect reality. Ever. Even when they do capitulate and sell positive, it will tend to be at the tail end of a bull market, when they get swept up in the euphoric zeitgeist—they're still playing to the crowd. They just sense reflexively that the crowd wants something different.

But the media does us all a huge service. They help show us where sentiment is! As we saw way back in Chapter 1, modern media's groupthink hyperbole reflects and influences the masses, making it a great way to spot widely held beliefs, false fears and changes in sentiment. If the media talks something to death, good or bad, markets probably priced it. You can game that.

To see this in action, let's look one more time at quantitative easing (QE) and the media's persistent warnings that Federal Reserve bond buying was the only thing propping up stocks. Throughout 2012, 2013 and even 2014, doomsayers claimed QE flooded us with money-creating low long-term rates, and when the music stopped, this hot money would pour out and stocks would crash. Meanwhile, inflation would soar from all that money. The fear was everywhere—a strong indication it was priced!

Moreover, the media ignored a pile of contrary evidence, like the fact monthly equity mutual fund net inflows were negative most of QE's first four years—a rough sign money wasn't flooding in. QE didn't flood liquidity—most of the "new money" was on deposit at the Fed as excess reserves. It technically and literally always takes net loan growth in the banking system to create new money, but loan growth was the slowest in six cycles—banks weren't using QE reserves as collateral to create new money. All broad measures of the quantity of money (like M2 or M4, the latter calculated by the Center for Financial Stability) had grown slower than in any modern economic expansion, raising the question "What money?" All publicly available information—elephant in the room! But ignored, and therefore underappreciated by markets and gameable. Media was showing sentiment leaning one way and not the other.

Gaming the media's false fear instead of following it was a winning move in 2013 and 2014. After then-Fed head Ben Bernanke first alluded to winding down QE on May 22, 2013, long-term interest rates jumped—markets started pricing in the program's eventual end. Rates rose over the rest of the year, and stocks didn't implode. Instead they rallied. Silly stocks. Bernanke finally announced the first reduction in monthly bond buying in December, and stocks again didn't crash—the S&P 500 finished 2013 up 32.4%![2] The Fed shaved $10 billion off QE at each of its biquarterly meetings in 2014, bringing it to a close in October. Stocks rose. They never even had a "normal" 10% correction! (Interest rates, on the other hand, fell, fooling most of us. Bond markets have strong TGH tendencies, too.) As I write this, the doomsayers are still at it, now saying the day of reckoning will come when the Fed starts shrinking its balance sheet; markets aren't fooled—they already know there's nothing there.

We've seen this time and again—in this book and in history. The more the media stews over potential worst-case scenarios, the more those are priced in. We saw it with QE. The Affordable Care Act, back in Chapter 6. The eurozone's widely feared (but never seen) collapse and China's mythical hard landing in Chapter 3. In all cases, the media helped keep sentiment down, giving reality an easy hurdle to clear. Stocks loved it.

Some posit gloomy media creates a negative sentiment spiral, pulling stocks down—a self-fulfilling prophecy. But what this really does is lower expectations and extend the proverbial wall of worry bull markets love to climb. The longer expectations stay low, the easier they are to beat, and the more positive surprises markets get.

I can't be sure, but I suspect the media's increased groupthink and heightened sensationalism are behind the longer market cycles of the past few decades. The 1990s bull market was history's longest. So was the ensuing bear market. The 2000s bull was probably about halfway through its natural lifecycle, as measured by sentiment, when FAS 157 killed it on its fifth birthday. That bear market was long too, fully 17 months. As I write, the current bull market is nearly six and also just past its sentiment halfway point. If we don't get walloped by a big unexpected, hence unpriced, negative, this may be a 10-year bull market, too. Maybe longer. TGH loves what few can conceive.

Cycles have elongated as the media has grown and herded. Because no one wants to stand out, they take longer to move past the deep pessimism of early bull markets, finding consensus as sentiment gradually changes over many years. This might very well extend Sir John Templeton's sentiment progression—pessimism to skepticism to optimism to euphoria, lengthening market cycles for good and ill. I think it does but can't prove it. Too few cycles for statistical validation.

Why Good Information Is Hard to Find

Our human infatuation with negative news isn't the only reason media is so dour. Google is infatuated with it, too!

Negative stories tend to rank highest in Google searches. Don't believe me? I just did a Google News search for "Apple." You can replicate it yourself, narrowing the search date range to 12/2/2014. Here are the leading headlines:

"Apple in the Dock: $1 Billion Antitrust Claim Casts Steve Jobs as Conspirator" (Karen Gullo, *Bloomberg*, 12/2/2014)

"Steve Jobs Emails Featured in Apple iPod US Antitrust Trial" (Dan Levine, *Reuters*, 12/2/2014)

"Star Witness in Apple Lawsuit Is Still Steve Jobs" (Brian X. Chen, *The New York Times*, 11/30/2014)

"Apple Misled iPod Owners, Plaintiffs Allege at Class Action Trial" (Nick Statt, *CNET*, 12/2/2014)

"GT Advanced Creditors Want to Question Apple Executive" (Joseph Checkler, *The Wall Street Journal*, 12/2/2014)

"The Stupidly Simple Reason That Apple Stock Is Overrated" (Susie Poppick, *Time*, 12/2/2014)

"6 Reasons Apple Could Have Fallen 6% Yesterday" (Peter Cohan, *Forbes*, 12/2/2014)

"Another Apple Analyst Suggests Selling Shares" (Jennifer Booton, *MarketWatch*, 12/2/2014)

Of the 18 articles on the first results page, just two paint Apple in an overtly positive light.

The results would be fairly similar for almost any search: floods of negative stories about companies, countries, people, economies, markets, you name it—unless it is a subject few care about, like the lifecycle of a rare Asian frog. But in the realm subject to mass interest, objective, factual, deeper, positive analysis rarely ranks. Whatever you consider to be important intellectual contributions probably don't rank. Search engine algorithms are as myopic as the humans who program them.

This gives media another big incentive to go negative. Not ranking on Google is the kiss of death! If you don't make page one, folks won't find you! For media and journalists, optimizing Google results means printing reams of bad news, slam pieces and dreary outlooks via sensationalism and hot "keywords."

The page-one negativity can help you discern sentiment and what's priced, as we just covered. But it can't help you spot the elephants—the ignored information that helps steer you in the right direction. That's always buried. You'll likely have to click through to the fourth or fifth page of results or beyond—or find it elsewhere in the real world. That's where the useful nuggets lurk. A pain! But again, a favor—Google's quirks keep negativity front and center, prepricing fears and giving contrarians opportunities to game the herd.

What the Media Always Misses

We chronicled several ways to rebut media gloom in Chapters 3 and 4, but I saved one for the end: the media's endless warnings that technology has reached its limits, dooming us to run out of resources in a generation or two.

The godfather of these fears was a gent named Al Gore—oops, my bad, I meant Thomas Malthus, an eighteenth-century philosopher who famously believed population growth would surpass food production, leaving humanity unable to cope and survive unless we allowed death rates to increase while reducing birth rates. Scary stuff! I won't bore you with the ins and outs of his theory. Suffice it to say, we have a few billion more people today, most of whom get enough food because we create a lot more of it now. A hugely higher percentage of the world is well-fed now than when I was young, a point few notice. Real starvation now is largely restricted to a few big geographies. Like most of Africa, where politics seems endlessly problematic and capable of holding back the future. But in most of the places where humans starved when I was young, they don't now, with vastly more humans. Ironically for a man who once claimed to be a disciple of Adam Smith, Malthus overlooked a few key things, like technology, capitalism and human creativity. Again, where starvation tragically exists, it's a function of corruption and trade barriers preventing markets from working, not actual shortages. North Korea's and other famines are man-made.

Malthus was wrong and died nearly two centuries ago, but his philosophy is alive and well and everywhere, and the media loves to hype it. What can get more eyeballs than stark warnings that Resource X is running out? Humans can't get enough of the stuff! We made the 1973 film *Soylent Green* a blockbuster and Rachel Carson's *Silent Spring* a 1960s bestseller! This stuff plays endlessly and never bores the forever-fearing human race.

Fear we're running out of resources is always wrong and likely always will be—but surely will be wrong in your lifetime, and the media will seldom tell us. Too Pollyanna-ish! It also takes faith in capitalism and human ingenuity to see our limitless long-term potential. Faith doesn't sell papers—cynicism does.

No one today can know exactly how technology, capitalism and innovative creativity will evolve to solve mankind's future problems. Our visions of the far future are hopelessly, often comically flawed. When *Back to the Future II* envisioned the year 2015 back in 1989, it foresaw flying cars and hoverboards but didn't envision laser printers, the Internet, iPhones, gene sequencing or a Tesla. Oops! But we don't need to predict the specifics—just have a little faith.

History backs this up. Consider the Great Horse Manure Crisis of 1894—an actual thing. You can look it up. Back then, as urbanization swelled in industrialized nations, a problem arose. The more people moved to the cities, the more horses were needed to carry goods and people across town. New York, London and other major cities each had tens of thousands of horses to power buggies, wagons and buses. But with tens of thousands of horses came millions of pounds of manure—per day. It had to be swept up and disposed of daily, lest flies and pestilence descend.

As you can imagine, fear of a manure-covered urban apocalypse swelled in tandem with the population. In 1894, one London *Times* writer predicted the whole of London would be buried under nine feet of manure within 50 years. City planners scrambled globally, holding crisis summits and planning conferences—not unlike today's climate-change frenzy. None could dream up a solution. Mankind was doomed!

But then the automobile happened. Technology solved the problem! Cars replaced horses. Crisis averted. The crisis is dead, long live the crisis.

Consider Peak Oil theory—the belief, championed in 1956 by geophysicist M. King Hubbert, that global oil production would peak at some point in the near future, then decline steadily until we ran out. At first, Hubbert predicted production would peak in 1970. But supply didn't tank, and the peak date was pushed out, again and again, to compensate for new finds and new technologies. But the theory gets recycled and re-popularized repeatedly because we have an impossibility foreseeing technologies well.

And then the shale boom happened. Geologists always knew shale oil was there. Peak Oil fretters just assumed it was untappable, because they underestimated technology. They forgot capitalism and didn't realize that, at some point, rising oil prices would provide huge incentives to invest in the technology to extract shale oil. That's exactly what happened. By the late 1990s, geologists had figured out how to collide two old technologies, hydraulic fracturing and horizontal drilling, to release the oil and natural gas trapped in shale formations. (Of course, Moore's Law helped a lot, too, with advanced electronics because there is a lot of data crunching in geophysical analysis.) It was expensive, but by the mid-2000s, high oil prices gave firms a big incentive to invest in this new technology and launch shale projects throughout Texas, North

Dakota, Pennsylvania and elsewhere. Now US production is surging past levels last seen in the early 1980s, and folks scoff at the notion of running out of oil any time soon. Peak Oil now looks like 1894's peak horse manure. Again.

Technology is limitless! We can't conceive of all the ways it will evolve and help use resources more efficiently, preserve the environment and feed us. Capitalism and free markets will make it happen, just as they did with manure and oil. Few fathom this, because few understand just how the market impacted US energy production in the 1980s and 1990s. As production declined, most took the Peak Oil view, assuming we were just plain running out. That was the accepted narrative for decades—few realized low oil prices were the real culprit. Figure 10.1 illustrates this. When oil crashed in the early 1980s and bounced around between $10 and $30 for nearly 15 years, it killed investment in domestic oil fields. It wasn't

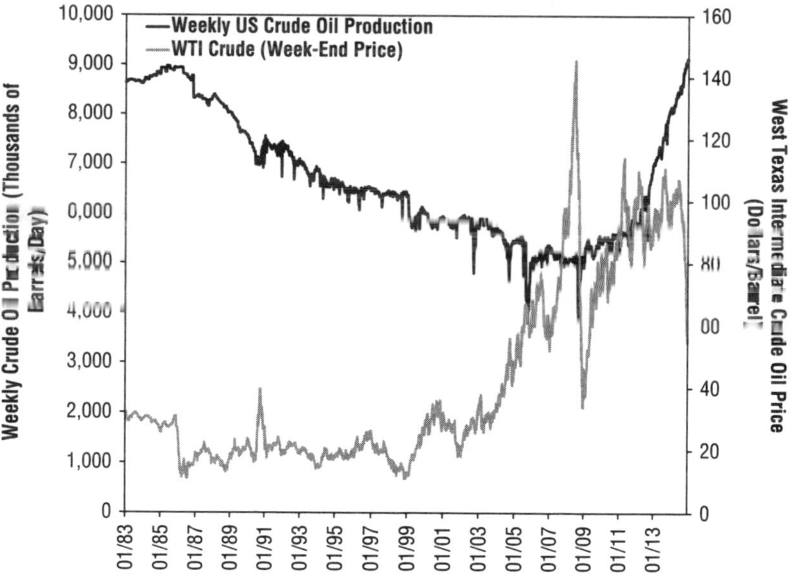

Figure 10.1 Crude Oil Prices and US Production

Source: FactSet, as of 1/6/2015. US Crude oil field production and West Texas Intermediate benchmark crude oil prices, 12/31/1982-12/31/2014.

profitable! Oil revenues have always been price-sensitive, not volume-sensitive, and fixed costs are high. For a long stretch, it simply wasn't economical to invest in new wells and goose production—importing was cheaper. So that's what we did. Once prices rose and it made sense to invest here again, firms did, and production shot up. Never underestimate profit motive! Never underestimate the long-term technology effect!

In Technology (and Capitalism) We Trust

The capitalist magic that drove technology from farming through the industrial age and beyond survives and thrives—as Steve Forbes said in the title of his great 2009 book in response to the 2007 recession, "capitalism will save us." Every day, technologies collide in marvelous ways we couldn't have dreamed of before. The potential here is endless. Life will get better in ways you can't imagine.

Today's myopic media trumpets Peak Innovation and Peak Technology, but don't believe it. Innovation hasn't stopped. We are no more in "secular stagnation" today than when the term was first coined by Alvin Hansen, America's then-leading Keynesian economist, in the late 1930s. Technology is getting faster and more amazing all the time—just not in ways as widely seen as the Internet. Think back to the techie trends we outlined back in Chapter 4—Moore's Law, which says microprocessing power roughly doubles every two years. Koomey's Law, which posits the same for energy efficiency in computing. Kryder's Law, which holds that data storage doubles every 13 months. The Shannon-Hartley Theorem, which says communication speed potential is limitless. Inventive users of these technologies constantly collide and compound them into wonderful, life-altering products.

Technology's limitless potential to better our quality of life and speed growth goes way beyond the pure tech world. Think about the vast applications for drone technology, if the Federal Aviation Administration (FAA) will allow it! Think about medical care! DNA sequencing is moving at Moore's Law–like speed! Imagine how this can collide with other technologies, allowing customizable medicine—cures and treatments coded specifically for each human. The medical world in a few decades will make today's treatments seem as modern as leeches. This isn't my field, of course, so I won't speculate on the specifics. If you want to give your imagination a boost, though, go read Ray Kurzweil's *The Singularity Is Near* (Viking Penguin, 2005). It goes too far to wing-nutty, far-fetched places, like assuming we'll have eternal life through machines, but if you can look past those flights of fancy, it is a phenomenal look at just how much we underestimate technology's potential. The future is far, far brighter than any of us can imagine.

But for investors, here's the best part: Stocks are your long-term way to own all this! The companies that create, adopt and collide new technologies will grow and profit—never-ending advancement is a never-ending source of earnings growth. It is both the technology creators and even more the creative, intelligent technology consumers. Only stocks represent colliding, compounding technologies past, present and future. This is why, historically, stocks have outpaced other similarly liquid assets. It's why stocks rise far more often than not. It's why you should forget and ignore all that media bunk about perma-stagnation and running out of X or Y. None of that matters for stocks now or in the far future! Technology and creativity will win out for as long as free markets exist—and the human spirit is amazing at preserving capitalism and building wealth. And at the end of the day, that's what the stock market is all about for future levels of wealth overall. Why wouldn't you want to own that?

Parting Thoughts

With that in mind, I can think of no better way to leave you than with the words my father left readers with in the conclusion to *Common Stocks and Uncommon Profits* in 1958:

> We are starting the second decade of a half century that may well see the standard of living of the human race advance more than it has in the preceding five thousand years. Great have been the investment risks of the recent past. Even greater have been the financial rewards for the successful. However, in this field of investment, the risks and rewards of the past hundred years may be small beside those of the next fifty.

Those words are as true today as they were when he wrote them in 1958. Moore's Law didn't even exist then! But Father trusted technology, creativity and free-market magic, and he knew the opportunities were endless—for society and for stocks.

When you're inundated with doom-and-gloom long-term forecasts, remember those words. When the media tells you the world is going to hell in a long-term handbasket, remember those words. When pundits claim this time it's different and we'll never recover from the next crisis, remember those words. Markets are beautiful, volatile, fickle, confounding, forward-looking and a lot of other things. But they accurately price the compounding wealth created by colliding technologies in ways the public and media, to date, have never fathomed. As ugly as the world can get sometimes, that limitless potential is always there, always lurking around the corner, always ready to spark a rebound before long and drive the world to ever-greater heights. It is, as Yogi Berra would say so famously, "déjà vu all over again."

Notes

1. "Grins, Gore, and Videotape—The Trouble With Local TV News," Eric Pooley, *New York*, October 9, 1989, 37–44.
2. FactSet, as of 9/30/2014. S&P 500 Total Return Index, 12/31/2012–12/31/2013.

Index

Index

Index